Reading Comprehension

LSAT Strategy Guide

This guide will teach you an effective technique for mastering LSAT Reading Comprehension and then sharpen your newfound skills with full passages and targeted drills. Learn to change the way you read, tackle the questions effectively, and apply your skills to a wide range of material.

Reading Comprehension LSAT Strategy Guide, 4th Edition

10-digit International Standard Book Number: 1-937707-76-8
13-digit International Standard Book Number: 978-1-937707-76-7
eISBN: 978-1-937707-81-1

Each copyrighted LSAT question that appears in this book is part of a section marked with the exam and exam section from which it was taken (e.g., PrepTest 43, Section 2). Each question is marked with the official question number of the particular question.

Layout Design: Dan McNaney and Cathy Huang
Cover Design: Dan McNaney and Frank Callaghan

INSTRUCTIONAL GUIDE SERIES

Logic Games
(ISBN: 978-1-937707-74-3)

Logical Reasoning
(ISBN: 978-1-937707-75-0)

Reading Comprehension
(ISBN: 978-1-937707-76-7)

PRACTICE BOOKS

10 Real LSATs Grouped by Question Type
Practice Book I
(ISBN: 978-1-937707-78-1)

15 Real, Recent LSATs
Practice Book II
(ISBN: 978-1-937707-39-2)

March 25, 2014

Dear Student,

Thank you for picking up a copy of LSAT *Reading Comprehension*. I hope this book provides just the guidance you need to get the most out of your LSAT studies.

As with most accomplishments, there were many people involved in the creation of the book you are holding. First and foremost is Zeke Vanderhoek, the founder of Manhattan Prep. Zeke was a lone tutor in New York when he started the company in 2000. Now, 14 years later, the company has instructors and offices nationwide and contributes to the studies and successes of thousands of LSAT, GMAT, GRE, and SAT students each year.

Our Manhattan Prep Strategy Guides are based on the continuing experiences of our instructors and students. We are particularly indebted to our instructors Mary Adkins, Brian Birdwell, Gilad Edelman, Dmitry Farber, Ian Jorgeson, Matt Sherman, Noah Teitelbaum, Patrick Tyrrell, and Tommy Wallach for their hard work on this volume. Special thanks to Dmitry Farber for providing the guiding vision behind this new edition. Dan McNaney and Cathy Huang provided their design expertise to make the books as user-friendly as possible, and Liz Krisher made sure all the moving pieces came together at just the right time. Beyond providing additions and edits for this book, Chris Ryan and Noah Teitelbaum continue to be the driving force behind all of our curriculum efforts. Their leadership is invaluable. Finally, thank you to all of the Manhattan Prep students who have provided input and feedback over the years. This book wouldn't be half of what it is without your voice.

At Manhattan Prep, we continually aspire to provide the best instructors and resources possible. We hope that you will find our commitment manifest in this book. If you have any questions or comments, please email me at dgonzalez@manhattanprep.com. I'll look forward to reading your comments, and I'll be sure to pass them along to our curriculum team.

Thanks again, and best of luck preparing for the LSAT!

Sincerely,

Dan

Dan Gonzalez
President
Manhattan Prep

www.manhattanprep.com/lsat 138 West 25th St., 7th Floor, NY, NY 10001 Tel: 646-254-6480 Fax: 646-514-7425

HOW TO ACCESS YOUR ONLINE RESOURCES

If you...

➤ are a registered Manhattan Prep student

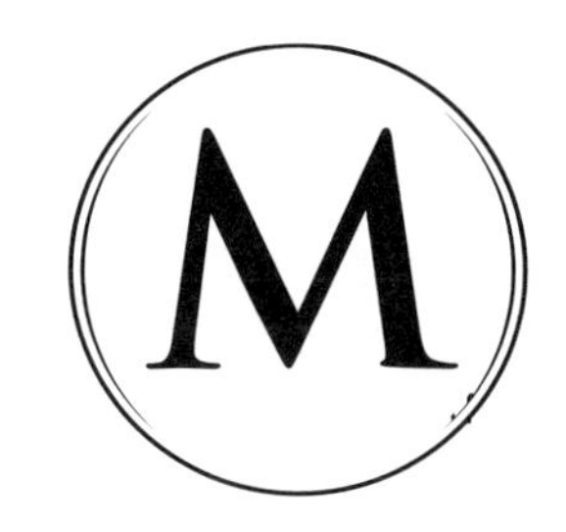

and have received this book as part of your course materials, you have AUTOMATIC access to ALL of our online resources. To access these resources, follow the instructions in the Welcome Guide provided to you at the start of your program.

Do NOT follow the instructions below.

➤ purchased this book from the Manhattan Prep online store or at one of our centers

1. Go to: www.manhattanprep.com/lsat/studentcenter.
2. Log in using the username and password used when your account was set up.

➤ purchased this book at a retail location

1. Create an account with Manhattan Prep at the website: www.manhattanprep.com/lsat/createaccount.
2. Go to: www.manhattanprep.com/lsat/access.
3. Follow the instructions on the screen.

Your one year of online access begins on the day that you register your book at the above URL.

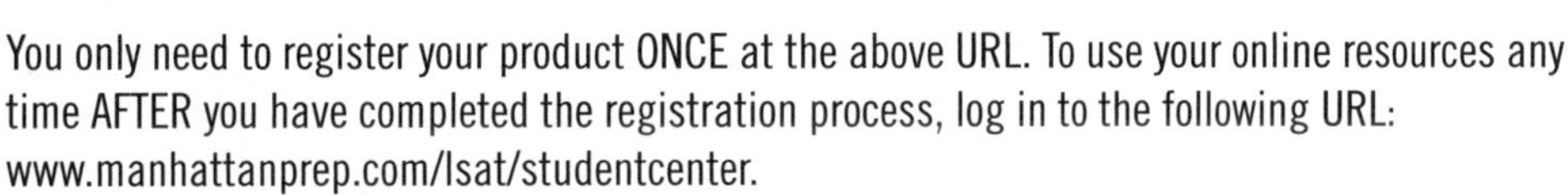

You only need to register your product ONCE at the above URL. To use your online resources any time AFTER you have completed the registration process, log in to the following URL: www.manhattanprep.com/lsat/studentcenter.

Please note that online access is nontransferable. This means that only NEW and UNREGISTERED copies of the book will grant you online access. Previously used books will not provide any online resources.

➤ purchased an eBook version of this book

1. Create an account with Manhattan Prep at the website: www.manhattanprep.com/lsat/createaccount.
2. Email a copy of your purchase receipt to lsat@manhattanprep.com to activate your resources. Please be sure to use the same email address to create an account that you used to purchase the eBook.

For any technical issues, email techsupport@manhattanprep.com or call 800-576-4628.

TABLE *of* CONTENTS

Chapter 1 of Reading Comprehension

Part 1: Change How You Read

Reading Comprehension Overview

Why Study Reading Comprehension?

I already know what reading comprehension is. What can this book do for me?
We strongly suspect that you already know how to read! Not only that, but your reading comprehension has probably been tested many times before, starting in elementary school and continuing on through the SAT and now the LSAT.

There is a reason for this: reading comprehension exams are a great way to test an individual's ability to absorb, comprehend, process, and respond to written information in a time-efficient manner. Of course, these are also skills you'll need as a law student and as a lawyer.

It seems to make sense, but is it really possible to accurately quantify a person's level of reading comprehension? Can't we all, by looking at our own lives and experiences, see that our own level of reading comprehension is something that *fluctuates* from situation to situation?

Let's look at a few scenarios:

1. Terry is an electrical engineer. She has been working in a niche industry for years, but it's very easy for her to understand and evaluate articles on engineering concepts that fall outside of her specialty, even when she isn't familiar with the specific terminology involved. She's recently become interested in the stock market and has been trying to read up on it. However, she's having a lot of trouble understanding and organizing the investment advice that she's read in various financial publications.
2. Chad is a freshman in high school. He has mastered the art of instant messaging, sending and receiving hundreds of messages a day. He filters and organizes them easily and is able to weave together a cohesive understanding of the lives of his friends. However, when he tries to organize the personalities and events of 18th-century Europe from his history textbook, he's hopelessly lost.
3. Jane is an English literature professor and a Luddite. She's finally getting around to using the internet to communicate with her students. She is surprised by the short, abrupt, and casual messages they send to her. She can quickly make sense of complex texts on abstract literary theory, but in this new format she is unable to catch subtleties and has difficulty interpreting the tone of the messages she receives. She tries to write short responses back but invariably ends up sending emails that are too long and take her too much time to put together.

It's easy to see how different types of reading comprehension exams would score Ted, Sally, and Jane very differently. The truth is, none of us has a definable (or quantifiable) level of reading comprehension. Put simply, our reading comprehension ability is highly variable. It depends on many factors, including our familiarity with the subject matter, the manner in which the material is written, our purpose for reading, and our overall interest and focus level.

For a few of you, the strengths you possess as readers already align with the skills tested by LSAT Reading Comprehension. In other words, your ability to read and comprehend LSAT passages is similar to Chad's ability to organize and synthesize his text messages. However, for most of us, the complex passages that appear on the LSAT do not naturally fall into our reading "sweet spot." So what do we do? We have to do much more than simply read a bunch of LSAT passages. We must work to become intimately familiar with the characteristics of LSAT passages and then refine our reading approach in response to these characteristics. In other words, we must expand our sweet spot to *include* the LSAT.

Your Path to Success

Do not believe those who say that you cannot improve your Reading Comprehension. You can, and if you do the work, you will. This book is designed to lead you through that process, one step at a time. If you are not already an "LSAT reader," you will become one by the time we are through. That said, mastering Reading Comprehension on the LSAT is not easy. It takes a lot of work to get to the point where you can read and understand an LSAT passage just as comfortably (or at least *almost* as comfortably) as you would the articles in your favorite magazine. Here are the steps we're going to take to get you there:

1. Define your reading perspective.

The perspective from which you read can have a huge impact on how you make sense of a given piece of text. Let's go back to high school for a minute. Imagine your English teacher has assigned you to read *Hamlet* and that your reading of the play will be evaluated in one of the following three ways:

1. You will be given a quote exam, during which you will be asked to identify certain lines taken from the text of the play.
2. You will be asked to write an essay about the major themes in the play.
3. You will be assigned one of the roles in a high school production of the play.

If you were asked to complete a quote exam, you would read with a particular focus on learning the characters and understanding the basic plot. If you were asked to write an essay on the major themes, you would interpret and extrapolate, attempting to uncover the author's implicit messages. If you were asked to act out the play, you would read with an eye towards character development, and you would pay close attention to the emotions of the characters at different points in the story. Needless to say, both your interaction with the text and your interpretation of the play would be greatly affected by the perspective that you adopted.

We'll spend a good deal of time in this book developing an advantageous perspective from which to read any LSAT passage: the perspective of a law student. We'll use the image of a scale to represent this perspective. Thinking in terms of the scale provides a clear and consistent approach to each passage and makes it easier to quickly recognize and organize the most important information.

2. Develop an effective routine.

Once you have your perspective set, you will want to develop a strong technique that you can bring to bear on each and every passage. Although the subject matter on the LSAT can range widely, you can create a consistent and successful reading experience for yourself by practicing the active reading techniques outlined in chapters 3 and 4.

3. Understand what the test is asking you to do.

Every Reading Comprehension question on the LSAT tests your ability to do one or more of the following: (1) **identify** a piece of supporting text, (2) **infer** from a piece of text, or (3) **synthesize** several parts of the text to come to a new understanding. It's important that you recognize your task in each case and that you know how to find support for each kind of question.

We'll spend chapter 5 looking at these core competencies. You'll develop a keen sense for what correct answers should accomplish.

4. Identify patterns in incorrect answer choices.

Success on Reading Comprehension questions depends, in large part, on your ability to eliminate incorrect answers. On a harder problem, the right answer may be far from ideal and impossible to predict. In fact, it is often easier to spot wrong answers than it is to spot the right answer. With this in mind, it is important that you develop a sense for how the test writers create those incorrect choices.

In chapter 6, we'll examine the common characteristics of incorrect answers and learn to use our understanding of these characteristics to work wrong-to-right, eliminating bad choices and narrowing the field down to those answers that are worthy of another look.

5. Prepare to handle any situation.

After you've learned our core techniques in the first six chapters, we'll take a brief "intermission" to examine your progress and talk about timing strategy. After that, you will get a chance to apply everything you've learned to a wide range of passages, and you'll receive guidance on how to handle extreme situations—the time crunch, the passage that confounds your expectations, or the passage that looks like it's in another language!

With all these tools in hand, you'll be ready to dominate LSAT Reading Comprehension. Before we get started with the process of expanding your reading sweet spot, let's discuss some of the logistics of the Reading Comprehension section of the test.

Reading Comprehension on the LSAT

Section Breakdown

The entire LSAT exam is comprised of the following sections (not necessarily in this order):

SECTION	QUESTIONS	SCORED?	TIME
Logic Games	22–23	yes	35 minutes
Reading Comprehension	26–28	yes	35 minutes
Logical Reasoning (1)	24–26	yes	35 minutes
Logical Reasoning (2)	24–26	yes	35 minutes
EXPERIMENTAL	22–28	no	35 minutes
Essay	1 essay	no	35 minutes

Note that every LSAT exam will contain one Reading Comprehension section that will count towards your final score. Thus, about one-quarter of the total scored questions on the LSAT will be Reading Comprehension questions.

Keep in mind that the Experimental section could end up being a Reading Comprehension section as well. If you do receive two RC sections on your exam, only one of those two sections will actually count towards your final score. Unfortunately, it's impossible to know if you're facing a "real" section while you're facing it.

Scoring

Every Reading Comprehension question, and every other question on the LSAT for that matter, is worth exactly 1 point. If you answer a question correctly, you will be credited 1 point for that question. If you answer the question incorrectly, or if you fail to answer the question, you will be credited 0 points for that question.

It is important to note that there is no guessing penalty on the LSAT. An incorrect answer is scored the same as no answer. Thus, it is to your advantage to answer every single question on the exam, even if some of those answers are guesses.

During the scoring of your exam, your points are totaled and then converted to a scaled score between 120 and 180. The conversion depends on the performance of all the other test-takers who took the same exam and on statistical data from past LSAT exams.

Subject Matter: Do I have to know about the law?

Every Reading Comprehension section contains four passages. You can expect to see one passage per section in each of the following four subject areas:

Subject Area	Expect to see passages on...
LAW	legal history, international law, legal theory, social ramifications of law
NATURAL SCIENCES	evolution, biology, chemistry, physics, agriculture
SOCIAL SCIENCES	history, political science, sociology, economics
HUMANITIES	literature, art, film

The LSAT does *not* expect that you have any prior knowledge when it comes to law, natural sciences, social sciences, or humanities. All the information you will need to answer the questions will be contained in the passage. That said, students with a certain level of familiarity with these subject areas will have a slight advantage. As we discussed earlier, the more familiar you are with the subject matter, the more likely you are to comprehend what you are reading. If you'd like to do a little outside reading to boost your background knowledge in a particular area, you can take a look at the reading list we provide in your online Student Center (go to page 7 for access instructions). However, you will probably want to devote most of your precious study time to LSAT-specific materials.

Pacing

You will have a total of 35 minutes to complete the four passages. This works out to an average of 8:45 per passage. However, you will need to be faster than 8:45 on easier passages in order to have the extra time necessary for the more difficult passages. Generally speaking, the four passages on the LSAT are arranged in order from easier to harder, but this is a rough approximation at best. Every section is different, and so is every reader! We recommend a flexible approach to timing—we'll go over this in detail in chapter 7—but here's a sample of what your time usage might look like on a typical Reading Comprehension section:

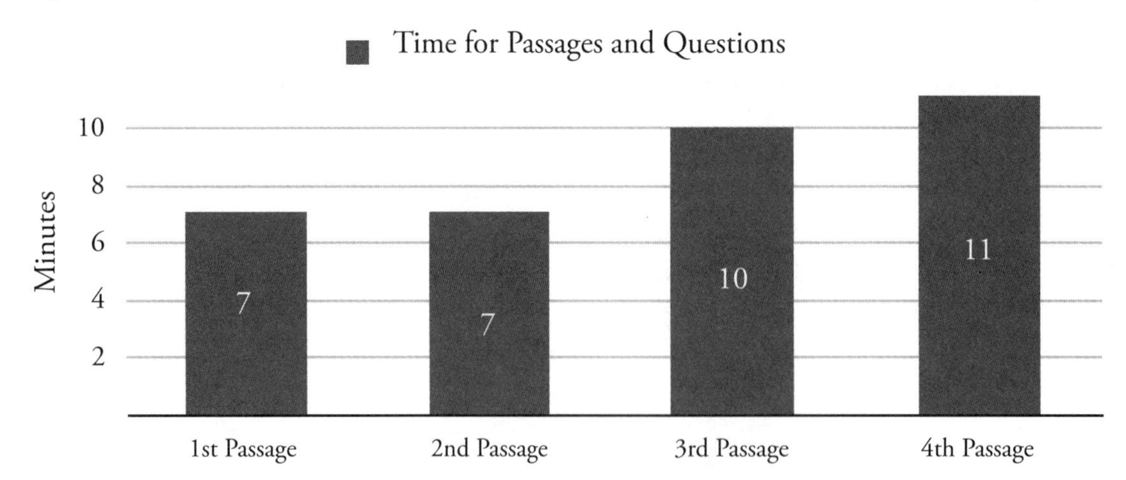

Within each passage, you will generally need to spend more time answering the questions than reading the text, but the precise ratio will depend on your own personal style and your particular strengths and weaknesses. There are no absolutes when it comes to timing. Use this book and your own practice to get a sense of how to allocate time between reading the text and answering the questions.

Let's get to work.

Chapter 2
of
Reading Comprehension

Reading for the Scale

Getting Familiar

Read the following passage untimed, notating however you would like. At the end of your reading process, look over the text again and try to create a quick summary of the passage in the box provided. Don't worry about writing in complete sentences, etc. Style is not important. Just try to identify the key points.

PrepTest 38, Section 3, Passage 2

Intellectual authority is defined as the authority of arguments that prevail by virtue of good reasoning and do not depend on coercion or convention. A contrasting notion, institutional authority, refers to the power of (5) social institutions to enforce acceptance of arguments that may or may not possess intellectual authority. The authority wielded by legal systems is especially interesting because such systems are institutions that nonetheless aspire to a purely intellectual authority. (10) One judge goes so far as to claim that courts are merely passive vehicles for applying intellectual authority of the law and possess no coercive powers of their own.

In contrast, some critics maintain that whatever (15) authority judicial pronouncements have is exclusively institutional. Some of these critics go further, claiming that intellectual authority does not really exist—i.e., it reduces to institutional authority. But it can be countered that these claims break down when a (20) sufficiently broad historical perspective is taken: Not all arguments accepted by institutions withstand the test of time, and some well-reasoned arguments never receive institutional imprimatur. The reasonable argument that goes unrecognized in its own time (25) because it challenges institutional beliefs is common in intellectual history; intellectual authority and institutional consensus are not the same thing.

But, the critics might respond, intellectual authority is only recognized as such because of institutional (30) consensus. For example, if a musicologist were to claim that an alleged musical genius who, after several decades, had not gained respect and recognition for his or her compositions is probably not a genius, the critics might say that basing a judgement on a unit of time— (35) "several decades"—is an institutional rather than an intellectual construct. What, the critics might ask, makes a particular number of decades reasonable evidence by which to judge genius? The answer, of course, is nothing, except for the fact that such (40) institutional procedures have proved useful to musicologists in making such distinctions in the past.

The analogous legal concept is the doctrine of precedent, i.e., a judge's merely deciding a case a certain way becoming a basis for deciding later cases (45) the same way—a pure example of institutional authority. But the critics miss the crucial distinction that when a judicial decision is badly reasoned, or simply no longer applies in the face of evolving social standards or practices, the notion of intellectual (50) authority is introduced: judges reconsider, revise, or in some cases throw out the decision. The conflict between intellectual and institutional authority in legal systems is thus played out in the reconsideration of decisions, leading one to draw the conclusion that legal (55) systems contain a significant degree of intellectual authority even if the thrust of their power is predominantly institutional.

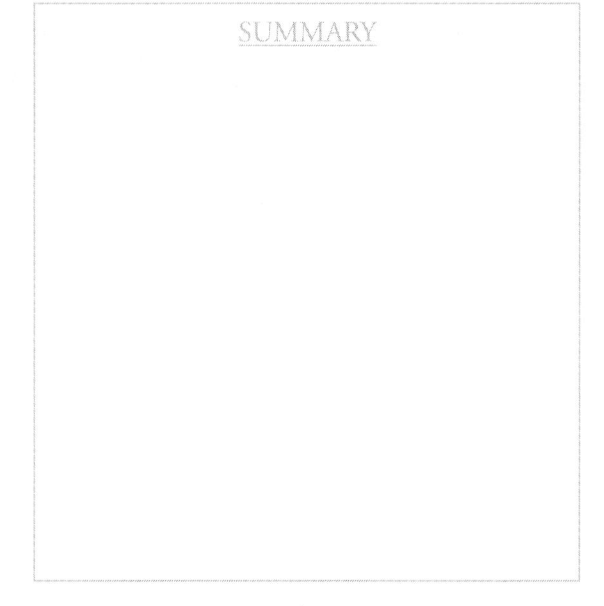

Identifying the Scale

Defining Your Perspective: Read Like a Law Student

We'll get back to the passage on the previous page soon enough, but first, let's fast-forward into the future. Imagine yourself as a law student, a legal scholar. There you sit, poring over legal cases, frantically scribbling notes, wondering if your name will be cold-called in tomorrow's lecture. You have so many cases to read and so little time.

While the reading will be challenging, and you'll often wonder if you'll be able to get through it all, your fundamental tasks for each case that you read can be thought of in very simple terms: (1) clearly define the two sides of a central argument, or case, (2) make note of the parties that fall on each side of the argument, and (3) consider any evidence that is presented in support of either side.

This all makes good sense. After all, law school is designed to prepare you for a career in law. In order for lawyers or judges to successfully prepare for a case, they must understand the two sides of a central argument in a clear and specific manner. This understanding creates the framework through which they can evaluate and organize the evidence and opinions that are presented.

It is no wonder, then, that the LSAT would test your ability to deconstruct a reading passage in just this way. Though LSAT Reading Comprehension passages vary a good deal in terms of subject matter, they are rather consistent when it comes to structure. Most LSAT passages provide exactly what you'd expect as a law student: information about two sides of an argument and supporting evidence for one or both sides.

In short, think of yourself as a law student as you read. It is from this perspective that you will most effectively organize and understand the information presented.

Visualizing the Scale

So how does a law student read a passage efficiently? Because the typical passage is organized around an argument, your top priority should be to identify, in a clear and specific way, the two sides of this argument. The image of a balance scale is a useful way to visualize how the competing sides of the argument are presented in the passage. Let's look at a few examples:

Some passages will give equal consideration to both sides of an argument.

Literature does not need to convey cultural roots.

It is important for literature to express its cultural roots.

Some passages will give consideration to both sides, but place emphasis on one side over the other.

As you can see, we are adding a tilt to the scale to indicate which side the passage discusses more. This tilt does not indicate which side the author agrees with, only which side receives more attention in the passage.

Some passages will introduce an argument but focus entirely on the evidence for one side.

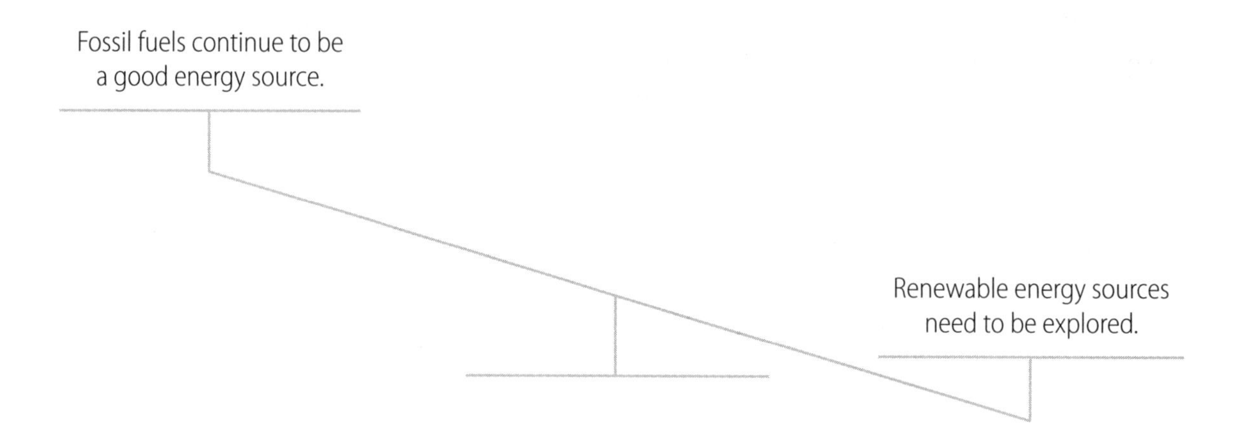

Although you won't want to take the time to draw a scale on your paper during the LSAT, the idea of a scale provides a simple way to organize the contents of each passage as you read. *Everything* in the passage exists in order to inform the sides of the argument in some way. By identifying the scale, you will have a structure on which to hang all of the other elements of the passage.

However, not every passage will have a clear scale. For instance, you will occasionally come across a passage that is strictly informative and contains no argument at all. Think of this as a refreshing break from all that arguing! We'll get into more detail on these passages in chapter 10, but for now, let's focus on the scale, which is going to serve you well on the vast majority of passages. Even when there is no argument, simply taking a moment to recognize that fact may give you an advantage when it comes to answering the questions.

The Challenges of Identifying the Scale

Now that we've defined our reading perspective, let's revisit the Getting Familiar passage from the start of the chapter and see if we can identify the scale.

Passage:

Intellectual authority is defined as the authority of arguments that prevail by virtue of good reasoning and do not depend on coercion or convention. A contrasting notion, institutional authority, refers to the power of social institutions to enforce acceptance of arguments that may or may not possess intellectual authority.

Comment:

Great! The passage immediately contrasts intellectual authority and institutional authority. But we have to be careful—we can't simply put these two kinds of authority on either side of the scale. They are contrasting ideas, but we have yet to be introduced to a debate.

It's important not to be in too much of a rush to finalize our scale. We will frequently need to fine-tune or overhaul the scale as we read on. In fact, trying to figure out the scale as we read is an important technique for staying alert throughout the passage!

Passage:

The authority wielded by legal systems is especially interesting because such systems are institutions that nonetheless aspire to a purely intellectual authority.

Comment:

We don't have an argument yet, but we seem to be narrowing the scope of the discussion. Do legal systems have intellectual or institutional authority? They are institutions, but apparently they "aspire" to intellectual authority. It's kind of strange for legal systems to have aspirations! So far, the author hasn't presented one side of a debate.

Passage:

One judge goes so far as to claim that courts are merely passive vehicles for applying the intellectual authority of the law and possess no coercive powers of their own.

Comment:

There we go—a concrete opinion: one judge claims that courts apply intellectual authority and have no institutional authority. Maybe we have one side of the scale?

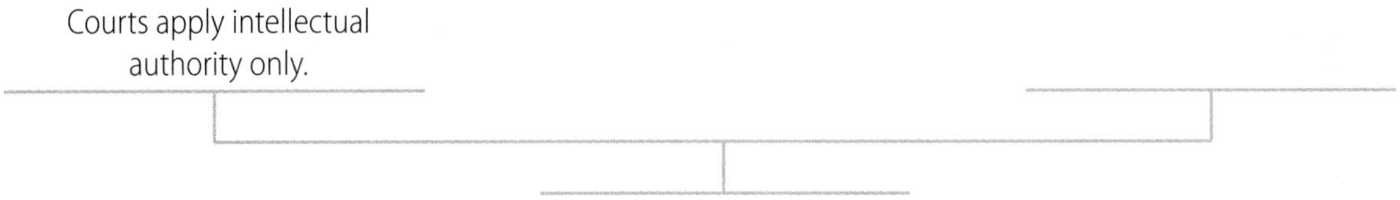

Courts apply intellectual authority only.

In contrast, some critics maintain that whatever authority judicial pronouncements have is exclusively institutional ...

Now that we have noted one opinion, it's not too surprising to see that someone else holds the opposite opinion. Now we have the two sides of an argument, so it feels pretty safe to set up our scale like this:

Courts apply intellectual authority only. | Courts apply institutional authority only.

At this point, take a look back at the passage summary you wrote on the first page of the chapter and compare it with this scale. Did you note a central argument? If not, what did you focus on? Note that we have not finished reading the passage, and our scale might change by the end (hint, hint), so don't worry if you included ideas that aren't captured by the above scale; we'll come back to that a little later in the chapter.

In the meantime, let's get some practice reading for the scale.

DRILL IT: Identifying the Scale

Each of the following is a truncated version of a Reading Comprehension passage from a past LSAT. Your goal is to correctly identify the two sides of the argument.

PrepTest 38, Section 3, Passage 1

The myth persists that in 1492 the Western Hemisphere was an untamed wilderness and that it was European settlers who harnessed and transformed its ecosystems. But scholarship shows that forests, in particular, had been altered to varying degrees well before the arrival of Europeans. Native populations had converted much of the forests to successfully cultivated stands, especially by means of burning. Nevertheless, some researchers have maintained that the extent, frequency, and impact of such burning was minimal. However, a large body of evidence for the routine practice of burning exists in the geographical record. One group of researchers found, for example, that sedimentary charcoal accumulations in what is now the northeastern United States are greatest where known native American settlements were greatest.

PrepTest 34, Section 1, Passage 3

In the eighteenth century the French naturalist Jean Baptiste de Lamarck believed that an animal's use or disuse of an organ affected that organ's development in the animal's offspring. Lamarck claimed that the giraffe's long neck, for example, resulted from its ancestors stretching to reach distant leaves. But because biologists could find no genetic mechanism to make the transmission of environmentally induced adaptations seem plausible, they have long held that inheritance of acquired characteristics never occurs. Yet new research has uncovered numerous examples of the phenomenon. For example, the inherited absence of cell walls in bacteria results from changes in the interactions among genes, without any attendant changes in the genes themselves.

The new evidence suggests that genes can be divided into two groups. Most are inherited "vertically," from ancestors. Some however, seem to have been acquired "horizontally," from viruses, plasmids, bacteria, or other environmental agents. Some horizontal transmission may well be the mechanism for inheritance of acquired characteristics that has long eluded biologists, and that may eventually prove Lamarck's hypothesis to be correct.

PrepTest 51, Section 2, Passage 4

Computers have long been utilized in the sphere of law in the form of word processors, spreadsheets, legal research systems, and practice management systems. Most exciting, however, has been the prospect of using artificial intelligence techniques to create so-called legal reasoning systems—computer programs that can help to resolve legal disputes by reasoning from and applying the law. But the practical benefits of such automated reasoning systems have fallen short of optimistic early predictions and have not resulted in computer systems that can independently provide expert advice about substantive law. Early attempts at automated legal reasoning systems underestimated the problems of interpretation that can arise at every stage of a legal argument. Proponents of legal reasoning systems now argue that accommodating reference to, and reasoning from, cases improves the chances of producing a successful system. But in order to be able to apply legal rules to novel situations, systems have to be equipped with a kind of comprehensive knowledge of the world that is far beyond their capabilities at present or in the foreseeable future.

PrepTest 39, Section 3, Passage 1

The contemporary Mexican artistic movement known as muralism, a movement of public art that began with images painted on walls in an effort to represent Mexican national culture, is closely linked ideologically with its main sponsor, the new Mexican government elected in 1920 following the Mexican Revolution. This government promoted an ambitious cultural program, and the young revolutionary state called on artists to display Mexico's richness and possibility. But the theoretical foundation of the movement was formulated by the artists themselves. While many muralist works express populist or nationalist ideas, it is a mistake to attempt to reduce Mexican mural painting to formulaic, official government art. It is more than merely the result of the changes in political and social awareness that the Mexican Revolution represented; it also reflected important innovations in the art world. Awareness of these innovations enabled these artists to be freer in expression than were more traditional practitioners of this style.

PrepTest 12, Section 3, Passage 4

How does the brain know when carbohydrates have been or should be consumed? The answer to this question is not known, but one element in the explanation seems to be the neurotransmitter serotonin, one of a class of chemical mediators that may be released from a presynaptic neuron and that cause the transmission of nerve impulse across a synapse to an adjacent postsynaptic neuron. In general, it has been found that drugs that selectively facilitate serotonin-mediated neurotransmission tend to cause weight loss, whereas drugs that block serotonin-mediated transmission often have the opposite effect: they often induce carbohydrate craving and consequent weight gain.

Serotonin is a derivative of tryptophan, an amino acid that is normally present at low levels in the bloodstream. The rate of conversion is affected by the proportion of carbohydrates in an individual's diet: carbohydrates stimulate the secretion of insulin, which facilitates the uptake of most amino acids into peripheral tissues, such as muscles. Blood tryptophan levels, however, are unaffected by insulin, so the proportion of tryptophan in the blood relative to the other amino acids increases when carbohydrates are consumed. Since tryptophan competes with other amino acids for the transport across the blood-brain barrier into the brain, insulin secretion indirectly speeds tryptophan's entry into the central nervous system, where, in a special cluster of neurons, it is converted into serotonin.

SOLUTIONS: Identifying the Scale

The parts of the passage that most clearly inform us of the central argument have been underlined.

PrepTest 38, Section 3, Passage 1

The myth persists that in 1492 the Western Hemisphere was an untamed wilderness and that it was European settlers who harnessed and transformed its ecosystems. But scholarship shows that forests, in particular, had been altered to varying degrees well before the arrival of Europeans. Native populations had converted much of the forests to successfully cultivated stands, especially by means of burning. Nevertheless, some researchers have maintained that the extent, frequency, and impact of such burning was minimal. However, a large body of evidence for the routine practice of burning exists in the geographical record. One group of researchers found, for example, that sedimentary charcoal accumulations in what is now the northeastern United States are greatest where known native American settlements were greatest.

Side A:
Native populations had little impact on the ecosystems of the Western Hemisphere.

Side B:
Western Hemisphere ecosystems, particularly forests, were significantly altered by native populations well before the arrival of Europeans.

PrepTest 34, Section 1, Passage 3

In the eighteenth century the French naturalist Jean Baptiste de Lamarck believed that an animal's use or disuse of an organ affected that organ's development in the animal's offspring. Lamarck claimed that the giraffe's long neck, for example, resulted from its ancestors stretching to reach distant leaves. But because biologists could find no genetic mechanism to make the transmission of environmentally induced adaptations seem plausible, they have long held that inheritance of acquired characteristics never occurs. Yet new research has uncovered numerous examples of the phenomenon. For example, the inherited absence of cell walls in bacteria results from changes in the interactions among genes, without any attendant changes in the genes themselves.

The new evidence suggests that genes can be divided into two groups. Most are inherited "vertically," from ancestors. Some however, seem to have been acquired "horizontally," from viruses, plasmids, bacteria, or other environmental agents. Some horizontal transmission may well be the mechanism for inheritance of acquired characteristics that has long eluded biologists, and that may eventually prove Lamarck's hypothesis to be correct.

Side A:
Lamarck's hypothesis of inheritance of acquired characteristics is incorrect.

Side B:
Lamarck's hypothesis is correct.

2

PrepTest 51, Section 2, Passage 4

Computers have long been utilized in the sphere of law in the form of word processors, spreadsheets, legal research systems, and practice management systems. Most exciting, however, has been the prospect of using artificial intelligence techniques to create so-called legal reasoning systems—computer programs that can help to resolve legal disputes by reasoning from and applying the law. But the practical benefits of such automated reasoning systems have fallen short of optimistic early predictions and have not resulted in computer systems that can independently provide expert advice about substantive law. Early attempts at automated legal reasoning systems underestimated the problems of interpretation that can arise at every stage of a legal argument. Proponents of legal reasoning systems now argue that accommodating reference to, and reasoning from, cases improves the chances of producing a successful system. But in order to be able to apply legal rules to novel situations, systems have to be equipped with a kind of comprehensive knowledge of the world that is far beyond their capabilities at present or in the foreseeable future.

Side A:
Legal reasoning systems may be able to provide independent expert legal advice.

Side B:
Legal reasoning systems are not likely to live up to their promise.

PrepTest 39, Section 3, Passage 1

The contemporary Mexican artistic movement known as muralism, a movement of public art that began with images painted on walls in an effort to represent Mexican national culture, is closely linked ideologically with its main sponsor, the new Mexican government elected in 1920 following the Mexican Revolution. This government promoted an ambitious cultural program, and the young revolutionary state called on artists to display Mexico's richness and possibility. But the theoretical foundation of the movement was formulated by the artists themselves. While many muralist works express populist or nationalist ideas, it is a mistake to attempt to reduce Mexican mural painting to formulaic, official government art. It is more than merely the result of the changes in political and social awareness that the Mexican Revolution represented; it also reflected important innovations in the art world. Awareness of these innovations enabled these artists to be freer in expression than were more traditional practitioners of this style.

Side A:
Mexican mural painting is formulaic, official government art.

Side B:
Mexican mural painting is more than that; it also reflected important innovations in the art world.

PrepTest 12, Section 3, Passage 4

How does the brain know when carbohydrates have been or should be consumed? The answer to this question is not known, but one element in the explanation seems to be the neurotransmitter serotonin, one of a class of chemical mediators that may be released from a presynaptic neuron and that cause the transmission of nerve impulse across a synapse to an adjacent postsynaptic neuron. In general, it has been found that drugs that selectively facilitate serotonin-mediated neurotransmission tend to cause weight loss, whereas drugs that block serotonin-mediated transmission often have the opposite effect: they often induce carbohydrate craving and consequent weight gain.

Serotonin is a derivative of tryptophan, an amino acid that is normally present at low levels in the bloodstream. The rate of conversion is affected by the proportion of carbohydrates in an individual's diet: carbohydrates stimulate the secretion of insulin, which facilitates the uptake of most amino acids into peripheral tissues, such as muscles. Blood tryptophan levels, however, are unaffected by insulin, so the proportion of tryptophan in the blood relative to the other amino acids increases when carbohydrates are consumed. Since tryptophan competes with other amino acids for the transport across the blood-brain barrier into the brain, insulin secretion indirectly speeds tryptophan's entry into the central nervous system, where, in a special cluster of neurons, it is converted into serotonin.

CURVEBALL: Strictly Informative

There is no argument here at all! Notice that the entirety of the text is factual. No claims or theories are described, nor does the author express an opinion.

Finding the Author

So now you've had some practice identifying the two sides of an argument, but what about the author's take on the matter? If you've had much experience with Reading Comprehension, you probably know that we are almost invariably asked for the main point of the passage, and we are often asked what the author might think about a particular idea.

Finding the author's opinion can be challenging, however, especially when it is surrounded by the opinions of others. LSAT passages are rarely written in the first person, so we have to use language cues to disentangle the author's opinion from the other views presented in the passage. Sometimes the author is kind enough to state an opinion outright:

Lichenometry has distinct advantages over radiocarbon dating.[1]

Since only the territoriality theory affords trademark owners any real legal protection against gray marketing practices ... it is inevitable as well as desirable that it will come to be consistently applied in gray marketing cases.[2]

Often, the author will show an opinion by citing someone else's work approvingly:

In one of the most illuminating discussions of the novel to date, Henry Louis Gates, Jr., states ...[3]

But present-day observations sometimes yield evidence that supports relict behavior hypotheses.[4]

Kogawa's use of motifs drawn from Christian rituals and symbols forms a subtle critique of the professed ethics of the majority culture that has shunned Naomi.[5]

However, most commonly the author will present an opinion by taking issue with someone else's. Either the author doesn't like what was said or the author thinks that it isn't careful or subtle or complete enough:

This assertion assumes the automatic dominance of the imported productions and their negative effect on the domestic culture. But the assertion is polemical and abstract, based on little or no research into the place held by imported programs in the economies of importing countries or in the lives of viewers.[6]

This version of history patronizes the Victorians.[7]

Aimed so squarely at the head, such books cannot stimulate students who yearn to connect to history emotionally as well as intellectually.[8]

Hopefully, an author who doesn't like the views discussed so far will be kind enough to provide a counterclaim. Sometimes, this happens immediately:

But the difficulty of the sources, while it might appear to explain why the relevant scholarship has not been undertaken, seems actually to have deterred few: the fact is that few historians have wanted to write anything approaching women's legal history in the first place.[9]

---

1 *PrepTest 62, Section 1, Passage 1*
2 *PrepTest 8, Section 3, Passage 2*
3 *PrepTest 17, Section 4, Passage 1*
4 *PrepTest 46, Section 1, Passage 3*
5 *PrepTest 46, Section 1, Passage 2*
6 *PrepTest 51, Section 2, Passage 3*
7 *PrepTest 41, Section 4, Passage 4*
8 *PrepTest 52, Section 4, Passage 2*
9 *PrepTest 29, Section 2, Passage 4*

But while such factors may help to explain the differences, it can be argued that these differences ultimately reflect different conceptions of the nature and purpose of fiction.[10]

Identifying the author's opinion is a crucial part of our process. Even on questions that don't ask for the main point or purpose of the passage, knowing the author's point of view can help us to identify the purpose and structure of certain lines or paragraphs, strengthen or weaken the author's argument, and make inferences about the author's attitude to specific elements of the text. Additionally, the process of looking for this opinion can help us to refine our scale. If the author doesn't seem to rest on either side, perhaps there is more to the issue than we realized and we need to take a moment to revise our scale.

Adding the Author

Let's revisit our Getting Familiar passage with an eye toward placing the author's opinion on the scale. At what point does the author express an opinion on the issue of intellectual vs. institutional authority? Before you keep reading, take a moment to flip back to page 20 and find the first clear expression of the author's opinion.

There are certainly plenty of opinion words—"claim," "in contrast," "But it can be countered"—but all of these seem to present a battle between two sides that the author is merely reporting on. It's not until we get to the final paragraph that the author presents any opinions of her own: "But the critics miss the crucial distinction ..." The author starts to show support for the notion that legal systems wield intellectual authority but then closes by slyly presenting her opinion in the third person: "... leading one to draw the conclusion that legal systems contain a significant degree of intellectual authority even if the thrust of their power is predominantly institutional."

What should we do with this? The author grants that the power of legal systems is mostly institutional, but she concludes that they have intellectual authority, too. One way we can represent this is to add the author's "middle way" to our existing scale:

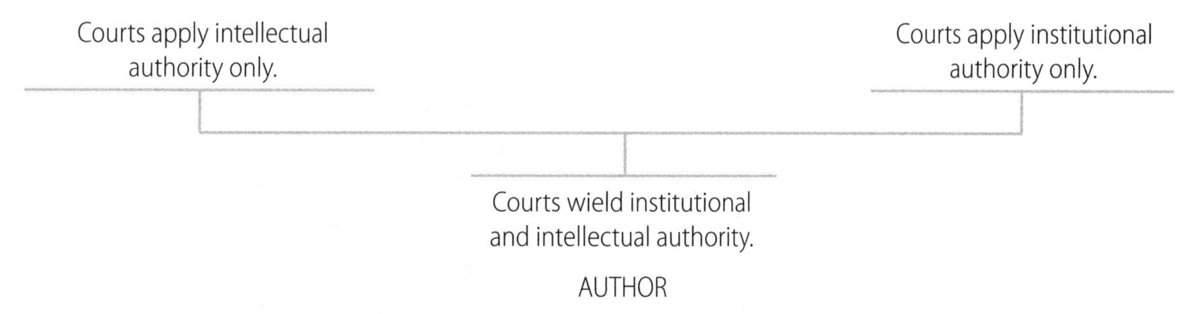

This captures all the major points of the passage and conveys the author's opinion. We could certainly attack the questions successfully with this scale. On the other hand, we could reframe the debate using a new scale concept:

10 *PrepTest 62, Section 1, Passage 4*

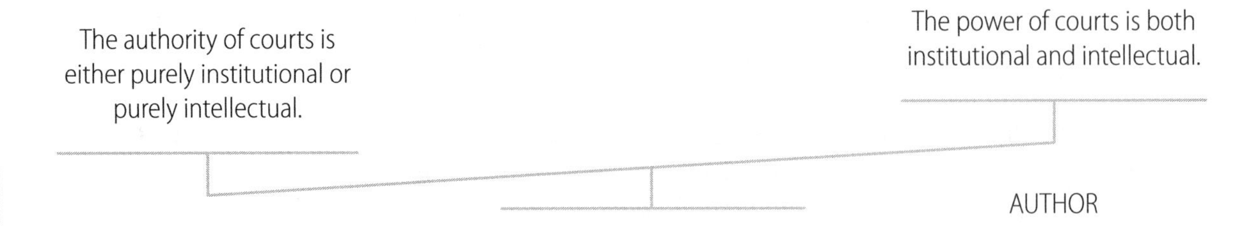

This approach has the advantage of representing the author's opinion on one side of the scale, with all of the one-sided critics on the other. This is not radically different from our first scale—the main difference is that we are now pitting the author against both camps. But is this what is really happening in the passage? Looking back, it seems that the passage spends a lot of time detailing the attacks on intellectual authority. Then, in the last paragraph, the author comes to intellectual authority's defense. Notice that there is no defense of institutional authority—the author acknowledges that it exists, and she even says that "the thrust of [courts'] power is predominantly institutional" (lines 56–57), but she does not seem to feel that that viewpoint needs defending. With this in mind, we can narrow the focus of our scale slightly:

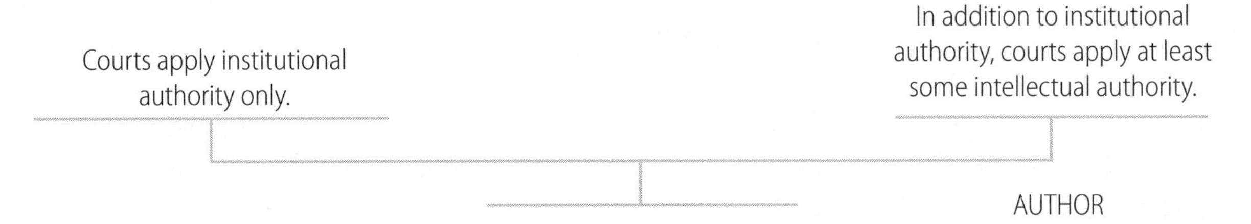

The last scale is the most nuanced of the three. Reading with this level of sophistication requires that you remain flexible and ready to change the scale as the passage and your understanding of it progress. There's a danger in shutting down too quickly and ignoring that a passage has shifted away from how you initially viewed it.

In the case of this passage, would it be a problem if you walked away from your read with either of the first two scales? No. Those first two represent a satisfactory level of comprehension. The truth is that among our teachers we sometimes see debates about what exactly a scale should be. That said, there are some scales that are definitely wrong, and the clearest examples are those in which we haven't correctly identified the author's point of view. In the end, the proof is in the questions: does your comprehension of the passage set you up for success in the questions that follow? If you have a clear sense of where the author stands in relation to the argument, you're going to be in much better shape when you get to the questions. You'll have a chance to try applying this scale to a couple of questions after the drill.

DRILL IT: Author's Opinion

Take a moment to return to the passage excerpts from the last drill starting on page 25. For each passage, identify which side of the scale the author falls on. What parts of the text would you cite to support your decision? If you're having a hard time placing the author on one side, why is that? Does our scale need to be revised?

SOLUTIONS: Author's Opinion

PrepTest 38, Section 3, Passage 1

The author firmly supports Side B. In the opening line, he refers to the idea that North America was unaltered before the Europeans came as a "myth." He then goes on to provide supporting research, saying that "scholarship shows" that forests were altered and that there is "a large body of evidence" for routine burning.

PrepTest 34, Section 1, Passage 3

The author does not support Side B completely, but rather states that Lamarck's hypothesis may eventually be proven correct, citing new research that supports the idea of the inheritance of acquired characteristics. Now that we've identified the author's opinion, we might revise the scale by softening Side B: "Lamarck's hypothesis may be correct in some instances."

PrepTest 51, Section 2, Passage 4

The author supports Side B. Although she says that the prospect of legal reasoning systems has been exciting, she goes on to say that these systems have fallen short of expectations, and ends by saying that these systems are unlikely to be capable of providing independent legal advice in the foreseeable future.

PrepTest 39, Section 3, Passage 1

The author supports Side B. In fact, we really get Side B directly from the author. He tells us that Side A—seeing Mexican murals as formulaic government art—is a mistake, and goes on to explain how the murals are more than that.

PrepTest12, Section 3, Passage 4

This passage is strictly informative, so the author has nothing to take sides about!

Did you notice in the drill above that the author tended to support Side B, that is, the second position described by the passage? Indeed, it's common for LSAT passages to be a complex version of "some people say X, but actually Y is true."

Reading for the Scale vs. Reading through the Scale

So far, we've looked for the scale and then gone back and placed the author on it. Later on, when we start reading full passages, we'll be taking what we read and categorizing it using the scale (e.g., "Is this support for seeing Mexican murals as formulaic government art or as something more?"). It's easy to lump all of these reading goals together as "reading for the scale," but it's actually a bit more complicated than that.

At the beginning of a passage, since you have no idea of what you're about to dive into, you're always working to figure out what the scale actually is. We can call this "reading *for* the scale." It's the great hunt! But what about when you've hit upon what seems like the scale? Now you can shift to "reading *through* the scale," meaning that you're using the scale you've developed to comprehend the rest of the passage.

However, because the author can swoop in late in the passage and change the scale ("But both arguments fail because..."), even if we think we've settled on *the* scale, we have to be able to shift gears from reading *through* the scale back to reading *for* it. This is one of several tensions that successful readers need to navigate skillfully.

TENSIONS

Success on the LSAT doesn't come from always doing the same exact thing. Rather, what is consistent in a top test-taker's form is the ability to shift gears as needed. In Reading Comprehension, that means knowing when to shift from one mode or perspective to another: from reading through the scale back to reading for it, or from reading for thorough comprehension to reading quickly enough to leave adequate time for the questions. The pull of these two possible approaches creates a tension. We'll be sure to point out similar tensions as the book progresses—after all, the first step in navigating these tensions is noticing that they exist!

The Benefits of Reading for the Scale

Later in the book, we will look at how reading for the scale gives you an advantage when it comes to answering particular types of questions, but for now, let's pause for a moment and quickly highlight some of the benefits of this reading stance.

1. Reading with a purpose keeps you engaged.

Imagine that every night for a month you have to attend a high society cocktail party and sit in on the conversations of people you don't know. Probably, you'd find it rather uninteresting or even overwhelming—unless you're actually an undercover detective, trying to figure out who is plotting against whom. How much more exciting to go night after night when you have a mission! Similarly, when you have no reason to read (other than trying to get a good LSAT score), it's difficult to stay engaged. Furthermore, you often have no background knowledge about the topics discussed in LSAT passages, which makes it even easier to keep the passage at arm's length and read passively. Having a perspective—must find that scale!—gives you a purpose and helps you stay engaged with any passage.

2. The method is a natural fit for the structure of the passages.

As mentioned earlier, these passages are designed to test the very same reading and recognition skills that will be required in law school, which, of course, is designed to give you the skills that will be required of you as a lawyer or a judge. Reading for the scale is a great way to jump-start your legal studies, but for now what's important is that *these passages are meant to be read this way.*

3. Most general questions depend on a clear understanding of the central argument in the passage.

If you can divide the passage into the two sides of the scale, you will be ready to answer most questions that pertain to the passage as a whole. Also, general questions will often require you to correctly incorporate and assign the various opinions, especially those of the author.

4. On questions about specific parts of the passage, knowledge of the scale often makes for easy eliminations.

While the devil is in the details, some devils are easy to spot when you have a strong grasp of the passage.

While we won't dig into questions until chapter 5, let's sneak in two quick ones now to see how the scale can help us.

First, let's look at a specific question from the Getting Familiar passage on page 20:

13. The author discusses the example from musicology primarily in order to

(A) distinguish the notion of institutional authority from that of intellectual authority.
(B) give an example of an argument possessing intellectual authority that did not prevail in its own time.
(C) identify an example in which the ascription of musical genius did not withstand the test of time.
(D) illustrate the claim that assessing intellectual authority requires an appeal to institutional authority.
(E) demonstrate that the authority wielded by the arbiters of musical genius is entirely institutional.

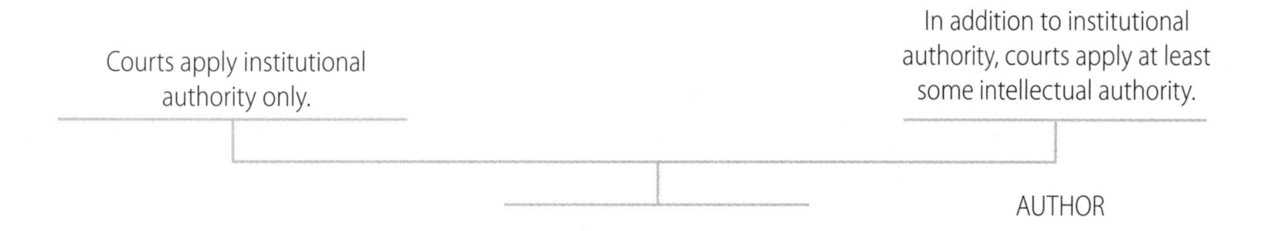

The question is asking us why the author brings up musicology in the middle of an argument about legal systems. (Perhaps you found yourself asking the same thing.) The quick answer to a question of this type is "To support the author's side of the scale." While that may be true, it doesn't do us much good here. None of the answers say that the example is there to defend intellectual authority. Why not? Let's look back at the immediately preceding text: "But, the critics might respond, intellectual authority is only recognized as such because of institutional consensus. For example …." Aha! This portion is actually providing an example to support the critics who are pushing the importance of institutional authority. In fact, the author lets the critics press forward on this point until midway into the last paragraph, when we're told that these critics are missing a "crucial distinction."

So how does having a grasp of the scale help us here? By getting some of the wrong answers out of our way! Is the author trying to make a point about music? No. Answer (C) is out. Answer (E) brings authority into the picture, but only in relation to music. Besides, it supports institutional authority 100%. We can cut that, too. The author accomplishes answer (A) at the very beginning of the passage and doesn't spend any more time explaining the difference. If we had kept our scale at just the words "institutional vs. intellectual," this might be tempting, but as it stands, we can eliminate (A).

By using our knowledge of the scale, we can cut the answer choices down to two. This is when we need to slow down and be more careful. Looking back, we don't see an example of an argument that didn't prevail in its own time, but we can see that our example follows a claim that intellectual authority relies on institutional authority. The correct answer is (D).

The moral of this story is that a little additional time spent understanding the passage up front can save you time on the questions while increasing your accuracy. As you progress, this up-front process should get faster, too. If this way of reading is not easy and comfortable yet, never fear! In the next few chapters, we'll delve deeper into the reading process and give you plenty of opportunity to practice and refine your approach.

Now let's look at a general question from the same passage:

9. Which one of the following most accurately states the main idea of the passage?

(A) Although some argue that the authority of legal systems is purely intellectual, these systems possess a degree of institutional authority due to their ability to enforce acceptance of badly reasoned or socially inappropriate judicial decisions.
(B) Although some argue that the authority of legal systems is purely institutional, these systems are more correctly seen as vehicles for applying the intellectual authority of the law while possessing no coercive power of their own.
(C) Although some argue that the authority of legal systems is purely intellectual, these systems in fact wield institutional authority by virtue of the fact that intellectual authority reduces to institutional authority.
(D) Although some argue that the authority of legal systems is purely institutional, these systems possess a degree of intellectual authority due to their ability to reconsider badly reasoned or socially inappropriate judicial decisions.

(E) Although some argue that the authority of legal systems is purely intellectual, these systems in fact wield exclusively institutional authority in that they possess the power to enforce acceptance of badly reasoned or socially inappropriate judicial decisions.

Notice the structure of the answer choices: each answer starts with "Although," and then gives us an opinion that is attributed to a vague group, "some"; next, an alternative opinion is given. Because this second opinion is not attributed to anyone, it should represent the author's side of the scale. When we think about our scale in these terms, the answer should read (in a general sense):

"Although some think the authority of legal systems is purely institutional, it is at least partly intellectual."

Working with this general understanding, we can quickly eliminate answer choices (A), (C), and (E) using the first part alone. Answers (C) and (E) also incorrectly place the author on the "institutional only" side of the scale. If we had a less precise scale, we might be tempted by (A). After all, it grants that courts might have both kinds of authority. However, if we have identified that the author is primarily concerned with defending the intellectual authority side, we can cross this one out. That's the power of nuance.

Speaking of nuance, now we have to cut out one more answer choices. Both (B) and (D) start the same way—some people go for "institutional only"—and then proceed to defend the notion of intellectual authority. So what's the difference? Answer choice (B) says that the intellectual side is correct and that courts have no coercive power. This places the author strictly on Side A of our old "intellectual vs. institutional" scale. It doesn't allow for both types. Remember, the author ends by acknowledging courts' institutional authority.

This leaves us with (D). Under time pressure, we might notice that this one defends the idea of intellectual authority in a fairly mild way (legal systems have "a degree of intellectual authority") and figure that this answer is the keeper. If we had more time, we could go back to the passage and confirm that, yes, in the final paragraph, the author uses the reconsideration of decisions as support for the notion of intellectual authority.

It's interesting to note that we can move much more quickly through the answer choices by having a clear sense of the scale. We didn't really have to delve into the reasoning in (A), (C), and (E) because we saw that they were going in the wrong direction. Similarly, once we got down to (B) and (D), our scale helped us to focus on the latter halves of the answer choices.

Changing How You Read: Time to Stop Timing

As we discussed in the first chapter, you can improve in this section, but it won't be easy! You've been reading academic texts in a specific way for a long time, perhaps with a great deal of success. Reading for the scale is not something you can simply turn on in a moment, so for now don't worry about timing your work. There will be plenty of time to read to the sweet tick-tocking melody of an analog watch, but what's most important at this early stage of your prep is that you disrupt your habitual reading style and get comfortable reading for the scale. Time-induced panic is your enemy! We'll start working on your timing after we build up your reading process in these first four chapters. Meanwhile, grab some brain fuel, because we are going deeper in the next chapter!

Chapter 3 of Reading Comprehension

PEAR

3

Introducing PEAR

You're hard at work when your boss appears ominously behind you. "When you've got a moment, can I see you up in my office?" he asks, and disappears without another word. You distractedly put the finishing touches on the report you were writing up and then make your way upstairs. On your way, you run through the possibilities; you're certainly not in line for a promotion, so it must be something bad. Was it that sketchy joke you made at the meeting yesterday, or the overly long lunches you've been taking from time to time? Maybe the company isn't doing as well as you thought, and as a junior employee you're the first on the chopping block. By the time you enter the office, you've pretty much convinced yourself that you're losing your job.

Thanks for coming up. Close the door, please, and sit down.

This can't be good. Why can't you talk with the door open?

You went to college, right?

Oh no, he's read your reports and they're full of errors.

What did you major in?

You tell him and he nods vaguely. It doesn't look like you're about to be laid off. What then?

You ever do any public speaking?

Hmm, maybe your performance at the meeting wasn't so bad after all. Are you being groomed for something?

Do you know the university lecture series we sponsor?

Wait, now you're going to lecture at the university? No, you're not an academic. It must be something else. You're going to introduce the speaker or something like that.

Normally, I go, say a few words, and try to stay awake through the lecture. I just don't think I can make it tonight. Do you think you're up for the job?

Hmm, does this mean you're making a good impression or is this just a job no one else will take and this is how you pay your dues?

If you have a good time, you can probably make this a monthly thing. You can fill me in later on what the lecture was about. Of course, you can bill for your time. We want to make a good showing, and I need someone who can show a little class.

Hey, look at that. He thinks you have class. And a few extra hours a week will help pay for that trip you've been planning. Maybe a promotion is in the works after all.

Just try not to say too much. I wanted to throw something at you in that meeting yesterday.

Ah well, one step at a time.

A few hours later, you're sitting in the front row of a crowded lecture hall. You made your best attempt at a short, gracious speech on behalf of the company, and now you're listening as a world-renowned expert on phytoplankton presents her surprising findings about the microscopic world beneath the waves. You want to have a good report for the boss tomorrow, so you're sitting attentively and trying to take it all in. Unfortunately, you sometimes notice that whole chunks of the lecture go by almost without your noticing them. She'll click to the next slide of her presentation and you'll realize you couldn't say one thing about what was on the last one. It's not that you can't understand what she's saying—most of it makes sense—it's that you're having a hard time knowing what to do with the information and it's hard to maintain your interest. After all, your boss is not going to be any more interested in the minute details than you are. After a while, you content yourself to let the lecture sort of wash over you, and you spend most of your energy simply trying to nod, laugh, or look curious in the right places. The next morning you've forgotten almost everything you "learned" about phytoplankton, but you can practically recite your conversation with the boss word-for-word.

So… what made the difference? Why did you take in what the boss said so well and have such trouble at the lecture? Think for a moment about the differences and then compare your thoughts to our list:

1. Familiarity

Your conversation with the boss was in a familiar setting with a person you know and was connected to topics you already knew about. At the lecture, everything was new and unfamiliar. While new experiences can certainly be memorable, they can also be hard to understand, because we have a harder time connecting them to what we already know and we struggle to identify what's important.

2. Engagement

You were actively conversing with your boss. He asked you questions and expected intelligent responses, so more of your mental resources were engaged in the task. Once the lecture began, you were a passive audience member and you were free to let most of your mind wander to other things.

3. Motivation

There was a productive tension in your meeting with the boss. Wondering about the status of your job can really focus your attention, and by actively balancing your concerns about what might happen with careful attention to what was actually happening in the room, you improved your comprehension and retention. During the lecture, your only goal was to have something to say the next day.

Hopefully you see where this is going. The material in LSAT passages is not usually familiar or engaging. You may be motivated to do well on the test, but you may still find large chunks of text passing by without making much of an impression on your brain. There's a big difference between simply reading all the words and actively *engaging* with the material. How can you approach each passage with the kind of focused attention you brought to the meeting with the boss?

Reading for the scale is a big help. Perhaps if you had been able to come up with a scale for the lecture on phytoplankton, you could have gotten a few of the professor's ideas to "stick" to that. But what if you're having a hard time getting deep enough into the passage to find the scale? Besides, you want to get more out of the passage than just the scale. There are a lot of juicy details in there craving your attention!

With that in mind, we'd like to introduce a process we call PEAR. Our goal is to give you some explicit steps to think about to make sure you're as actively engaged with your reading as you were with your boss. Here are the steps:

Pause

Take a moment to stop and process what you've read so far. When you're under pressure to read quickly, it's tempting to cut out the time you would normally spend reflecting on the material. This is a crucial mistake—don't let the passage pass by without you on board! You need to pause and digest what you've read so that you understand sentences in relation to the whole passage, not just to those immediately preceding or following. A natural stopping point is the end of each paragraph, but you might stop more often than that if the text is really rich with ideas or significance for the scale. Early in the passage, you might find yourself pausing briefly after each sentence.

Evaluate

Take stock of what you've just read. Do you have an idea of the scale, or do you need to revise your existing scale? Why is the author presenting this particular content? How does it relate to the larger issue at hand? If an opinion is presented, whose is it? Is there any indication of what the author thinks? Are there any concepts here you're having trouble with? You may need to reread or you may just want to plow ahead and see if the next portion clarifies these ideas for you.

Anticipate

Where do you think the passage is going? Has the author given any hints of what's coming next? This might not seem like a crucial step—after all, you're going to read the whole passage anyway—but think about how you approached the meeting with the boss. You were making predictions the whole time! Most of them weren't right, but that's not the point. Anticipating what was coming next kept you focused and alert throughout the conversation. It's the same way you probably approach any content that's meaningful to you—a chat with a family member, a thrilling book or movie, or even a well-told joke. Your brain is constantly making predictions based on your understanding of the present situation, and that active participation makes the entire experience more engaging, meaningful, and memorable. We're not really suggesting anything new; we're just encouraging you not to turn that part of your brain off during the LSAT!

Reassess

As the passage unfolds, be ready to change your view of the content. With each pause, you want to compare the reality with your predictions in order to improve the accuracy of your next prediction. (Notice that your accuracy got a bit better as the talk with your boss progressed.) The author may take you in directions you didn't anticipate at all, and you want to maintain the flexibility to deal with that. You may need to change your scale or revise your understanding of the content. Maybe after a paragraph or two you realize you've misunderstood a central term ("Oh! Prairie dogs aren't really dogs at all!") and you need to do a bit of rereading with this new perspective. Maybe you realize that two concepts you've separated are really the same thing ("Oh! Diatoms are just a kind of phytoplankton!") and you can simplify your view a bit.

DRILL IT: Anticipate!

At the beginning of a passage, you are most definitely reading *for* the scale. While the scale may become clear early on, you should be open to the strong possibility that your initial concept of the scale will be refined or completely revised as you read on. PEAR reading helps you to maintain this flexible attention.

Below you will find the opening lines of several LSAT passages. Your job here is to evaluate the given text and anticipate what might come next. See if you can imagine a few different paths the subsequent text could take—what different scales we might eventually encounter—and then decide which seems most likely to you.

Be sure to check the solutions after each sample. What matters in this drill is not that you are able to correctly predict where the passage actually goes, but that you become comfortable making reasonable predictions.

1. *PrepTest 29, Section 2, Passage 4*

Until about 1970, anyone who wanted to write a comprehensive history of medieval English law as it actually affected women would have found a dearth of published books or articles concerned with specific legal topics related to women and derived from extensive research in actual court records.

2. *PrepTest 31, Section 4, Passage 1*

By the year 2030, the Earth's population is expected to increase to 10 billion; ideally, all would enjoy standards of living equivalent to those of present-day industrial democracies.

3. *PrepTest 32, Section 2, Passage 4*

Most scientists who study the physiological effects of alcoholic beverages have assumed that wine, like beer or distilled spirits, is a drink whose only active ingredient is alcohol.

4. *PrepTest 19, Section 3, Passage 3*

When the same habitat types (forests, oceans, grasslands, etc.) in regions of different latitudes are compared, it becomes apparent that the overall number of species increases from pole to equator.

5. *PrepTest 7, Section 3, Passage 1*

The labor force is often organized as if workers had no family responsibilities.

SOLUTIONS: Anticipate!

1. *PrepTest 29, Section 2, Passage 4*

As soon as we see those opening words, "Until about 1970," we know that the author is describing something that changed. So, after 1970 there must have been an improvement in the situation—someone started publishing material on the effect of English law on women that satisfied the author's criteria.

But where is the author going to go from here? Perhaps we'll get a survey of these post-1970 works. On the other hand, we may get a rundown of the work published prior to 1970 and its many flaws. The author might choose to select one particular scholar and analyze that person's work. Bravo if you anticipated any of the above, though the actual passage takes a rather unexpected turn. (If you plan to take these LSATs and are worried about knowing too much, feel free to skip the italicized last paragraph of each of these solutions; that's where we reveal the actual main thrust of each passage.)

It turns out there is a key in the word "actually." The author wants to know how the law "actually affected women" and spends the rest of the passage discussing why scholarship has focused only on how the law was intended to affect women. Other than a brief mention at the end that the situation is slowly improving, there is actually no mention of post-1970 work!

2. *PrepTest 31, Section 4, Passage 1*

In this opener, the most important word is "ideally." An *ideal* situation is one that is unlikely to occur because of practical issues. Therefore, we would expect the passage to somehow contradict the idea that 10 billion people will enjoy a high standard of living.

The passage is most likely to go one of two ways from this opening. It could give a rather negative and pessimistic take on the future, giving a bunch of reasons why a high standard of living can't be maintained by such a huge population. But what's more likely (because the LSAT isn't usually so bleak!) is that some kind of plan will be suggested for reaching the "ideal situation."

Indeed, the passage does end up going this second route. The next paragraph actually begins "These estimates are not meant to predict a grim future," opening the door for a long description of a new model of industrial activity that might allow for the realization of the ideal situation. While it's unlikely we ever could have predicted the specific content of this model, we definitely could have expected the general thrust of this passage—from an ideal situation, to the problems with that ideal, to possible solutions to those problems.

3. *PrepTest 32, Section 2, Passage 4*

The first sentence of this passage sets us up pretty strongly for a contradiction. "Most people believe X is true, but actually Y is true" is a very common opening on LSAT RC passages. It's very likely (practically certain) that the next few paragraphs will tell us that scientists have discovered how wine is different from beer and distilled spirits, probably because it has some active ingredients other than alcohol. All of this is implied by the first sentence.

Looking forward, we see that the passage goes just where we thought it would. The second paragraph describes how most alcoholic beverages have deleterious effects on health, but wine has some salutary effects. The third paragraph then lists out these salutary effects in more detail. What a great passage for anticipation. (And it pairs pretty well with antipasto, too!)

4. PrepTest 19, Section 3, Passage 3

This opener is slightly more interesting than the last few in that it doesn't set up any obvious contradiction. While it's possible that the next sentence might go that route (e.g., "For a long time, it was believed this latitudinal gradient was caused by X."), we couldn't anticipate that with any confidence at this stage.

Going on just this sentence, which doesn't yet contain any kind of hypothesis, the most likely follow-up is more of a topical passage, rather than a highly opinionated passage. This kind of subtlety becomes more common in the third and fourth passages of an RC section. We might expect a hypothesis to be described, explored, and possibly questioned, but not fully endorsed or dismissed.

In fact, this particular passage goes on to give us no fewer than four possible theories for why there are more species closer to the equator than at the poles. At the end, it argues that one of these four is more likely than the others. We couldn't have predicted this exact structure, but we certainly could have been ready for something more complex than a simple "Used to believe X, now believe Y" pattern.

5. PrepTest 7, Section 3, Passage 1

Once again, we're looking at some kind of contradiction setup. The word "often" here works a lot like the phrase "most scientists" in example 3; the LSAT loves to argue with the majority! Anytime the author sets up something as the status quo, you can expect that "something" to be refuted!

We can also use a little real-world knowledge here. We know that workers *do* have family responsibilities, so if the labor force is organized in a way that isn't consonant with this, we can guess the passage is going to call it out for being problematic.

The actual passage ends up taking a bit of a left turn after the first paragraph; it is primarily about how the organization of labor affects women, even though the introduction doesn't mention anything about gender. However, no one could see that coming. If we've anticipated that the passage will be a takedown of the current way of organizing labor, that's more than good enough.

Log in to your Student Center for more questions for this drill (look at page 7 for instructions on how to do that). Throughout the book, 📶 means a drill has more questions online.

DOES ACCURACY COUNT?

When checking the solutions in the last drill, you probably found yourself mentally scoring your work against our notes about the actual direction that each passage took. When asked to make a prediction, it's natural to set accuracy as the goal, but here, *reasonability* is more important. That said, even though predicting correctly isn't the main event, the more you do this, the more accurate you will become. There are structural tendencies in LSAT passages that you can learn to recognize. We're not suggesting that you memorize the dozen or so typical structures; instead, let hours of active reading naturally improve your ability to see where passages are likely to go. At the same time, don't lose your innocence! Even the most seasoned LSAT teacher can be surprised by where a passage goes, so stay on your toes.

PEAR in Action

Now that you've had the chance to build up your anticipation muscles, let's take some time to put the entire PEAR process to work. We'll present an LSAT passage in small chunks, with prompts for you to answer. Once you've taken a moment to answer, compare your responses to our thoughts on the right. You're unlikely to see a precise match, and that's fine. The overall goal is to practice pausing and taking stock in a meaningful way.

PrepTest 30, Section 3, Passage 2

Tragic dramas written in Greece during the fifth century B.C. engender considerable scholarly debate over the relative influence of individual autonomy and the power of the gods on the drama's action. One early scholar, B. Snell, argues that Aeschylus, for example, develops in his tragedies a concept of the autonomy of the individual.

Confused already? It's important not to lose the thread early in the passage, so reread if necessary. Once you get what's been said, take a shot at an initial scale. What seems to be at issue so far? (Remember, decide for yourself before looking at our reaction.)

Okay, so we already have a debate. Maybe the scale is "individual autonomy vs. the power of the gods." But then again, we just know that Snell is interested in individual autonomy. That doesn't mean that he doesn't also think the power of the gods is important. Is it going to be a battle of which is more important or is it going to be something more subtle about how they relate?

In these dramas, the protago nists invariably confront a situation that paralyzes them, so that their prior notions about how to behave or think are dissolved. Faced with a decision on which their fate depends, they must reexamine their deepest motives, and then act with determination. They are given only two alternatives, each with grave consequences, and they make their decision only after a tortured internal debate. According to Snell, this decision is "free" and "personal" and such personal autonomy constitutes the central theme in Aeschylean drama, as if the plays were devised to isolate an abstract model of human action. Drawing psychological conclusions from this interpretation, another scholar, Z. Barbu, suggests that "[Aeschylean] drama is proof of the emergence within ancient Greek civilization of the individual as a free agent."

Evaluate: Any sign of the author's opinion yet?
Reassess: Is our initial scale holding up?
Anticipate: Where do you think this is going?

Hmm, nothing at all here about the gods. Snell just seems interested in the characters' internal decision process, and Barbu seems to think that this focus represents a change in Greek civilization. Maybe the gods only play a role in earlier Greek works? But what does the author think? We have "free" and "personal" in quotes, followed by "as if." Maybe the author isn't a fan of this approach?

To A. Rivier, Snell's emphasis on the decision made by the protagonist, with its implicit notions of autonomy and responsibility, misrepresents the role of the superhuman forces at work, forces that give the dramas their truly tragic dimension.

Notice what just happened? How do Rivier's views relate to Snell's? Consider how this would affect the scale and whether you need to revise it.

Ooh, now we have a fight! Rivier thinks Snell is wrong to leave out the gods and doesn't seem to think that the protagonist has autonomy. Our initial scale idea—individual autonomy vs. power of the gods—is looking pretty good. Now we'll probably see why the gods make the dramas so tragic.

These forces are not only external to the protagonist; they are also experienced by the protagonist as an internal compulsion, subjecting him or her to constraint even in what are claimed to be his or her "choices." Hence all that the deliberation does is to make the protagonist aware of the impasse, rather than motivating one choice over another. It is finally a necessity imposed by the deities that generates the decision, so that at a particular moment in the drama necessity dictates a path. Thus, the protagonist does not so much "choose" between two possibilities as "recognize" that there is only one real option.

That was pretty dense! You don't need every detail, but how does it relate to what you've read so far? Can you place it on one side or the other of your scale?

Rivier is on the "power of the gods" side—and this presents more details about how that works. Our prediction seems about right. In general, it seems Rivier is saying that the gods give the protagonist only one way to deal with a hard situation.

A. Lesky, in his discussion of Aeschylus' play *Agamemnon*, disputes both views.

Uh-oh! Now what?

Agamemnon, ruler of Argos, must decide whether to brutally sacrifice his own daughter. A message from the deity Artemis has told him that only the sacrifice will bring a wind to blow his ships to an important battle. Agamemnon is indeed constrained by a divine necessity. But he also deeply desires a victorious battle: "If this sacrifice will loose the winds, it is permitted to desire it fervently," he says. The violence of his passion suggests that Agamemnon chooses a path—chosen by the gods for their own reasons—on the basis of desires that must be condemned by us, because they are his own. In Lesky's view, tragic action is bound by the constant tension between a self and superhuman forces.

What was that example an example of?

It looks like Lesky is in the middle of the scale. Agamemnon does what the gods want, but he does it for his own selfish reasons, so we still get to judge him. So in Lesky's view, our original scale itself is what Greek drama is about. However, we're now at the end and the author hasn't weighed in. Perhaps giving Lesky the last word was a nod in that direction, but we can't know for sure. The author seems content to let us watch the debate unfold.

3

Are you surprised to see a three-part scale? We are too! (And the fact that the author never spoke up was surprising as well.) We're not introducing this here to add a new type of scale to your arsenal. Rather, we want to emphasize that reading for the scale is a process to improve your reading. The goal is not to squeeze every passage into a neat and tidy package. We could have said that the debate here is whether Greek dramas are about both autonomy *and* the power of the gods or just one of them, but that feels a bit forced considering the amount of discussion devoted to the individual ideas. So go ahead and land on the occasional oddball scale as long as your process and final vision of the passage lead you to success on the questions.

What If I Just Don't Get It?

Okay, by now you've had some decent practice building up your understanding of a passage piece by piece. Hopefully, you're comfortable reading for the scale, anticipating what's ahead, and reassessing as you go. But what if you hit a snag? What if there's a part of the passage—a word, a sentence, a whole paragraph—that you just can't seem to understand? Maybe English is not your native language or maybe some of the technical language looks like it's not in English. Here are a few tips for the moments when you find yourself befuddled:

1. Work with the context.

What is happening *around* this confusing portion? Is the author presenting an opinion or defining some complex terminology or articulating one side of the scale? By knowing how this section relates to the rest of the passage, you may be able to get by without actually understanding the pesky details. For example, the first few words of a sentence may make it clear that what follows serves as an example of something mentioned earlier or as a contrast to an initial opinion. In that case, you at least know what side of the scale it goes on—even if you don't quite understand why. In other cases, a little bit of context might actually make the meaning of the part you're missing fairly clear. We'll get some practice looking for context in the next drill.

2. Contain the damage.

While you can often use context clues to piece together a general sense of what a complex detail is doing in the passage, sometimes it's clear that you're missing an important piece of the puzzle. Try rereading the sentence, but if it's still a mystery, admit it. Perhaps the most dangerous move you can make when confused is to pretend that you're not! During a conversation, it might work to pretend you know what's going on, but during the LSAT, honesty is the only policy. Pretending to understand leads you to add in ideas that are not in the passage, and that turns you into a sitting duck for trap answers. Instead, confess your ignorance and put a fat question mark next to the confusing bit of text. When you take a moment to map the passage before moving to the answer choices (we'll discuss how to do this in the next chapter), see if you can piece together a more accurate understanding.

3. Rename complex ideas.

One danger of stumbling on a tricky word or line is that it can throw you off for the rest of the passage. You don't want to say, "I don't know what an organophosphate is, and I can't pronounce it, so I can't understand this paragraph." Keep reading and, if necessary, come up with a shorter nickname for any tough words. Maybe you'll read on and find that the passage is mostly concerned with DNA, which you're told is an organophosphate, and you won't need to deal with the term at all. Or maybe you can simply note that "DNA is an O" and move on from there. Another similar tactic is to assign basic categories to confusing terms. Is the organophosphate a "good guy" or a "bad guy" in this passage?

4. Visualize.

The world's top memory champions are able to memorize mind-numbingly long lists of numbers, or the order of two shuffled decks of cards, and we can learn from their techniques. These mental athletes almost all resort to using mental imagery. This is because our brains are much better at remembering images and stories than words or numbers. Obviously, we're not trying to memorize the LSAT passages that we read, but we should be able to recall the basic gist of what we have read at the end of a paragraph or passage. So, capitalize on what our brains do best and form a mental image of what you're reading. If you learn that DNA is an organophosphate composed of nucleotides, picture the double helix covered in O's and crawling with little N's. As you read about the current state of research on how medieval English law affected women, picture a student looking at a book with a picture of women in medieval gowns standing in front of a judge reading a scroll (add one of those wigs with curls if you like). If it turns out that the laws are intended to suppress women, picture the men writing the laws laughing as women cower. Stick to what the text tells you, but freely add color and don't hesitate to be outrageous—nobody is watching. This all may sound silly, but visualization is actually a powerful tool to improve your retention of the material you read.

5. Identify the problem.

This last one is a study tip. If you find yourself getting stuck on certain content, take note of the problem. What is it that's causing the difficulty? Is it vocabulary, tricky sentence structure, or a certain type of material? For instance, some people are intimidated by science passages, while others have trouble with literary theory. If this is the case, it might be a good idea to spend some extra time reading outside of your comfort zone. We maintain a list of reading recommendations in our Student Center. If your difficulty is with sentence structure, try to look for structural words in these tough sentences that you might lean on (or memorize). If there are specific vocabulary words getting in your way, it's hard to improve on that directly because of the tremendous range of material the LSAT might draw from. You'll be much better off practicing how to use context clues than drilling vocabulary directly. At the same time, the more you read and analyze what you're reading, the more your vocabulary will grow!

With that in mind, let's get some practice working with context clues.

DRILL IT: Read around the Blanks

In this drill, we've taken some pretty complex text from academic texts (cited at the end of the chapter) and replaced some of the words with random Turkish words, with some Danish ones throw in for good measure. As you read, see how much you can figure out about the replaced words by using the context of each short passage. Take some brief notes on your best educated guesses at the meaning of each word, and after each passage check your ideas against the solutions that follow. (By the way, we didn't use literal translations, so don't try to learn Turkish here.)

1. When placed on a surface containing a high concentration of VUNDET, worms become BRUGEN. In the present study, the authors found that this paralysis could be overcome by mutating the gene OMHULLEN the *ser-2* KITAP. They also found another gene with the same effect, suggesting its involvement in the same GUC.[1]

VUNDET:
BRUGEN:
OMHULLEN:
KITAP:
GUC:

2. While critics contend that the views expounded on in *Against Method* are SKREVET to scientific anarchism, its author Paul Feyerabend maintains that his views stem not from a desire to promote scientific OPRINDELSE so much as from a recognition that many of the fundamental DIZGIYE of science—rationality, RASTGELE, and objectivity, for example—are as seriously flawed as the "subjective" paths to truth that scientists are quick to UZANAN.[2]

SKREVET:
OPRINDELSE:
DIZGIYE:
RASTGELE:
UZANAN:

1 *Robinson R. (2013). How the Worm Turns, in Molecular Detail. PLoS Biol 11(4): e1001526. doi:10.1371/journal.pbio.1001526*
2 *This is from our own title: 5lb Book of GRE Practice Problems.*

3. Certainly children, whose CEVIZI arise not only from their OKYANUS impulses, but also from the world in which they have lived from the beginning, will be eager to know the past that is of YÜZME concern to the present. It is a clear gain in the psychology of instruction if history is a socially live thing. The children will be more eager to MUZ knowledge; they will hold it longer, because it is EKMEK.[3]

CEVIZI:
OKYANUS:
YÜZME:
MUZ:
EKMEK:

4. The recent genealogical NEHIR of human populations is a complex BOYAMA formed by individual migration, large-scale population MESAFE, and other RÜYA events. Population genomics YELKENCILIK can provide a window into this recent history, as rare traces of recent shared genetic ancestry are ADA due to long segments of shared genomic material.[4]

NEHIR:
BOYAMA:
MESAFE:
RÜYA:
YELKENCILIK:
ADA:

5. A flowering plant generates many different BÖCEK such as KELEBEK, KARASINEK, and KARGA, each with a particular function and shape. These types of organ are thought to represent variations on a DÜNYEVI underlying developmental program. However, it is unclear how this program is ÖNEMLI under different selective constraints to generate the diversity of forms observed.[5]

BÖCEK:
KELEBEK:
KARASINEK:
KARGA:
DÜNYEVI:
ÖNEMLI:

---

3 *Hartwell, Ernest C. The Teaching of History. Boston, New York, and Chicago: Houghton Mifflin, 1913. Project Gutenberg. Web.*
4 *Ralph P, Coop G. (2013). The Geography of Recent Genetic Ancestry across Europe. PLoS Biol 11(5): e1001555. doi:10.1371/journal.pbio.1001555.*
5 *Sauret-Güeto S, Schiessl K, Bangham A, Sablowski R, Coen E. (2013). JAGGED Controls Arabidopsis Petal Growth and Shape by Interacting with a Divergent Polarity Field. PLoS Biol 11(4): e1001550. doi:10.1371/journal.pbio.1001550.*

SOLUTIONS: Read around the Blanks

1. When placed on a surface containing a high concentration of VUNDET, worms become BRUGEN. In the present study, the authors found that this paralysis could be overcome by mutating the gene OMHULLEN the *ser-2* KITAP. They also found another gene with the same effect, suggesting its involvement in the same GUC.

VUNDET must refer to some sort of chemical that has the effect of making the worms BRUGEN. In the second sentence, we learn that VUNDET causes paralysis, so we'll call VUNDET "bad stuff," and BRUGEN must be a synonym for paralyzed. Meanwhile some gene is doing something called OMHULLEN to the *ser-2* KITAP (whatever that is), and this stops the paralysis. We'll accept that we don't know what all this is, but we know it's something that makes worms move. We don't know what GUC is, but it seems to be about a process or mechanism that's the same as in the last sentence. So we know that there are two genes that affect the *ser-2* KITAP and thereby overcome paralysis.

Actual words: tyramine, immobilized, encoding, receptor, pathway

2. While critics contend that the views expounded on in *Against Method* are SKREVET to scientific anarchism, its author Paul Feyerabend maintains that his views stem not from a desire to promote scientific OPRINDELSE so much as from a recognition that many of the fundamental DIZGIYE of science—rationality, RASTGELE, and objectivity, for example—are as seriously flawed as the "subjective" paths to truth that scientists are quick to UZANAN.

At first, the only thing that jumps out is that SKREVET describes how Feyerabend's views relate to scientific anarchism. From the title, *Against Method,* and the complaints of critics, can we assume that he is being accused of anarchism? If so, then SKREVET would mean "the same as," but if we're wrong it could mean "opposed to." Now, he's defending himself, so if we're right about SKREVET, then OPRINDELSE would mean something similar to "anarchism." "Fundamental" and the subsequent list of lofty ideals tell us that DIZGIYE means rule or principle. RASTGELE is a principle of science—something about being scientific! The last sentence makes it clear that Feyerabend believes the principles of science are flawed, making it a bit clearer that SKREVET means that his ideas are similar to or leading to scientific anarchism. Now what does UZANAN mean? It seems that the fundamentals of science are just as flawed as the subjective ways that scientists are quick to… what? Criticize? That's certainly a common phrase, and from the context, we can guess that we are looking at something scientists don't like, especially since—as we've just been reminded—scientists tend to value objective rather than subjective data. UZANAN must be a synonym for "criticize."

Actual words: tantamount, chaos, tenets, empiricism, repudiate

3. Certainly children, whose CEVIZI arise not only from their OKYANUS impulses, but also from the world in which they have lived from the beginning, will be eager to know the past that is of YÜZME concern to the present. It is a clear gain in the psychology of instruction if history is a socially live thing. The children will be more eager to MUZ knowledge; they will hold it longer, because it is EKMEK.

At first, we don't have enough context to guess what CEVIZI means. Skipping to OKYANUS, the "not only X, but also Y" structure suggests that it's different from "the world in which they have lived from the beginning." So OKYANUS probably means something like "inherent," as opposed to something you learn from the outside world. Going back to CEVIZI, we can guess that it refers to something that arises from inherent impulses; maybe it's something like "desires." Since we've just read about the connection between children and the world they live in, we can infer that the author believes they'll be interested in history that connects to the present, so YÜZME means something like "significant." The middle sentence states that there will be gains in the psychology of instruction. The last sentence appears to be describing what those gains will be. If children's eagerness to MUZ knowledge counts as a gain in the psychology of instruction, MUZ must mean "obtain," since education aims to have children obtain knowledge. From the last sentence, it's clear that if something is EKMEK, you will want to hold it longer, so EKMEK probably means "valuable."

Actual words: interests, innate, dominant, acquire, significant

4. The recent genealogical NEHIR of human populations is a complex BOYAMA formed by individual migration, large-scale population MESAFE, and other RÜYA events. Population genomics YELKENCILIK can provide a window into this recent history, as rare traces of recent shared genetic ancestry are ADA due to long segments of shared genomic material.

All we know about NEHIR so far is that it's something that recently happened with human populations—perhaps a change, growth, or event. BOYAMA is complex, and is the product of migration and other events. Since we're talking about recent population changes, this must mean something like "mixture." (Here, we can also use our awareness that standardized test passages often focus on diversity.) "Large-scale population MESAFE" is in the same category of causes as individual migration, so MESAFE probably means something quite close to "migration." Since the first two elements in the list are about people moving around, RUYA probably means "related to people moving around." Population genomics YELKENCILIK must be some sort of analytical or scientific technique—let's just call it "the technique." The phrase "this recent history" allows us to go back and fill in the meaning of NEHIR: it must be history, since the word "this" signals that "recent history" has already been mentioned in the passage. Now, we know the technique provides a window into recent history because "rare traces of recent shared genetic ancestry are ADA." So those "rare traces" are evidence, and ADA must mean something like "revealed."

Actual words: history, mosaic, movements, demographic, datasets, detectable

5. A flowering plant generates many different BÖCEK such as KELEBEK, KARASINEK, and KARGA, each with a particular function and shape. These types of organ are thought to represent variations on a DÜNYEVI underlying developmental program. However, it is unclear how this program is ÖNEMLI under different selective constraints to generate the diversity of forms observed.

The first sentence gives us no context for the mystery terms other than that they are things generated by a flowering plant. But the phrase "these types of organ" in the second sentence has to refer back to what we just read, so we know BÖCEK means "organs" and the "three K's" are specific types of plant organs. DÜNYEVI describes the underlying program on which these organs are variations, so it must mean something like "uniform." ÖNEMLI is what happens to the program. We know that what happens is that variations on the program produce different organs, so ÖNEMLI must mean something like "altered."

Actual words: organs, leaves, petals, stamens, common, modulated

 For more practice, log in to your Student Center!

Changing How You Read: Focus on Process, Not Questions (for now)

Reading with true comprehension is an incredibly complex task, particularly when facing random LSAT passages with a ticking time clock overhead. Just as with reading for the scale, implementing PEAR does not happen overnight. Go ahead and do some practice LSAT passages, but be very deliberate with your goal. At this point, your focus should be on adjusting how you read to make it fit with the challenges of the LSAT. As we said at the end of the last chapter, don't worry about your timing yet; rather, worry about whether you're actually pausing, evaluating, anticipating, and reassessing. Are you able to remain engaged with the passage? Are you maintaining a healthy inner dialogue about the scale?

Do the questions that follow whatever passage you read, but know that your goal is not to ace the questions but to have the most productive read possible. That said, you should find that the questions become somewhat easier as your grasp of the passages improves.

In the next chapter, we'll finish our work on how to read for the LSAT by looking at what sort of notations on our page will further our ability to read for the scale, and we'll also look at how to seal in what we've gathered during our read so that we're ready to take on the questions with confidence. Important stuff!

Chapter 4 of Reading Comprehension

Annotation and Passage Mapping

Annotation

As a college student, did you develop the habit of highlighting and taking notes in your textbooks? Although it may not have endeared you to the next readers of your books, notating text as you go is a good way to encourage the type of reading that will get you through a rigorous assignment with a strong grasp of the big picture. Let's take some time to review whether what you've been doing—underlining?—can help you to implement PEAR and read for the scale on LSAT passages.

Ideally, you want to walk into the exam with an annotation system that you've practiced and feel very comfortable with. The process of annotating, or marking the passage with notes, signs, or underlines, can help you in several ways. For one, most of us read much more actively and carefully when we take notes. The very act of marking the passage forces us to make decisions about what information is important and how parts of the passage relate to one another.

That said, passage annotation can quickly become counterproductive if you're not careful. We'll present our recommended annotation approaches in a minute, but first a few words of warning. As you work on your own annotation process, keep the following in mind:

1. Annotation is a means to an end.

Never let the *process* of annotation become more important than actually *understanding* the passage. You must remember that the process is meant to serve your understanding of the central argument and its associated parts. The end goal is always comprehension. In fact, many successful annotators never look back at what they've written. Some people are so comfortable with the idea that their notes are for deepening comprehension, not for rereading later, that their notes are usually illegible to them. These students haven't wasted time by taking notes; the annotation process itself has helped them both to grasp the argument's scale and to remember the order in which information was presented in the passage, making it easier to locate the answers to specific questions. Remember, your annotation process should be helping you to understand the central argument and answer the questions effectively. If it isn't, then change it.

2. There is no such thing as correct or incorrect annotation.

Each of us will annotate differently, meaning that each of us will end up with a unique set of notes. The annotation in and of itself is not what's important. Rather, you should evaluate your notation system in terms of how much it helps you to read carefully and retain information. Again, if your annotation process isn't helping you, then change it.

3. Your annotation will be a record of your *evolving* understanding of the passage.

You may mark up the beginning of the passage based on some premature understanding of the central argument, only to discover later that you need to revise that understanding. Does this mean that your initial markings are wrong or need to be erased? No! Leave them as is. Remember, you *should* be guessing and then reassessing your understanding of the passage. That's part of an engaged reading experience. Let your notes be a record of that process.

4. You do not need to annotate to be a strong LSAT reader.

Some strong LSAT test-takers rarely or never put pencil to paper while they read passages. And for those who do regularly mark up passages, often one passage will be densely marked up while another will remain untouched. This makes perfect sense: the difficulty of the passage should dictate the degree to which you annotate. If a passage is difficult, it makes sense to slow down and spend more time gathering meaning. However, if a passage is easy to comprehend, then notation might be a waste of time. Similarly, you might find that you need to do less notating as you become a stronger LSAT reader. Annotation is a tool, and as with every other tool, you want to be deliberate about when you use it.

Keeping these factors in mind, you will want to develop your own annotation style, and you may decide that you don't need to do any annotating. The goal is to come up with a clear and efficient way to identify important information so that you can approach the questions with a strong grasp of the passage. What's the important information? Anything that helps you to identify the sides of the scale and see how the different parts of the passage relate to that scale.

Annotation Styles

With the above ideas in mind, let's consider a few possible annotation styles from which you can assemble your own approach:

1. Underline and mark up continuously as you read.

This is probably the most obvious method, but be careful: very few of us can underline effectively *as we read*. The reason is that it's very difficult to assess the purpose or the importance level of a sentence without knowing what follows it. It's like keeping a diary throughout the day—you may not end up recording the most significant events of the day—versus only filling in an entry at the end of the day when you have had a chance to put everything in perspective.

If you underline as you read, it's easy to end up passively underlining too much, or getting into a rhythm and thinking you have to underline once every few sentences. There is also the danger that you'll get so involved in deciding what to underline that you get distracted from actually processing and comprehending the passage. For these reasons, marking continuously is effective only for a small percentage of test-takers: generally, these are very strong readers who notate selectively.

2. Underline and mark up at the end of each paragraph.

Once you are done with a paragraph, skim back through and decide what is worth taking note of. This fits in very nicely with PEAR—your mark-up process is there to support you as you pause and evaluate what you've read. You certainly don't have to wait for the end of a paragraph—you can stop and underline at any significant pause point—but because a paragraph break typically indicates a shift in the passage, this is a natural point at which to stop and take stock.

3. Take notes on the side.

Writing notes in your own words will take a little more time than underlining will. However, for some people, it's exactly what they need to truly digest what they're reading. Putting ideas into your own words forces you to absorb the text. Furthermore, writing notes allows you to be more specific about the purpose of each part of the passage. If you find that you're walking away confused from passages, definitely try paraphrasing what you're reading on the side (this is a strategy similar to visualizing what you're reading). Don't worry if your notes aren't very neat, because you won't spend much time looking back at them—it's the *act* of taking notes that provides most of the benefits.

4. Focus on structural sign posts.

Every strong reader knows that "however" or "but" indicates a shift in the discussion, and some readers find it useful to circle such key words. "For example" is another important phrase in an LSAT passage that might deserve a circle or some other sort of marking: the passage is telling us the role the next bit of the passage plays—supporting what comes before the "for example"—so make sure you know what you're reading an example of. Similarly, some readers like to note the members of each side of a debate. And what is the most important opinion to note? The author's, of course! Make sure to mark it with an "AO" so you can find it again quickly.

RHETORICAL MARKERS

While you don't need to memorize the following list, it is useful to familiarize yourself with the different kinds of structural language that are likely to appear in RC passages.

The words below are your best friends when it comes to getting a feel for when the passage makes an important claim, supports a claim, continues the same trajectory, or alters course.

Shift in view: but, yet, however, nevertheless, rather, instead
These markers normally come after a claim has been made and before an important point the author wants to make. The first but/yet/however of the passage frequently sets up the scale or introduces the main point.

Support: first, second, moreover, furthermore, also, additionally, finally
When you see one of these markers, a series of points is being made to support some larger contention. You can speed up a bit on this portion of the reading, knowing that the author will be staying on the same trajectory, but make sure you know what the overarching point is.

Supporting example: for example, because, since, after all
These will come after a general point and introduce a specific illustration of that point. Any time you see this language, you should stop to make sure you know the general point this specific evidence is intended to illustrate.

Author's view: conveniently, fortunately, regretfully, correctly
Adverbs such as these very subtly express the author's opinion or attitude. They are easy to miss while you're reading unless you're very attuned to noticing tone, but in some cases these words are the only textual justification we have on questions related to the author's opinion.

Concession: despite, although, while, granted, of course, naturally, true, indeed
These generally mean that the author is conceding a point to the opposing side of the argument. The most important part of this sentence will be the second half: the author will acknowledge the merit of the opposing view before telling us what she ***really*** wants to say. These qualified statements also give us a sense of the nuances of the author's opinion, helping us to avoid answers that are too extreme.

4

Reading for Content vs. Reading for Structure

Whatever annotation style you use, it should support you in your attempts to build the scale and understand the support for both sides. However, when you are trying to decide which parts of the passage are important, you may find yourself pulled in two different directions. Some material seems to indicate the author's purpose and direction, while other material presents details that may prove to be important. Where do we focus our attention, on *what* is being said or on *how* the passage is structured? What do we mark up? Welcome to the tension of annotation! For instance, take a look at this sample and see what you think is important:

> The advantages of Ozawa's plan were evident. Providing students and parents with a clear schedule of assignments in advance eliminated many of the existing concerns about fairness, prevented distracting negotiations over due dates, and enabled students to develop a sense of responsibility for their work over a longer term. However, by preventing the individual teacher from responding flexibly to student needs by revising, extending, or eliminating assignments to reflect the progress made in class, the plan undermined one of the primary stated goals of the school.

One reader might focus immediately on structural language that gives us a sense of the author's opinion:

> The advantages of Ozawa's plan were evident. Providing students and parents with a clear schedule of assignments in advance eliminated many of the existing concerns about fairness, prevented distracting negotiations over due dates, and enabled students to develop a sense of responsibility for their work over a longer term. However, by preventing the individual teacher from responding flexibly to student needs by revising, extending, or eliminating assignments to reflect the progress made in class, the plan undermined one of the primary stated goals of the school.

The underlined portions definitely seem important. Ozawa's plan looked good on paper, but apparently it went against the school's mission, and the author doesn't seem to approve. But doesn't this omit some important details? Don't we need to know *what* the plan was and *why* it undermined the school's goal? Another reader might produce this:

> The advantages of Ozawa's plan were evident. Providing students and parents with a clear schedule of assignments in advance eliminated many of the existing concerns about fairness, prevented distracting negotiations over due dates, and enabled students to develop a sense of responsibility for their work over a longer term. However, by preventing the individual teacher from responding flexibly to student needs by revising, extending, or eliminating assignments to reflect the progress made in class, the plan undermined one of the primary stated goals of the school.

Now we have Ozawa's plan, and the objection to it. This might be good, as we have something for both sides of a potential scale. Should we schedule all the assignments in advance? The author says no.

Here's a way someone might use notation to capture both the central content and the passage's structure:

O's plan: advance sched. = good

> The advantages of Ozawa's plan were evident. Providing students and parents with a clear schedule of assignments in advance eliminated many of the existing concerns about fairness, prevented distracting negotiations over due dates, and enabled students to develop a sense of responsibility for their work over a longer term. However, by preventing the individual teacher from responding flexibly to student needs by revising, extending, or eliminating assignments to reflect the progress made in class, the plan undermined one of the primary stated goals of the school.

Problem! Too rigid.

The paraphrasing notes help the reader to "own" the content, and the circle around "however" highlights the turn in subject.

Developing Your Own Annotation Style

You should have noticed by now that we're not advocating one specific annotation style over another. What we want is for you to evaluate what sort of notations you tend to make in terms of whether that system is useful for what the LSAT demands of you. Students often find that changing their annotation style is part of a radical improvement on LSAT Reading Comprehension, so take this seriously. Are you over-annotating? Are you not annotating enough?

To help you evaluate your style, below is an LSAT passage for you to read and annotate (or not) as you normally would. Somehow put aside the feeling that there's a team of LSAT teachers watching your every notation and instead slip back into whatever normal annotation habits you have.

PrepTest 12, Section 3, Passage 3

Although the legal systems of England and the United States are superficially similar, they differ profoundly in their approaches to and uses of legal reasons: substantive reasons are more common
(5) than formal reasons in the United States, whereas in England the reverse is true. This distinction reflects a difference in the visions of law that prevail in the two countries. In England the law has traditionally been viewed as a system of rules; the
(10) United States favors a vision of law as an outward expression of the community's sense of right and justice.

Substantive reasons, as applied to law, are based on moral, economic, political, and other
(15) considerations. These reasons are found both "in the law" and "outside the law," so to speak.

Substantive reasons inform the content of a large part of the law: constitutions, statutes, contracts verdicts, and the like. Consider, for example, a
(20) statute providing that "no vehicles shall be taken into public parks." Suppose that no specific rationales or purposes were explicitly written into this statute, but that it was clear (from its legislative history) that the substantive purpose of the statute
(25) was to ensure quiet and safety in the park. Now suppose that a veterans' group mounts a World War

II jeep (in running order but without a battery) as a war memorial on a concrete slab in the park, and charges are brought against its members. Most (30) judges in the United States would find the defendants not guilty because what they did had no adverse effect on park quiet and safety.

Formal reasons are different in that they frequently prevent substantive reasons from coming (35) into play, even when substantive reasons are explicitly incorporated into the law at hand. For example, when a document fails to comply with stipulated requirements, the court may render the document legally ineffective. A will requiring (40) written witness may be declared null and void and, therefore, unenforceable for the formal reason that the requirement was not observed. Once the legal rule—that a will is invalid for lack of proper witnessing—has been clearly established, and the (45) legality of the rule is not in question, application of that rule precludes from consideration substantive arguments in favor of the will's validity or enforcement.

Legal scholars in England and the United States (50) have long bemused themselves with extreme examples of formal and substantive reasoning. On the one hand, formal reasoning in England has led to wooden interpretations of statutes and an unwillingness to develop the common law through (55) judicial activism. On the other hand, freewheeling substantive reasoning in the United States has resulted in statutory interpretations so liberal that the texts of some statutes have been ignored altogether.

If you did notate the passage, take a moment to review what you did. Does it reflect an effort to read for the scale? Were those markings helpful or just force of habit?

Take a look at how a hypothetical reader might have notated this passage. Because underlining is the most common annotation system, we've intentionally chosen to demonstrate some other techniques. We're not presenting this in order for you to grade your own style against it; rather, this is offered as a small buffet of possible annotation "moves" that you might want to try out on future passages. On the right side of the page are some notes explaining and discussing the notations.

PrepTest 12, Section 3, Passage 3

Although the legal systems of England and the United States are superficially similar, they differ profoundly in their approaches to and uses of legal reasons: substantive reasons are more common (5) than formal reasons in the United States, whereas in England the reverse is true. This distinction reflects a difference in the visions of law that prevail in the two countries. In England the law has traditionally been viewed as a system of rules; the (10) United States favors a vision of law as an outward expression of the community's sense of right and justice.

Sub. (US) vs Formal (UK)

Defining the terms (and countries) is a smart move with unfamiliar ideas.

Substantive reasons, as applied to law, are based on moral, economic, political, and other (15) considerations. These reasons are found both "in the law" and "outside the law," so to speak.

Sub. = other considerations

Substantive reasons inform the content of a large part of the law: constitutions, statutes, contracts verdicts, and the like. Consider, for example, a (20) statute providing that "no vehicles shall be taken into public parks." Suppose that no specific rationales or purposes were explicitly written into this statute, but that it was clear (from its legislative history) that the substantive purpose of the statute (25) was to ensure quiet and safety in the park. Now suppose that a veterans' group mounts a World War II jeep (in running order but without a battery) as a war memorial on a concrete slab in the park, and charges are brought against its members. Most (30) judges in the United States would find the defendants not guilty because what they did had no adverse effect on park quiet and safety.

Sub. Exmpl.

Labeling this section as an example makes its role clear.

Spirit of law, ~~letter~~

The example showed what substantive reasoning means, so this reader paraphrased it to aid retention.

Formal reasons are different in that they frequently prevent substantive reasons from coming (35) into play, even when substantive reasons are explicitly incorporated into the law at hand. For example, when a document fails to comply with stipulated requirements, the court may render the document legally ineffective. A will requiring (40) written witness may be declared null and void and, therefore, unenforceable for the formal reason that

Frml block sub?

Frml exmpl

the requirement was not observed. Once the legal
rule—that a will is invalid for lack of proper
witnessing—has been clearly established, and the
(45) legality of the rule is not in question, application of
that rule precludes from consideration substantive
arguments in favor of the will's validity or
enforcement.

Legal scholars in England and the United States
(50) have long bemused themselves with extreme
examples of formal and substantive reasoning. On
the one hand, formal reasoning in England has led
to wooden interpretations of statutes and an
unwillingness to develop the common law through
(55) judicial activism. On the other hand, freewheeling
substantive reasoning in the United States has
resulted in statutory interpretations so liberal that
the texts of some statutes have been ignored
altogether.

??

The reader was unclear what exactly was meant here. Noting confusion is a way of "containing the damage," and is far better than adding ideas that aren't actually present in the passage.

Extreme effects of both

Passage Mapping

Let's fast forward to test day: it's section five of your real live actual LSAT! Your proctor keeps sneezing and the guy next to you has the hiccups, but you're staying in the zone. You crack open the first page of that final section and find RC! The first two passages go smoothly, and you're feeling pretty confident until you turn the page and dive into a passage about literary theory and its relationship to the phenomenology of epistemology. But you are not going to be taken down by a lit theory passage! You turn up the dial on your PEAR reading, start taking short notes to help you digest the unfamiliar material, and are able to make slow but steady progress through the many twists of the passage. You finally make it through that trial by fire, and every fiber of your law-school-loving body and soul urges you to rush into the questions so you can get to that last passage.

Can you use your PEAR anticipation skills to guess what's coming next?

As you probably anticipated, we're now going to tell you that you shouldn't launch immediately into the questions: Instead, take 10 seconds or so to gather your thoughts and create a **passage map**. A passage map is a mental summary of what happened in each part of the passage. Like The Big Pause in our Logic Games strategy, the little moment you take to create a passage map helps you to capitalize on your work by pulling any loose threads into a cohesive vision of what you just read.

To be clear, creating a passage map is not a reread, it's not a skim, and it's not something that requires you to actually write or draw anything. It is a quick internal process of reminding yourself what major point was made in each paragraph and what role each paragraph plays in the passage. When the test-day pressure is on, it's easy to fall prey to panic, and having a routine that includes stopping and thinking can be a score-saver. This brief pause can help you to avoid charging into the questions with an incomplete picture of what you just read. A passage map will strengthen your performance on general questions, and it will make it much easier for you to remember where in the passage to look when you need specific details.

Take another look at the passage we just read and create a passage map. What was the role of each paragraph and what was discussed? When you're done, take a look at what we think the passage map might look like.

PrepTest 12, Section 3, Passage 3

Although the legal systems of England and the United States are superficially similar, they differ prof... al reas... han form... ngland the ... rence in th... tries.

Introduction of two approaches.
Substantive bigger in the U.S.; formal bigger in England.

In England the law has traditionally been viewed as a system of rules; the United States favors a vision of law as an outward expression of the community's sense of right and justice.

Substantive reasons, as applied to law, are based on moral, economic, political, and other considerations. These reasons are found both "in the law" and "outside the law," so to speak.

Substantive reasons inform the content of a large part of the law: constitutions, statutes, contracts verdicts, and the l... g that "no ... pose that ... tly writ... n its legis... the statu... Now

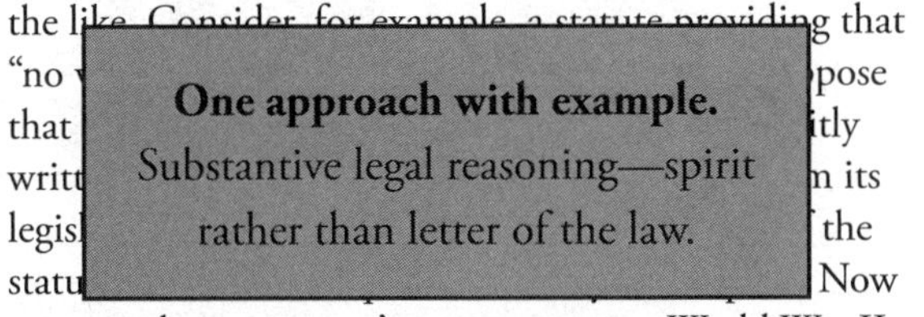

suppose that a veterans' group mounts a World War II jeep (in running order but without a battery) as a war memorial on a concrete slab in the park, and charges are brought against its members. Most judges in the United States would find the defendants not guilty because what they did had no adverse effect on park quiet and safety.

Formal reasons are different in that they frequently prevent substantive reasons from coming into play, even when substantive reasons are explicitly incorporated into the law at hand. For example, when a document fails to con... t may render... quiring writte... d, theref... at the requir... le—

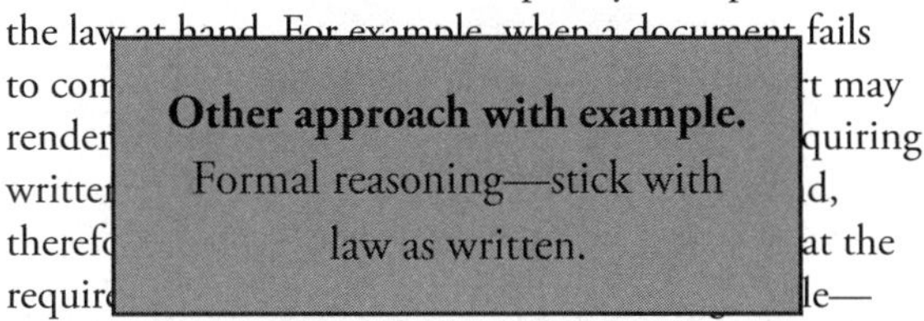

that a will is invalid for lack of proper witnessing—has been clearly established, and the legality of the rule is not in question, application of that rule precludes from consideration substantive arguments in favor of the will's validity or enforcement.

Legal scholars in England and the United States have long bemused themselves with extreme examples of fo... hand... h inte... deve... On ... reasoning in the United States has resulted in statutory interpretations so liberal that the texts of some statutes have been ignored altogether.

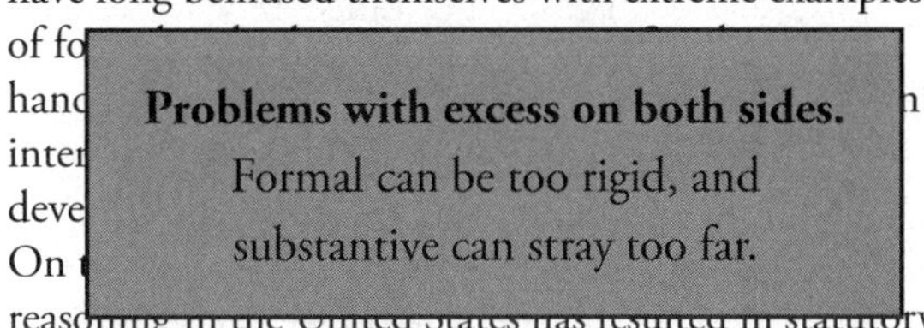

As usual, don't worry if your wording was different. Simply be sure you were able to identify the content of each section and describe that content's relationship to the central scale (which you probably agree is formal vs. substantive legal reasoning).

DRILL IT: Annotation and Passage Mapping

Let's practice the two strategies we've discussed in this chapter. Read each passage (untimed) and experiment with your annotation style as you go. At the end of each passage, force yourself to make a passage map. The passage map is normally a mental understanding, like the scale, but for this drill, actually write down the content of your passage map and check it against the solutions.

PrepTest 24, Section 1, Passage 3

In recent years, scholars have begun to use social science tools to analyze court opinions. These scholars have justifiably criticized traditional legal research for its focus on a few cases that may not be representative (5) and its fascination with arcane matters that do not affect real people with real legal problems. Zirkel and Schoenfeld, for example, have championed the application of social science tools to the analysis of case law surrounding discrimination against women in (10) higher education employment. Their studies have demonstrated how these social science tools may be used to serve the interests of scholars, lawyers, and prospective plaintiffs as well. However, their enthusiasm for the "outcomes analysis" technique (15) seems misguided.

Of fundamental concern is the outcomes analysts' assumption that simply counting the number of successful and unsuccessful plaintiffs will be useful to prospective plaintiffs. Although the odds are clearly (20) against the plaintiff in sex discrimination cases, plaintiffs who believe that their cause is just and that they will prevail are not swayed by such evidence. In addition, because lawsuits are so different in the details of the case, in the quality of the evidence the plaintiff (25) presents, and in the attitude of the judge toward academic plaintiffs, giving prospective plaintiffs statistics about overall outcomes without analyzing the reason for these outcomes is of marginal assistance. Outcomes analysis, for example, ignores the fact that in (30) certain academic sex discrimination cases—those involving serious procedural violations or incriminating evidence in the form of written admissions of discriminatory practices—plaintiffs are much more likely to prevail.

(35) Two different approaches offer more useful applications of social science tools in analyzing sex discrimination cases. One is a process called "policy capturing," in which the researcher reads each opinion; identifies variables discussed in the opinion, such as (40) the regularity of employer evaluations of the plaintiff's performance, training of evaluators, and the kind of evaluation instrument used; and then uses multivariate analysis to determine whether these variables predict the outcome of the lawsuit. The advantage of

(45) policy-capturing research is that it attempts to explain the reason for the outcome, rather than simply reporting the outcome, and identifies factors that contribute to a plaintiff's success or failure. Taking a slightly different approach, other scholars have adopted a technique that (50) requires reading complete transcripts of all sex discrimination cases litigated during a certain time period to identify variables such as the nature of the allegedly illegal conduct, the consequences for employers, and the nature of the remedy, as well as the (55) factors that contributed to the verdict and the kind of evidence necessary for the plaintiff to prevail. While the findings of these studies are limited to the period covered, they assist potential plaintiffs and defendants in assessing their cases.

PrepTest 50, Section 1, Passage 3

As the twentieth century draws to a close, we are learning to see the extent to which accounts and definitions of cultures are influenced by human biases and purposes, benevolent in what they include, (5) incorporate, and validate, less so in what they exclude and demote. A number of recent studies have argued that the anxieties and agendas of the present exert an extraordinary influence on the national identities we construct from the cultural past. For example, Greek (10) civilization was known originally to have had roots in Egyptian and various other African and Eastern cultures, but some current scholars charge that its identity was revised during the course of the nineteenth century to support an image of European (15) cultural dominance—its African and other cultural influences either actively purged or hidden from view by European scholars. Because ancient Greek writers themselves openly acknowledged their culture's hybrid past, nineteenth-century European (20) commentators habitually passed over these acknowledgments without comment.

Another example is the use of "tradition" to determine national identity. Images of European authority over other cultures were shaped and (25) reinforced during the nineteenth century, through the manufacture and reinterpretation of rituals, ceremonies, and traditions. At a time when many of the institutions that had helped maintain imperial societies were beginning to recede in influence, and (30) when the pressures of administering numerous overseas territories and large new domestic constituencies mounted, the ruling elites of Europe felt the clear need to project their power backward in time, giving it a legitimacy that only longevity could (35) impart. Thus in 1876, Queen Victoria of England was declared empress of India and was celebrated in numerous "traditional" jamborees, as if her rule were not mainly a matter of recent edict but of age-old custom.

(40) Similar constructions have also been made by native cultures about their precolonial past, as in the case of Algeria during its war of independence from France, when decolonization encouraged Algerians to create idealized images of what they believed their (45) culture to have been prior to French occupation. This strategy is at work in what many revolutionary poets say and write during wars of independence elsewhere, giving their adherents something to revive and admire.

(50) Though for the most part colonized societies have won their independence, in many cultures the imperial attitudes of uniqueness and superiority underlying colonial conquest remain. There is in all nationally defined cultures an aspiration to (55) sovereignty and dominance that expresses itself in definitions of cultural identity. At the same time, paradoxically, we have never been as aware as we are now of the fact that historical and cultural experiences partake of many social and cultural (60) domains and even cross national boundaries, despite the claims to the contrary made by purveyors of nationalist dogma. Far from being unitary, monolithic, or autonomous, cultures actually include more "foreign" elements than (65) they consciously exclude.

SOLUTIONS: Annotation and Passage Mapping

Since many annotation styles can be used successfully (including not doing anything), a "solution" is impossible. We are presenting one possible set of annotations for these passages, but regardless of the annotation style you used, hopefully you were able to develop a passage map similar to what follows. If you notice significant differences, reread the passage to see where your comprehension might have faltered.

PrepTest 24, Section 1, Passage 3

In recent years, scholars have begun to use social
science tools to analyze court opinions. These scholars
have justifiably criticized traditional legal research for
its focus on a few cases that may not be representative
(5) and its fascination with arcane matters that do not
affect real people with real legal problems. Zirkel and
Schoenfeld, for example, have championed the
application of social science tools to the analysis of
case law surrounding discrimination against women in
(10) higher education employment. Their studies have
demonstrated how these social science tools may be
used to serve the interests of scholars, lawyers, and
prospective plaintiffs as well. However, their
enthusiasm for the "outcomes analysis" technique
(15) seems misguided.

THESIS ☆ ☆

Of fundamental concern is the outcomes analysts'
assumption that simply counting the number of
successful and unsuccessful plaintiffs will be useful to
prospective plaintiffs. Although the odds are clearly
(20) against the plaintiff in sex discrimination cases,
plaintiffs who believe that their cause is just and that
they will prevail are not swayed by such evidence. In
addition, because lawsuits are so different in the details
of the case, in the quality of the evidence the plaintiff
(25) presents, and in the attitude of the judge toward
academic plaintiffs, giving prospective plaintiffs
statistics about overall outcomes without analyzing the
reason for these outcomes is of marginal assistance.
Outcomes analysis, for example, ignores the fact that in
(30) certain academic sex discrimination cases—those
involving serious procedural violations or
incriminating evidence in the form of written
admissions of discriminatory practices—plaintiffs are
much more likely to prevail.

Problems:
① Plaintiffs won't be convinced
② ignores reason for outcomes
↓ e.g.

(35) Two different approaches offer more useful applications of social science tools in analyzing sex discrimination cases. One is a process called "policy capturing," in which the researcher reads each opinion; identifies variables discussed in the opinion, such as
(40) the regularity of employer evaluations of the plaintiff 's performance, training of evaluators, and the kind of evaluation instrument used; and then uses multivariate analysis to determine whether these variables predict the outcome of the lawsuit. The advantage of
(45) policy-capturing research is that it attempts to explain the reason for the outcome, rather than simply reporting the outcome, and identifies factors that contribute to a plaintiff 's success or failure. Taking a slightly different approach, other scholars have adopted a technique that
(50) requires reading complete transcripts of all sex discrimination cases litigated during a certain time period to identify variables such as the nature of the allegedly illegal conduct, the consequences for employers, and the nature of the remedy, as well as the
(55) factors that contributed to the verdict and the kind of evidence necessary for the plaintiff to prevail. While the findings of these studies are limited to the period covered, they assist potential plaintiffs and defendants in assessing their cases.

2 better approaches!

① policy capturing

explains reasons

② reading complete transcripts

limited, but helpful

P1: Introduction and approval of general goal; criticism of specific technique. Though social science tools may be useful, Z and S's "outcome analysis" isn't great for analyzing sex discrimination cases.

P2: Flaws of technique. Plaintiffs won't be convinced, and it ignores the reasons for outcomes.

P3: Two more useful approaches. Policy capturing and reading complete transcripts are better methods.

PrepTest 50, Section 1, Passage 3

As the twentieth century draws to a close, we are
learning to see the extent to which accounts and
definitions of cultures are influenced by human biases
and purposes, benevolent in what they include,
(5) incorporate, and validate, less so in what they exclude
and demote. A number of recent studies have argued
that the anxieties and agendas of the present exert an
extraordinary influence on the national identities we
construct from the cultural past. For example, Greek
(10) civilization was known originally to have had roots in
Egyptian and various other African and Eastern
cultures, but some current scholars charge that its
identity was revised during the course of the
nineteenth century to support an image of European
(15) cultural dominance—its African and other cultural
influences either actively purged or hidden from view
by European scholars. Because ancient Greek writers
themselves openly acknowledged their culture's
hybrid past, nineteenth-century European
(20) commentators habitually passed over these
acknowledgments without comment.

Present views warp past, sense of ID

Ex: Eurocentric view of Greeks

Another example is the use of "tradition" to
determine national identity. Images of European
authority over other cultures were shaped and
(25) reinforced during the nineteenth century, through the
manufacture and reinterpretation of rituals,
ceremonies, and traditions. At a time when many of
the institutions that had helped maintain imperial
societies were beginning to recede in influence, and
(30) when the pressures of administering numerous
overseas territories and large new domestic
constituencies mounted, the ruling elites of Europe
felt the clear need to project their power backward in
time, giving it a legitimacy that only longevity could
(35) impart. Thus in 1876, Queen Victoria of England was
declared empress of India and was celebrated in
numerous "traditional" jamborees, as if her rule were
not mainly a matter of recent edict but of age-old
custom.

Ex: "Tradition"

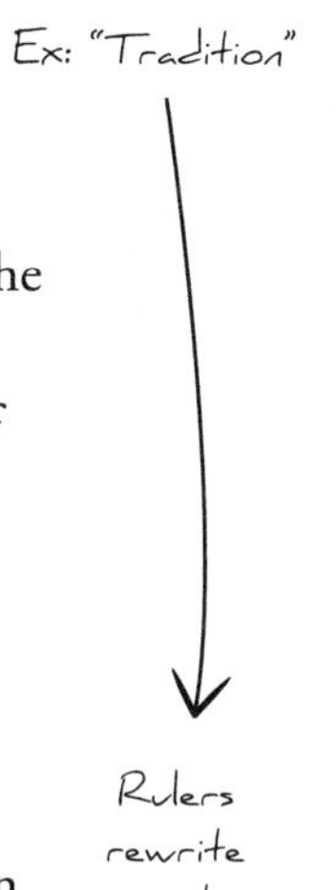

Rulers rewrite past

(40) Similar constructions have also been made by
native cultures about their precolonial past, as in the

Native cultures do it, too

4

case of Algeria during its war of independence from
France, when decolonization encouraged Algerians to
create idealized images of what they believed their
(45) culture to have been prior to French occupation. This
strategy is at work in what many revolutionary poets
say and write during wars of independence elsewhere,
giving their adherents something to revive and
admire.

Idealize past

(50) Though for the most part colonized societies
have won their independence, in many cultures the
imperial attitudes of uniqueness and superiority
underlying colonial conquest remain. There is in all
nationally defined cultures an aspiration to
(55) sovereignty and dominance that expresses itself in
definitions of cultural identity. At the same time,
paradoxically, we have never been as aware as we
are now of the fact that historical and cultural
experiences partake of many social and cultural
(60) domains and even cross national boundaries,
despite the claims to the contrary made by
purveyors of nationalist dogma. Far from being
unitary, monolithic, or autonomous, cultures
actually include more "foreign" elements than
(65) they consciously exclude.

Natl. cult. prone to dominant stance

But cultures are a mix!

(Main point?)

P1: Introduction of phenomenon with example. People's current biases affect how they interpret the past to construct national identities.

P2: Another example of the phenomenon. Imperial European powers used "traditions" to project power backward in time.

P3: Phenomenon extended. This isn't just about those in power: native cultures also construct idealized images of their precolonial past.

P4: Conclusion/synthesis. Cultures are not monolithic, and usually include many foreign elements.

Changing How You Read: *Really* Passage Mapping

Hopefully, you are now convinced that the passage map is a great tool. However, it's just as likely that you're going to not use it! Why? Because you've been reading academic texts for a long time without such a routine. Furthermore, plenty of LSAT passages are easy enough that when you do stop to make a passage map, it will seem too easy and not worth your time. Ignoring this passage map idea is fine if you're already scoring well enough on your RC sections. But if you're reading this book, clearly you are looking to improve the situation! Force yourself to use this strategy for a while to determine if it's helpful. At first, it might be awkward and formal-seeming, but work past that until you're comfortable enough that when you finish reading a passage, you could narrate its structure aloud. You might find that creating a passage map is almost automatic with easier passages, and that's great, but it's on the hard-to-map passages that this strategy really pays dividends. When things get tough, taking the time to build a mental passage map can help you to avoid a panicked, half-blind rush into the questions. It can also support your process of anticipating correct answers and avoiding traps. More on that in the next chapter...

Chapter 5 of

Reading Comprehension

Part 2: **Master the Questions**

Questions

The Search for Correct Answers

Okay, you've read the passage, you understand the argument, and you understand how everything else in the passage relates to that argument. Now what?

Now comes the payoff! You don't get points for reading; you get points for answering questions correctly. While a strong initial understanding of the passage will certainly set you up for success, the questions aren't going to give up the right answers without a fight. The question stems are often trickily worded, and it's sometimes hard to spot the little differences that make one answer right and the others wrong. On top of that, the clock is ticking and you have to work the tension between answering from your existing understanding of the passage and looking back to improve that understanding. Here are some opening tips for tackling the questions effectively:

1. Recognize the common characteristics of correct answers.

Exactly what skills is the LSAT testing? The test-taker can have an advantage if he or she knows what types of mental processes are tested and what types are not. This chapter will help you to identify and drill the key skills involved in producing correct answers to LSAT Reading Comprehension questions.

2. Recognize the common characteristics of incorrect answer choices.

Imagine that the people who write the LSAT start off each question with five *correct* answer choices. One by one, they introduce flaws into four of the choices. What types of flaws do they introduce? What can you look out for that will tip you off to a wrong answer? As we mentioned above, right answers are not always straightforward. The only way to get a high percentage of questions correct is to be able to confidently eliminate incorrect choices. We will discuss this at length in the next chapter.

3. Know where to look for support.

The most general questions will be all about the scale and passage map and may not require you to look back at the passage at all. On more specific questions, it can be dangerous to rely on memory, since there are so many trap answers out there. You will generally want to go back to the passage and find specific support for your answers. Having a strong mental map of the passage will make this process much faster and easier.

4. Use a consistent approach.

If you read passages in a passive, aimless manner and choose answers on vague "gut feelings," you are asking way too much of your intuition! You may be a strong enough reader to survive the RC section with this approach, but you are not giving yourself a real chance to improve. A systematic approach gives you a way to *organize* the various thought processes you must go through in order to successfully attack a question. Furthermore, a consistent process will help you to identify your flaws so that you can correct them. After chapter 6, we'll take a moment to check in on your RC progress. If you find that there are elements of the process that you struggle with, you will want to spend some time drilling down and honing your approach.

Question Types

A great deal of your success on LSAT Reading Comprehension questions will come from finding support for your chosen answer. We can divide the questions into three general categories—Identification, Inference, and Synthesis—based on the kind of support required.

Identification

According to the passage, Kolchin's study asserts that which one of the following was true of Russian nobles during the nineteenth century?[1]

According to the passage, King differed from most transcendentalists in that he[2]

According to the passage, Title VII of the 1964 Civil Rights Act differs from Executive Order 11,246 in that Title VII[3]

Identification questions ask you about something that is specifically stated in the passage. About 1–2 questions per passage depend solely on your ability to identify and understand the meaning of a specific piece of text. These questions will tend to involve content that is difficult to find or answers that you might not expect. For instance, the question might be phrased in such a way that you're unsure which part of the passage to refer to, or the answer may use very different wording from that used in the passage. For Identification questions, you nearly always need to find specific supporting text to verify your answer choice.

Inference

It can be inferred from the passage that the author would be most likely to agree with which one of the following characterizations of scientific truth?[4]

The passage suggests which one of the following about the kind of jazz played by Miles Davis prior to 1948?[5]

The author of the passage uses the word "criticism" in lines 46–56 primarily in order to[6]

Inference questions are the most common type of question that you will see. Expect 2–5 Inference questions per passage. Except perhaps for the most straightforward Identification questions, all Reading Comprehension questions can be seen as asking us to draw an inference. (In fact, some of our more mystical LSAT teachers have suggested that the entire LSAT is about making inferences.) In one sense, all RC questions are a variation on "From what you just read, what do you know regarding...?" But, for

1 *PrepTest 14, Section 3, Question 26*
2 *PrepTest 11, Section 3, Question 5*
3 *PrepTest 15, Section 1, Question 22*
4 *PrepTest 18, Section 3, Question 8*
5 *PrepTest 20, Section 2, Question 3*
6 *PrepTest 14, Section 3, Question 10*

the purpose of understanding the different types of work we'll be doing during the questions, Inference questions are those that ask you to go a step further than Identification questions. Inference questions ask you to identify a piece of text and then derive other truths from it. The correct answer may require you to take an unexpected logical step, but it will always be a *valid step*. In any case, we will often have to go back to the passage to find support for our inferences.

Synthesis

Which one of the following best expresses the main idea of the passage?

Which one of the following best describes the organization of the passage?

Which of the following best describes the function of the third paragraph?

Which one of the following expresses a view that the author of the passage would most probably hold concerning legal principles and legal rules?[7]

Some questions require you to take ideas from several places in the text and synthesize them into some greater understanding. Expect to see 1–4 Synthesis questions per passage.

For example, if we learn in the first paragraph that "critics don't like the plan because it is not cost-effective," and we learn in the third paragraph that "the few parents who support the plan represent a minority who disagree with the idea that the plan is bad for children," we can connect these two ideas and conclude that "critics and most parents share a common opinion, though their reasons for that opinion may differ." Incorrect answers to Synthesis questions will often infer correctly from one piece of information but not the other, or they will combine ideas in an incorrect manner. Most Synthesis questions pertain to the passage as a whole, and a structural understanding of the passage relative to a central argument is a tremendous asset for answering these questions. Looking back at the text is often unnecessary, but in some cases we will have to go back to the passage to fine-tune our understanding or find support for one detail over another.

7 *PrepTest 17, Section 4, Question 11*

How These Skills Relate to One Another

Notice how these three core skills build upon one another. In order to infer correctly, you must first identify the relevant piece of text. In order to synthesize, you must be able to identify and infer.

COMPREHENSION SKILLS

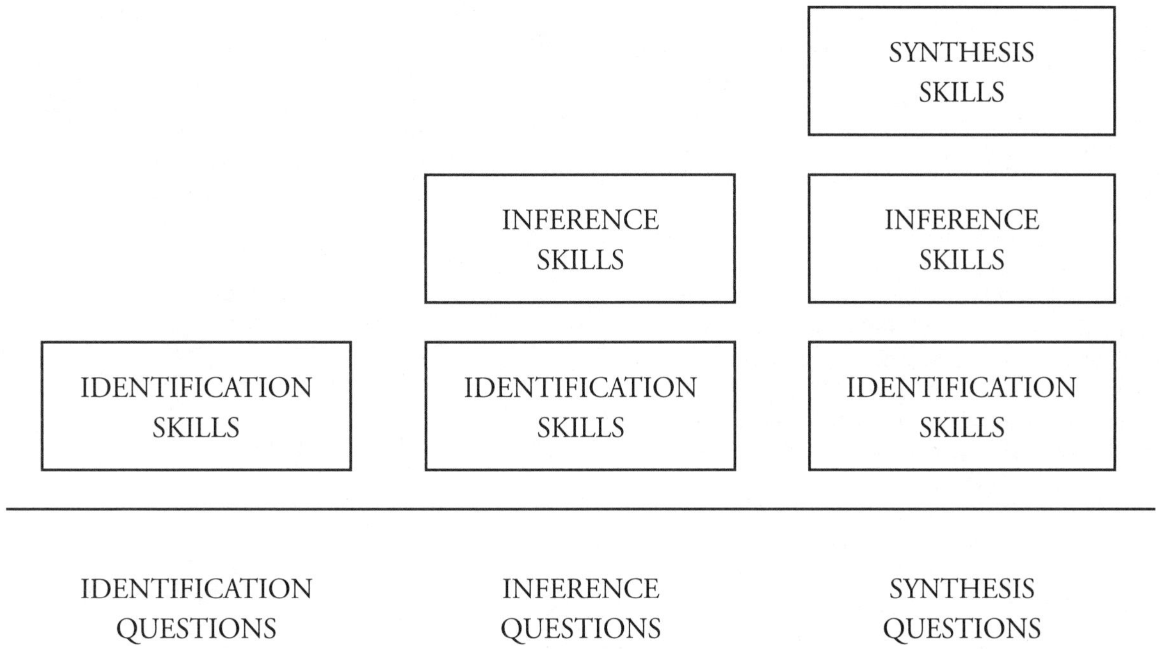

		SYNTHESIS SKILLS
	INFERENCE SKILLS	INFERENCE SKILLS
IDENTIFICATION SKILLS	IDENTIFICATION SKILLS	IDENTIFICATION SKILLS
IDENTIFICATION QUESTIONS	INFERENCE QUESTIONS	SYNTHESIS QUESTIONS

DRILL IT: Question Types in Action

Let's see how the question types look in action. Read the following passage and answer the three questions to the best of your ability. Identify the specific line numbers that support your answer to each question. Aim to finish within seven minutes.

PrepTest 42, Section 3, Passage 1

Most of what has been written about Thurgood Marshall, a former United States Supreme Court justice who served from 1967 to 1991, has just focused on his judicial record and on the ideological content of his (5) earlier achievements as a lawyer pursuing civil rights issues in the courts. But when Marshall's career is viewed from a technical perspective, his work with the NAACP (National Association for the Advancement of Colored People) reveals a strategic and methodical (10) legacy to the field of public interest law. Though the NAACP, under Marshall's direction, was not the first legal organization in the U.S. to be driven by a political and social agenda, he and the NAACP developed innovations that forever changed the landscape of (15) public interest law: during the 1940s and 1950s, in their campaign against state-sanctioned racial segregation, Marshall and the NAACP, instead of simply pursuing cases as the opportunity arose, set up a predetermined legal campaign that was meticulously (20) crafted and carefully coordinated.

One aspect of this campaign, the test case strategy, involved sponsoring litigation of tactically chosen cases at the trial court level with careful evaluation of the precedential nuances and potential impact of each (25) decision. This allowed Marshall to try out different approaches and discover which was the best to be used. An essential element in the success of this tactic was the explicit recognition that in a public interest legal campaign, choosing the right plaintiff can mean the (30) difference between success and failure. Marshall carefully selected cases with sympathetic litigants, whose public appeal, credibility, and commitment to the NAACP's goals were unsurpassed.

In addition, Marshall used sociological and (35) psychological statistics—presented in expert testimony, for example, about the psychological impact of enforced segregation—as a means of transforming constitutional law by persuading the courts that certain discriminatory laws produced public harms in violation (40) of constitutional principles. This tactic, while often effective, has been criticized by some legal scholars as a pragmatic attempt to give judges nonlegal material with which to fill gaps in their justifications for decisions where the purely legal principles appear (45) inconclusive.

Since the time of Marshall's work with the NAACP, the number of public interest law firms in the U.S. has grown substantially, and they have widely adopted his combination of strategies for litigation, (50) devoting them to various public purposes. These strategies have been used, for example, in consumer advocacy campaigns and, more recently, by politically conservative public interest lawyers seeking to achieve, through litigation, changes in the law that they have not (55) been able to accomplish in the legislature. If we focus on the particular content of Marshall's goals and successes, it might seem surprising that his work has influenced the quest for such divergent political objects, but the techniques that he honed— (60) originally considered to be a radical departure from accepted conventions—have become the norm for U.S. public interest litigation today.

7. According to the passage, some legal scholars have criticized which of the following?

(A) the ideology Marshall used to support his goals
(B) recent public interest campaigns
(C) the use of Marshall's techniques by politically conservative lawyers
(D) the use of psychological statistics in court cases
(E) the set of criteria for selecting public interest litigants

supporting line numbers:_______

5. The passage provides the most support for which one of the following statements?

(A) The ideological motivations for Marshall's work with the NAACP changed during his tenure on the U.S. Supreme Court.
(B) Marshall declined to pursue some cases that were in keeping with the NAACP's goals but whose plaintiffs' likely impression on the public he deemed to be unfavorable.
(C) Marshall's tactics were initially opposed by some other members of the NAACP who favored a more traditional approach.
(D) Marshall relied more on expert testimony in lower courts, whose judges were more likely than higher court judges to give weight to statistical evidence.
(E) Marshall's colleagues at the NAACP subsequently revised his methods and extended their applications to areas of law and politics beyond those for which they were designed.

supporting line numbers:_______

1. Which one of the following most accurately expresses the main point of the passage?

(A) In his role as a lawyer for the NAACP, Marshall developed a number of strategies for litigation which, while often controversial, proved to be highly successful in arguing against certain discriminatory laws.
(B) The litigation strategies that Marshall devised in pursuit of the NAACP's civil rights goals during the 1940s and 1950s constituted significant innovations that have since been adopted as standard tactics for public interest lawyers.
(C) Although commentary on Marshall has often focused only on a single ideological aspect of his accomplishments, a reinvestigation of his record as a judge reveals its influence on current divergent political objectives.
(D) In his work with the NAACP during the 1940's and 1950's, Marshall adopted a set of tactics that were previously considered a radical departure from accepted practice, but which he adapted in such a way that they eventually became accepted conventions in the field of law.
(E) Contrary to the impression commonly given by commentary on Marshall, his contributions to the work of the NAACP have had more of a lasting impact than his achievements as a U.S. Supreme Court justice.

supporting line numbers:_______

5

SOLUTIONS: Question Types in Action

Scale and Passage Map

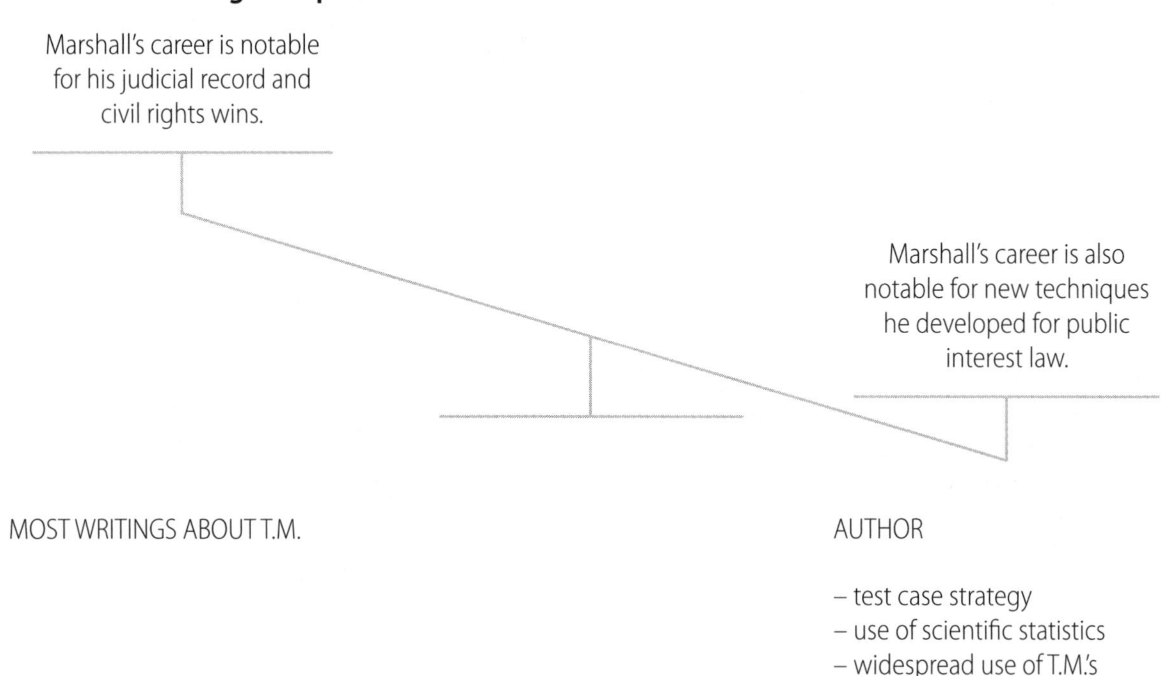

P1: Challenge to standard viewpoint. Evaluations of T.M.'s work usually focus on judicial record, but technical developments as civil rights lawyer were significant.

P2: One aspect of new viewpoint. T.M. developed the test case strategy.

P3: Second aspect of new viewpoint. T.M. controversially used sociological and psychological statistics.

P4: Direct support for author's point. Widespread adoption of T.M.'s techniques proves they were important.

Notice how heavily weighted the scale is here. The author mentions previous work on Marshall at the beginning, but doesn't spend much time on this. Rather, the passage ends up being about Marshall's innovations and their effect on public interest litigation. The scale informs and organizes the rest of the passage, but the author doesn't spend much time pitting the two sides against each other.

Identification

7. According to the passage, some legal scholars have criticized which of the following?

(A) the ideology Marshall used to support his goals
(B) recent public interest campaigns
(C) the use of Marshall's techniques by politically conservative lawyers
(D) the use of psychological statistics in court cases
(E) the set of criteria for selecting public interest litigants

Referenced text:

In addition, Marshall used sociological and
(35) psychological statistics—presented in expert testimony,
for example, about the psychological impact of
enforced segregation—as a means of transforming
constitutional law by persuading the courts that certain
discriminatory laws produced public harms in violation
(40) of constitutional principles. **This tactic**, while often
effective, has been criticized by some legal scholars ...

It's easy to work too hard on Identification questions. The right answer should provide a strong match between the text and the question, with little or no need for interpretation. Here, we want to look for material that matches "legal scholars have criticized." We can find this in the third paragraph. A good general understanding from the initial read should make it easier to find the relevant piece of text quickly. In other words, the stronger your passage map, the easier your search will be.

The LSAT has tried to make this question more difficult by using the relative phrase "this tactic" in the text. It requires a little extra work to confirm that "this tactic" refers to the use of sociological and psychological statistics.

The other answers are mentioned in the text, and it's not unreasonable to think that some of them can or should be criticized. However, the only one that is specifically stated as having been criticized is (D).

Tips for Identification Questions

1. Look for language cues.

Use the question stem and the answer choices as clues to help you recognize the question type and figure out where to look. Here, "according to the passage" tips us off that this is probably Identification rather than Inference, and "legal scholars" and "criticized" narrow our scope. Furthermore, every item in the answer choices is something that is explicitly mentioned in (rather than inferred from) the passage. Together, all these clues tell us that the question is just asking us to find something in the text.

2. Watch out for false matches.

Don't pick an answer just because you vaguely remember reading something similar in the text. Confirm that the text does match up specifically with the particular question stem and answer choice. In the case of the question above, all the other answers are mentioned in the text, but they are not what the legal scholars have criticized.

3. Connect with the text.

If you are stuck, don't spend extra time comparing answers against one another. Instead, spend that time going back through the passage to locate the relevant text. Nothing in the answer choices in and of themselves will tip you off. It's only by connecting the choices with the text that you can confirm your answer.

Inference

5. The passage provides the most support for which one of the following statements?

(A) The ideological motivations for Marshall's work with the NAACP changed during his tenure on the U.S. Supreme Court.
(B) Marshall declined to pursue some cases that were in keeping with the NAACP's goals but whose plaintiffs' likely impression on the public he deemed to be unfavorable.
(C) Marshall's tactics were initially opposed by some other members of the NAACP who favored a more traditional approach.
(D) Marshall relied more on expert testimony in lower courts, whose judges were more likely than higher court judges to give weight to statistical evidence.
(E) Marshall's colleagues at the NAACP subsequently revised his methods and extended their applications to areas of law and politics beyond those for which they were designed.

Referenced text:

... can mean the
(30) difference between success and failure. Marshall
carefully selected cases with sympathetic litigants,
whose public appeal, credibility, and commitment to
the NAACP's goals were unsurpassed.

The phrase "most support" tips us off that we may be looking to do something more than just identify. We need to use something in the text to prove something else. If we've done a good job of mapping, perhaps we remember that the test case strategy was the first innovation mentioned. When we get to (B), this knowledge will enable us to quickly find the relevant text to support this answer choice.

Answer choice (A) is simply not mentioned in the text. Answers (C), (D), and (E) stray too far from what we've been given. If we know that Marshall screened cases to find sympathetic litigants, we can logically deduce that he declined some cases involving unsympathetic litigants.

Tips for Inference Questions

1. Identify before you infer.

Infer only after you've found the relevant part of the text. It will make your work much easier!

2. Eliminate attractive wrong answers by comparing them to specific, relevant parts of text.

You may not have time to double-check every answer choice, but you do want to confirm or deny the most attractive answers by comparing them against the relevant parts of the text. For instance, (C) seems plausible—perhaps others in the NAACP were initially opposed to Marshall's tactics because these tactics were new and innovative. However, this is never directly or indirectly supported by the text. Answer (E) is also attractive. It's easy to misread the end and assume that the NAACP extended his work into other areas, but a rereading of the last paragraph reveals that there is no support for this inference. Marshall's tactics have been put to work for other purposes, but we're not told that this work has been done by the NAACP.

3. Don't infer too much!

Many of the wrong choices sound attractive because they are (1) reasonable and (2) in some indirect way connected to the text. Right answers to Inference questions need to be more than that—they should be fairly provable using the text. Resist answers that require assumptions or illogical leaps from the text.

Synthesis

1. Which one of the following most accurately expresses the main point of the passage?

(A) In his role as a lawyer for the NAACP, Marshall developed a number of strategies for litigation which, while often controversial, proved to be highly successful in arguing against certain discriminatory laws.

(B) The litigation strategies that Marshall devised in pursuit of the NAACP's civil rights goals during the 1940s and 1950s constituted significant innovations that have since been adopted as standard tactics for public interest lawyers.

(C) Although commentary on Marshall has often focused only on a single ideological aspect of his accomplishments, a reinvestigation of his record as a judge reveals its influence on current divergent political objectives.

(D) In his work with the NAACP during the 1940's and 1950's, Marshall adopted a set of tactics that were previously considered a radical departure from accepted practice, but which he adapted in such a way that they eventually became accepted conventions in the field of law.

(E) Contrary to the impression commonly given by commentary on Marshall, his contributions to the work of the NAACP have had more of a lasting impact than his achievements as a U.S. Supreme Court justice.

Referenced text:

... But when Marshall's career is
viewed from a technical perspective, his work with the
NAACP (National Association for the Advancement of
Colored People) reveals a strategic and methodical
(10) legacy to the field of public interest law ...

and social agenda, he and the NAACP developed
innovations that forever changed the landscape of
(15) public interest law...

... such divergent political
objects, but the techniques that he honed—
(60) originally considered to be a radical departure from
accepted conventions—have become the norm for U.S.
public interest litigation today.

Synthesis questions often test your understanding of the passage as a whole (or parts of the passage relative to the whole), but the difference between correct and incorrect answers may hinge on subtle details. If you read in a casual fashion, several of these answers may seem so similar that you struggle to choose one over the others.

At first glance, answer choice (B) might not seem that close to our scale, but did you notice how heavily weighted the scale is? The other side barely gets a mention! The author wants to focus on an aspect of Marshall's career that apparently hasn't gotten much attention, and then the rest of the passage stays on that theme. Answer (B) pushes the idea of innovation and mentions that those innovations have been adopted widely, as we noted in our scale.

Answer choice (A) speaks to the success of the strategies, and while it's true that success is mentioned in the passage, this answer choice fails to note the transformative impact that Marshall had on public interest litigation. Thus, while (A) is a provable statement, its scope is too narrow to accurately express the main point of the passage. Answer (C) incorrectly focuses on his experiences as a judge, whereas the bulk of the passage is about his work with the NAACP. Answer (D) is very attractive, but incorrect in its details. He did not adapt the tactics, he invented them ("developed innovations"). And the passage does not talk about his tactics becoming accepted conventions for the entire field of law, but rather for the niche of public interest work. Answer (E) seems to stick to our scale, but notice that it's saying that one part of Marshall's life was actually more important than another; the passage itself does not make any such comparison. As we noted in the scale, the passage just tells us that Marshall's work is also interesting for its technical innovations.

Tips for Synthesis Questions

1. Be flexible.

Understanding the argument structure is crucial, but so is flexibility. The correct answer is often not an ideal one, and it's often quite different from the answer you might predict. For instance, a correct answer might provide a decent overview of the passage, but leave out an element we would expect to see in a summary. Keep an open mind, and eliminate only those choices that you are certain are incorrect.

2. See the forest *and* the trees.

Yes, these questions are primarily about general understanding, but right and wrong answers are often determined by subtle details. If two or three different answers seem the same to you, look for small differences in the wording between them and compare these differences against the text.

3. Keep the author's opinion in mind.

Incorrect choices often misrepresent the author's opinion, both in terms of what side of the argument it falls on and how subtle or strong that opinion is. A correct understanding of the author's opinion will often help you pick the correct answer.

4. Watch out for "narrow scope" answers.

In the next chapter, we'll look at the characteristics of incorrect answers. For now, know that many incorrect answers to Synthesis questions are actually true in terms of their content (e.g., answer choice (A) on the last question), but too narrow in scope to accurately express the main point of the passage. One particularly tricky version of this trap can occur when a passage includes a "curved tail" at the end—a short application or prediction relating to the passage's main topic. Unless forcefully put and given a bit of support, these final points will not be considered the main point of the passage.

5. Notice the scale's balance.

If a scale is relatively balanced, meaning that both sides were discussed in some depth, the answer to a main idea/point question should directly or indirectly reference both sides of the scale. However, if the scale is heavily weighted and one side is barely discussed, as in the Thurgood Marshall passage above, it's likely that the right answer will reference only the "heavier" side.

SPECIFIC QUESTION TYPES

For those who appreciate a more detailed breakdown, the following is a complete list of the specific RC question types we've identified on the LSAT. You don't need to memorize this list, but it may help you to identify your task more quickly on some questions. We also use these categories in some of our materials, such as the explanations in *10 Real LSATs Grouped by Question Type.*

As you work with these categories, you might find that some of them could reasonably be broken down into further subcategories. There's a tension here—recognizing categories can be useful, but if we break things down too far, we risk cluttering our minds with terminology and failing to see the connections between questions. In the end, the bulk of your improvement will come from improving your core skills and recognizing which skills to apply to each question.

Analogy/Application
These questions require you to use your knowledge of the passage to identify a parallel situation, strengthen/weaken an argument, or apply a criterion in the passage to the answer choices. You may notice some overlap with Logical Reasoning Strengthen, Weaken, Principle, and Match the Reasoning questions.

Author General Opinion
These questions ask you to use your general understanding of the author's opinion. If you were able to develop a scale and place the author on it, you may well be able to answer from memory without looking back at the passage at all.

Author Local Opinion
These questions ask you about the author's opinion concerning one specific element of the passage. On these, it pays to look back at the relevant text and make sure you have a clear understanding of the author's opinion on that particular point before determining the answer.

Function/Structure

These questions ask about the overall organization of the passage or about the role that one particular portion of the text, from an individual word to a whole paragraph, serves in the passage. Your scale and passage map will be important here: on overall questions, you'll want the answer to track pretty closely to your passage map, and on more specific questions, while you'll certainly want to look back at the indicated portion, you'll also want to relate that text to the author's overall purpose and opinion.

General Inference/Local Inference

General Inference questions require you to infer something from the passage as a whole or from several different points within the passage. Local Inference questions require you to infer something from a specific part of the passage. However, you won't always know which type you're dealing with from the question alone. The question might simply read, "Which one of the following can most reasonably be inferred from the passage?" In that case, you will have to look at the answer choices to determine whether you are making a General or a Local Inference.

Identify Information

These questions are pure Identification. You will be asked for a specific piece of information from the passage, and you just have to go and find it. Get your hunting cap on!

Non-Author Opinion

These are similar to author opinion questions, except that you are asked about an opinion that is described in the passage—the author may or may not agree with that opinion. These are generally fairly local opinions, but if the entire passage is devoted to discussing the views of one person or group of people, you might see a more general Non-Author Opinion question.

Point/Purpose of Passage

These are general questions that ask you for either the main point of the passage or the author's point in writing the passage. In either case, these are similar to Author General Opinion questions in that if you've worked out the scale, you should be able to answer them without looking back to the passage. The difference between these and Author General Opinion questions is that the author's point or purpose in writing the passage is not always opinion-based. Maybe this author just wants to describe the three different types of dust she has observed, and while she may have an opinion ("Dust is not all the same!"), that opinion may not be the overall point of the passage.

DRILL IT: Inference

Let's take some time to train up those inference muscles! Each of the following mini-passages will be followed by a series of statements. Your job is to determine which of the statements can be properly inferred. In each set, there may be many correct inferences, or there may be none! Simply mark each statement yes or no.

Mini-Passage A:

Before the age of space exploration, astronomers assumed that the Moon's core was smaller than the Earth's, in both relative and absolute terms—the radius of the Earth's core is 55 percent of the overall radius of the Earth and the core's mass is 32 percent of the Earth's overall mass—but they had no way to verify this. Two sets of data gathered by Lunar Prospector have now given astronomers the ability to determine that the Moon's core accounts for 20 percent of the Moon's radius and for a mere 2 percent of its overall mass.

A1. Astronauts who landed on the Moon took measurements that allowed astronomers to revise estimates of the mass and radius of the Moon's core.

- ☐ Yes
- ☐ No

A2. New data suggests that the Moon's core is smaller in radius and in mass than was previously assumed.

- ☐ Yes
- ☐ No

A3. Most of the Earth's mass is located outside of its core.

- ☐ Yes
- ☐ No

A4. The Earth's core is bigger than the Moon.

- ☐ Yes
- ☐ No

A5. The age of space exploration began, in part, because of a desire to make measurements of the Moon's core.

- ☐ Yes
- ☐ No

A6. The two sets of data gathered by Lunar Prospector did not present any contradictory measurements.

- ☐ Yes
- ☐ No

A7. Scientific assumptions are not always undermined by an increase in data.

- ☐ Yes
- ☐ No

Mini-Passage B:

Despite its 1979 designation as a threatened species, the desert tortoise has declined in numbers by ninety percent since the 1980s. Although federal protection made it illegal to harm desert tortoises or remove them from the southwestern North American deserts, this measure has been insufficient to reverse the species' decline. The lack of recovery is partly due to the desert tortoise's low reproductive potential. Females breed only after reaching fifteen to twenty years of age, and even then may only lay eggs when adequate forage is available. The average mature female produces only a few eggs annually. From these precious eggs, hatchlings emerge wearing soft shells that will take five years to harden into protective armor. The vulnerable young are entirely neglected by adult tortoises, and only five percent ultimately reach adulthood.

B1. Poachers have largely ignored the threatened species status of the desert tortoise.

☐ Yes
☐ No

B2. Not all tortoises live in marshlands.

☐ Yes
☐ No

B3. A young desert tortoise's shell becomes fully formed more than two decades after the tortoise's mother was born.

☐ Yes
☐ No

B4. Had the penalties for violating federal protection regulations been stiffer, there would have been less of a decline in desert tortoise populations.

☐ Yes
☐ No

B5. An average mature female desert tortoise's output of eggs in any given year is unlikely to result in any new adult members of the species.

☐ Yes
☐ No

B6. Young tortoises are forced to seek protection by forming small groups.

☐ Yes
☐ No

B7. Within the first few years of life, a hatchling's shell conveys no survival advantage.

☐ Yes
☐ No

B8. The desert tortoise's low reproductive potential has contributed more to the species' decline than has lack of food for foraging.

☐ Yes
☐ No

SOLUTIONS: Inference

A1. **No, Cannot be inferred**
Astronauts who landed on the Moon took measurements that allowed astronomers to revise estimates of the mass and radius of the Moon's core.

We only know that the data came from Lunar Prospector. We don't know whether any humans had to land on the Moon in order for Lunar Prospector to gather its data.

A2. **No, Cannot be inferred**
New data suggests that the Moon's core is *smaller* in radius and in mass *than was previously assumed.*

Previously, scientists assumed the Moon's core was smaller than the Earth's. The new data confirms that they were correct.

A3. **Yes, Can be inferred**
Most of the Earth's mass is located outside of its core.

The passage tells us that the Earth's core makes up 32 percent of the Earth's mass, so the other 68 percent must be located outside of the core.

A4. **No, Cannot be inferred**
The Earth's core is *bigger than the Moon.*

We don't have the information needed to compare the size of the Earth's core to the size of the entire Moon. Sure, we know that the Earth's core makes up more than half the Earth's diameter, and in real life we may know that that's bigger than the Moon, but now we're not inferring from the passage anymore. The LSAT won't require us to bring in any knowledge of astronomical measurements.

A5. **No, Cannot be inferred**
The age of space exploration began, in part, *because of a desire* to make measurements of the Moon's core.

Even though it seems plausible to think that the space program was driven in part by curiosity about the Moon, it's pure speculation in terms of what we've been told. Be careful about assuming the motivation behind the facts presented.

A6. **No, Cannot be inferred**
The two sets of data gathered by Lunar Prospector did not present *any* contradictory measurements.

The word "any" is too extreme. Since scientists were able to determine facts about the Moon's core from these two sets of data, they couldn't completely contradict each other, but it's certainly possible that *some* measurements within the two sets of data contradicted each other.

A7. **Yes, Can be inferred**
Scientific assumptions are not always undermined by an increase in data.

Astronomers assumed that the Moon's core was smaller than the Earth's in relative terms. The two sets of data from Lunar Prospector (an increase in data) allowed astronomers to determine that their assumption was correct (the Moon's core is only 20 percent of the Moon's radius, while the Earth's core is 55 percent of the Earth's radius). Since this increase in data strengthened rather than undermined the assumption, it's safe to say that a scientific assumption doesn't have to be undermined by an increase in data.

B1. **No, Cannot be inferred**
Poachers have largely *ignored* the threatened species status of the desert tortoise.

Even though we learn that federal protection has done little to slow the decline of the species, we can't infer anything about whether hunters have anything to do with the decline.

B2. **Yes, Can be inferred**
Not all tortoises live in marshlands.

"Not all" statements can be translated as "some aren't/some don't," so this statement means "some tortoises do *not* live in marshlands." From the fact that the desert tortoise is not allowed to be removed from southwestern North American deserts, we know that some tortoises live in the desert. The LSAT allows us to use common sense definitions, so it's safe to say that desert is not the same as marshland.

B3. **Yes, Can be inferred**
A young desert tortoise's shell becomes fully formed more than two decades after the tortoise's mother was born.

We're told that female desert tortoises can't breed until they are 15–20 years of age. We're also told that a hatchling's shell does not become protective armor for at least 5 years. So if a female was 15 years old when she had a baby, that baby's shell would not become protective armor until the mother was at least 20 years old.

B4. **No, Cannot be inferred**
Had *the penalties* for violating federal protection regulations been stiffer, there would have been less of a decline in desert tortoise populations.

"The penalties for violating federal protection" are out of scope. In general, it's very dangerous on any Inference question to predict the outcome of a hypothetical. Had the passage said something like "weak federal penalties led to more violations, which accelerated the decline of tortoises," we would have more support for this, but it's still dangerous to assume what would have happened in a counterfactual.

B5. **Yes, Can be inferred**
An average mature female desert tortoise's output of eggs in any given year is unlikely to result in any new adult members of the species.

We know that a mature female will lay only a few eggs annually, and that's only if forage is available. We also know that only five percent of young tortoises reach adulthood. Even if a female were to have a banner year and lay five eggs, that would still only lead to an adult 25 percent of the time. We're safe calling something "unlikely" as long as its likelihood is less than 50 percent.

B6. **No, Cannot be inferred**
Young tortoises are forced to seek protection by *forming small groups*.

Though we know that the adults neglect the young, we are told nothing about how the young cope with this. Maybe each little turtle tries to go it alone.

B7. **No, Cannot be inferred**
Within the first few years of life, a hatchling's shell *conveys no survival advantage.*

While we know that the shell hasn't hardened into protective armor, it may still provide some advantages. Perhaps it keeps in moisture or shields the tortoise against UV rays.

B8. **No, Cannot be inferred**
The desert tortoise's low reproductive potential *has contributed more* to the species' decline than has lack of food for foraging.

We are only told that low reproductive potential is "partly responsible" for the species' decline, so we cannot make the leap of saying that it has contributed more to the tortoises' decline than something else.

For more practice, log in to your Student Center!

Finding Support

As we mentioned earlier, on some questions you will want to go back and find support in the passage, while on others you should be able to rely on your general understanding of the passage. However, in some cases the path may not be entirely clear. For instance, you may come across an Identification question for which you're pretty sure you know the answer or you may be asked about the author's opinion on a passage where you didn't think the author expressed an opinion. There is a tension here—should you go back and look for support or should you have a look at the answer choices and see if the right answer pops out at you? While there's no perfect answer to that question, in general it's wise to err on the side of going back too much until you are comfortable knowing when that's not needed. While this can certainly eat up your time if you're not careful, many LSAT questions are designed to take advantage of those who have a loose grasp of the passage and don't want to take the trouble to verify.

In the end, of course, the proof is in your performance. Look at what you're doing when you get the questions right (especially under time pressure), and also take note of the types of questions you're getting wrong. When you're *sure* about a detail, do you generally turn out to be correct? Does the test sometimes manage to trick you by using language similar to that used in the passage or by cleverly rephrasing an idea from the passage to make it unrecognizable? Make this kind of analysis a consistent part of your review process and develop a proven sense of when you do need to go back and when you don't. Also keep a lookout for questions that are so tough that an extra minute doesn't help—those are the questions from which you'll want to move on quickly to leave time for easier ones.

Whether you get a question right or wrong, when you review your work, go back and make sure you know where in the passage the correct answer is supported—actually find the text! In many cases, you will also be able to find some text that contradicts one or more of the wrong answers. If more than one answer seems to be supported, well, it's time to use your finely-honed inference skills to see which answer is the real thing.

DRILL IT: Finding Support

Take up to four minutes to read the following passage and develop a scale and passage map. Afterward, you will be presented with a series of statements. Mark each statement S, U, or C, to indicate whether it is supported, unsupported (meaning it's not addressed), or contradicted by the passage. If the statement is supported or contradicted, indicate which line(s) in the text either support or contradict the statement.

PrepTest 6, Section 1, Passage 2

In the late nineteenth century, the need for women physicians in missionary hospitals in Canton, China, led to expanded opportunities for both Western and Chinese women. The presence of (5) Western women as medical missionaries in China was made possible by certain changes within the Western missionary movement. Beginning in the 1870s, increasingly large numbers of women were forming women's foreign mission societies (10) dedicated to the support of women's foreign mission work. Beyond giving the women who organized the societies a formal activity outside their home circles, these organizations enabled an increasing number of single women missionaries (15) (as opposed to women who were part of the more typical husband-wife missionary teams) to work abroad. Before the formation of these women's organizations, mission funds had been collected by ministers and other church leaders, most of whom (20) emphasized local parish work. What money was spent on foreign missions was under the control of exclusively male foreign mission boards whose members were uniformly uneasy about the new idea of sending single women out into the mission field. (25) But as women's groups began raising impressive amounts of money donated specifically in support of single women missionaries, the home churches bowed both to women's changing roles at home and to increasing numbers of single professional (30) missionary women abroad.

Although the idea of employing a woman physician was a daring one for most Western missionaries in China, the advantages of a well-trained Western woman physician could not be (35) ignored by Canton mission hospital administrators. A woman physician could attend women patients without offending any of the accepted conventions of female modesty. Eventually, some of these women were able to found and head separate (40) women's medical institutions, thereby gaining access to professional responsibilities far beyond those available to them at home.

These developments also led to the attainment of valuable training and status by a significant (45) number of Chinese women. The presence of women physicians in Canton mission hospitals led many Chinese women to avail themselves of Western medicine who might otherwise have failed to do so because of their culture's emphasis on physical (50) modesty. In order to provide enough women physicians for these patients, growing numbers of young Chinese women were given instruction in medicine. This enabled them to earn an independent income, something that was then (55) largely unavailable to women within traditional Chinese society. Many women graduates were eventually able to go out on their own into private practice, freeing themselves of dependence upon the mission community.

(60) The most important result of these opportunities was the establishment of clear evidence of women's abilities and strengths, clear reasons for affording women expanded opportunities, and clear role models for how these abilities and responsibilities (65) might be exercised.

	Supported (S), Unsupported (U), or Contradicted (C)?	**Line Numbers (for S and C)**
1. There were very few women involved in foreign missionary work before the 1870s.	____	__________
2. In nineteenth-century China, the number of Western female doctors was not sufficient to provide care for all the women who wished to be seen by a female doctor.	____	__________
3. In the late nineteenth century, opportunities for women physicians were greater in Western countries than in China.	____	__________
4. The majority of professional women missionaries working abroad before the 1870s were located in Canton, China.	____	__________
5. In late-nineteenth-century Canton, China, it was not customary for female patients to be treated by male physicians.	____	__________
6. Most women missionaries working abroad before the 1870s were married to men who were also missionaries.	____	__________
7. The presence of Western women as medical missionaries in China was made possible primarily through fundraising initiated by church leaders.	____	__________
8. In late-nineteenth-century Canton, China, medical care was more often administered in the home than in hospitals.	____	__________

SOLUTIONS: Finding Support

1. There were very few women involved in foreign missionary work before the 1870s.

Unsupported. Lines 7–11 say that there was an increase in the number of women's missionary societies in the 1870s, but we don't know how many such societies there were before. In any case, the question is about the number of women missionaries, not the number of societies. Lines 15–16 tell us that husband-wife teams were typical, so there were at least some women missionaries, but we're unsure of the numbers.

2. In nineteenth-century China, the number of Western female doctors was not sufficient to provide care for all the women who wished to be seen by a female doctor.

Supported. Lines 50–53 indicate that many young Chinese women were trained in medicine in order to meet the demand from women seeking care from a female doctor.

3. In the late nineteenth century, opportunities for women physicians were greater in Western countries than in China.

Contradicted. Lines 38–42 describe female physicians in China who gained "access to professional responsibilities far beyond those available to them at home."

4. The majority of professional women missionaries working abroad before the 1870s were located in Canton, China.

Unsupported. Although the opening lines mention that demand in Canton created opportunities for women, this is a far cry from saying that "the majority of professional women missionaries" were located there. Notice that this doesn't just say the majority of those in China, but the majority of those "working abroad" in general. We don't even know about the distribution of missionaries in China, let alone the rest of the world!

5. In late-nineteenth-century Canton, China, it was not customary for female patients to be treated by male physicians.

Supported. Lines 36–38 and 45–50 tell us that before the arrival of female doctors, a culture of physical modesty prevented many female patients from seeking Western medical treatment.

6. Most women missionaries working abroad before the 1870s were married to men who were also missionaries.

Supported. Lines 15–16 tell us that women typically went on missions as part of a husband-wife team.

7. The presence of Western women as medical missionaries in China was made possible primarily through fundraising initiated by church leaders.

Contradicted. Church leaders emphasized local work (lines 19–20). The fundraising that led to an increase in women working abroad was performed by women's groups (lines 25–30).

8. In late-nineteenth-century Canton, China, medical care was more often administered in the home than in hospitals.

Unsupported. We simply know nothing about this. Lines 36–38 and 45–50 make it clear that not all women received Western-style medical treatment, but this doesn't tell us that they (or anyone else) were receiving medical care at home.

Prephrasing the Answer

In the drill above, we were looking at isolated statements and deciding whether they were supported or not. However, since the answers we choose from on the LSAT are always answers to a question, it's important to make sure we're getting as much from that question stem as possible. In many cases, we can get a fairly good sense of what the answer should be before we've even seen the answer choices. As is often the case on this test, a little up-front work can save us a lot of time by making it easier to eliminate wrong answers. Before we take a look at the answer choices, we will usually want to accomplish the following:

1. Read and interpret the question.

What type of question is this—Identification, Inference, or Synthesis? What exactly do I need to find out? Do I already know the answer? If not, where in the passage should I look?

2. Read and interpret the relevant supporting text *(as needed).*

Unless the question is fairly general or you've become very familiar with the needed details, it's best to go back and find the applicable text. Depending on the question and your grasp of that section of the passage, you may just need to remind yourself of what you read or you may need to go back and reread.

3. Prephrase an answer to the question.

How would you answer the question in your own words? What are you going to be looking for in the answer choices?

If you successfully complete these three steps, you will be in a good position to handle the answer choices without getting sidetracked by every out-of-scope answer choice. You won't *always* be able to prepare in this manner—sometimes the question is so vague or open-ended that all you can do is go straight to the answer choices. When you have a great prephrase, you can sometimes zip to the right answer, and you will feel very clever, but because it's so easy to get fooled by tiny little shifts in wording, your default approach should be to **work wrong-to-right**. This means actively working over the answer choices, eliminating where possible and deferring judgment when you don't see an obvious flaw. We'll discuss working wrong-to-right in great detail in the next chapter.

DRILL IT: Prephrasing the Answer, Part 1

Take about 3:30 to read the following passage and develop a scale and passage map. You will then be presented with a series of questions for prephrasing. For each question, determine where to go for support—can you answer this one directly from the scale and your general understanding of the passage or do you need to go back to some particular part(s) of the text? Take the necessary steps and do your best to prephrase an answer. What will you be looking for when you get to the answer choices in the second part of this drill?

PrepTest 16, Section 4, Passage 1

Three kinds of study have been performed on Byron. There is the biographical study—the very valuable examination of Byron's psychology and the events in his life; Escarpit's 1958 work is an example (5) of this kind of study, and biographers to this day continue to speculate about Byron's life. Equally valuable is the study of Byron as a figure important in the history of ideas; Russell and Praz have written studies of this kind. Finally, there are (10) studies that primarily consider Byron's poetry. Such literary studies are valuable, however, only when they avoid concentrating solely on analyzing the verbal shadings of Byron's poetry to the exclusion of any discussion of biographical considerations. A (15) study with such a concentration would be of questionable value because Byron's poetry, for the most part, is simply not a poetry of subtle verbal meanings. Rather, on the whole, Byron's poems record the emotional pressure of certain moments (20) in his life. I believe we cannot often read a poem of Byron's, as we often can one of Shakespeare's, without wondering what events or circumstances in his life prompted him to write it.

No doubt the fact that most of Byron's poems (25) cannot be convincingly read as subtle verbal creations indicates that Byron is not a "great" poet. It must be admitted too that Byron's literary craftsmanship is irregular and often his temperament disrupts even his lax literary method (30) (although the result, an absence of method, has a significant purpose: it functions as a rebuke to a cosmos that Byron feels he cannot understand). If Byron is not a "great" poet, his poetry is nonetheless of extraordinary interest to us because (35) of the pleasure it gives us. Our main pleasure in reading Byron's poetry is the contact with a singular personality. Reading his work gives us illumination—self-understanding—after we have seen our weaknesses and aspirations mirrored in (40) the personality we usually find in the poems. Anyone who thinks that this kind of illumination is not a genuine reason for reading a poet should think carefully about why we read Donne's sonnets.

It is Byron and Byron's idea of himself that hold (45) his work together (and that enthralled early-nineteenth-century Europe). Different characters speak in his poems, but finally it is usually he himself who is speaking: a far cry from the impersonal poet Keats. Byron's poetry alludes to (50) Greek and Roman myth in the context of contemporary affairs, but his work remains generally of a piece because of his close presence in the poetry. In sum, the poetry is a shrewd personal performance, and to shut out Byron the man is to (55) fabricate a work of pseudocriticism.

Write in your prephrases (when possible) for each of the following questions:

1. Which one of the following titles best expresses the main idea of the passage?

2. The author's mention of Russell and Praz serves primarily to

3. Which one of the following would the author most likely consider to be a valuable study of Byron?

4. Which one of the following statements best describes the organization of the first paragraph of the passage?

5. The author mentions that "Byron's literary craftsmanship is irregular" (lines 27–28) most probably in order to

6. According to the author, Shakespeare's poems differ from Byron's in that Shakespeare's poems

7. The author indicates which one of the following about biographers' speculation concerning Byron's life?

8. The passage supplies specific information that provides a definitive answer to which one of the following questions?

SOLUTIONS: Prephrasing the Answer, Part 1

Scale and Passage Map

If it took a while for you to find a scale here, you're not alone. The author describes three kinds of study—does that mean we need a three-part scale? Then we're told that studies of Byron's poetry are only valuable if they *don't* ignore his life. So the author isn't saying the third kind is good or bad, only that it needs to bring in his life because his poems aren't that great on their own. Does that mean that the author doesn't like Byron's poetry? Well, notice that we see "great" in quotes. The author is saying that Byron is not great in the way that people might say other poets, such as Shakespeare and Keats, are great. Rather, his poems are enjoyable and illuminating because they show us the man himself. Notice that there has been no further mention of the other types of study—apparently, the author doesn't take issue with those, just with studies of Byron's poetry that don't look at his life—so we can leave them off the scale. In the end we might produce something like this:

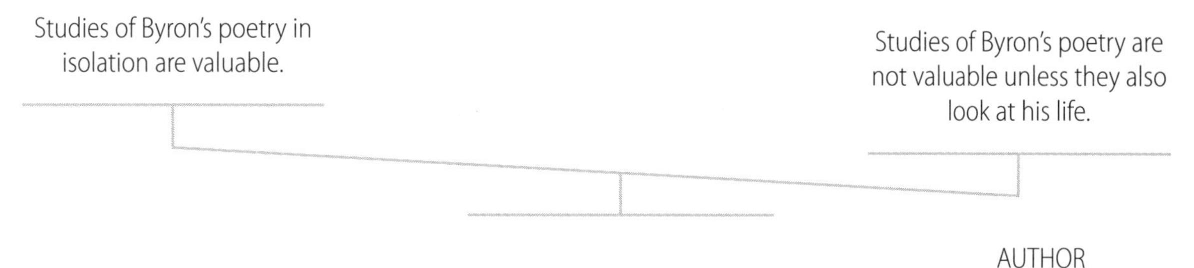

P1: Introduction of different approaches & author opinion. We need to study Byron's life when we study his poetry.

P2: Contrasting characterizations. Byron is not "great" because he doesn't have strong literary craftsmanship, but his work is fun & illuminating to read because we can see his personality.

P3: Elaboration of author's point. Byron himself is the central voice of his poems, so to ignore him when studying his poetry is to miss the point.

1. Which one of the following titles best expresses the main idea of the passage? *(Synthesis)*

This form of main point question asks us to express the main point in terms of a title for the passage. While it would be hard to predict the exact style of the title, it's going to have to be something that stresses the importance of Byron as a person, not just as a poet.

Prephrase: *To study Byron's poetry correctly, one must also study Byron himself.*

2. The author's mention of Russell and Praz serves primarily to *(Inference)*

Hmm, all we know about Russell and Praz is that they wrote a study of Byron's place in the history of ideas, and the author seems to find this kind of thing valuable. So we could say it's an example of one useful kind of study.

Prephrase: *Provide an example of a useful kind of study.*

3. Which one of the following would the author most likely consider to be a valuable study of Byron? *(Synthesis)*

The author approves of the first two kinds of study (biography and history of ideas), but the main focus is on studies of Byron's poetry that include his life and personality, so the answer seems most likely to focus on that.

Prephrase: *Probably something that looks at his poetry by examining his life.*

4. Which one of the following statements best describes the organization of the first paragraph of the passage? *(Synthesis)*

The author describes some useful ways to study Byron and one not-so-useful way, then says why you need to consider Byron's life when you study his poetry.

Prephrase: *A few ways to study Byron, then a focus on studies of his poetry and why it's important to include his life.*

5. The author mentions that "Byron's literary craftsmanship is irregular" (lines 27–28) most probably in order to *(Inference)*

The author seems to acknowledge some of Byron's faults here, but the overall point is not that he is a bad poet, just that he isn't great in the same way as some other poets. So perhaps the purpose here is to concede a point to critics of Byron, but this part also sets us up for the author to tell us what *is* good about Byron in the second half of the paragraph.

Prephrase: *To concede a criticism of Byron before moving ahead and complimenting him.*

6. According to the author, Shakespeare's poems differ from Byron's in that Shakespeare's poems *(Identification)*

The author thinks that we can read Shakespeare's poems without wondering what led him to write them, but we can't do the same with Byron's. Why? If we go with the information right before this, we see that Byron's work is not about subtle verbal meanings but about his life. Maybe Shakespeare's poems are verbally subtle and not overly biographical, but the author doesn't say that for sure. It seems like a bit of a stretch.

Prephrase: *We can read Shakespeare's poems without thinking about his life.*

7. The author indicates which one of the following about biographers' speculation concerning Byron's life? *(Identification)*

We don't have a whole lot to go on here. The second sentence tells us that this speculation is valuable and that biographers continue to engage in it.

Prephrase: *It's valuable and it continues.*

8. The passage supplies specific information that provides a definitive answer to which one of the following questions? *(Identification)*

This doesn't give us much to go on, does it? Well then…

Prephrase: *Straight to the answer choices!*

 For more practice, log in to your Student Center!

DRILL IT: Prephrasing the Answer, Part 2

Now that you've had a chance to prephrase the answers, let's take a look at the real test questions. There's no need for a strict time limit here, but it may be useful to track how long the full set takes. You're likely to find that the prephrases make the process a lot quicker! In some cases, your prephrase may match the correct answer quite closely. In others, you will still have your wrong-to-right work cut out for you, but hopefully your prephrasing work will give you some idea of what to look for and what to eliminate. Here we go!

1. Which one of the following titles best expresses the main idea of the passage?

(A) An Absence of Method: Why Byron Is Not a "Great" Poet
(B) Byron: The Recurring Presence in Byron's Poetry
(C) Personality and Poetry: The Biographical Dimension of Nineteenth-Century Poetry
(D) Byron's Poetry: Its Influence on the Imagination of Early-Nineteenth-Century Europe
(E) Verbal Shadings: The Fatal Flaw of Twentieth-Century Literary Criticism

2. The author's mention of Russell and Praz serves primarily to

(A) differentiate them from one another
(B) contrast their conclusions about Byron with those of Escarpit
(C) point out the writers whose studies suggest a new direction for Byron scholarship
(D) provide examples of writers who have written one kind of study of Byron
(E) give credit to the writers who have composed the best studies of Byron

3. Which one of the following would the author most likely consider to be a valuable study of Byron?

(A) a study that compared Byron's poetic style with Keats' poetic style
(B) a study that argued that Byron's thought ought not to be analyzed in terms of its importance in the history of ideas
(C) a study that sought to identify the emotions felt by Byron at a particular time in his life
(D) a study in which a literary critic argues that the language of Byron's poetry was more subtle than that of Keats' poetry
(E) a study in which a literary critic drew on experiences from his or her own life

4. Which one of the following statements best describes the organization of the first paragraph of the passage?

(A) A generalization is made and then gradually refuted.
(B) A number of theories are discussed and then the author chooses the most convincing one.
(C) Several categories are mentioned and then one category is discussed in some detail.
(D) A historical trend is delineated and then a prediction about the future of the trend is offered.
(E) A classification is made and then a rival classification is substituted in its place.

5. The author mentions that "Byron's literary craftsmanship is irregular" (lines 27–28) most probably in order to

(A) contrast Byron's poetic skill with that of Shakespeare
(B) dismiss craftsmanship as a standard by which to judge poets
(C) offer another reason why Byron is not a "great" poet
(D) point out a negative consequence of Byron's belief that the cosmos is incomprehensible
(E) indicate the most-often-cited explanation of why Byron's poetry lacks subtle verbal nuances

6. According to the author, Shakespeare's poems differ from Byron's in that Shakespeare's poems

(A) have elicited a wider variety of responses from both literary critics and biographers
(B) are on the whole less susceptible to being read as subtle verbal creations
(C) do not grow out of, or are not motivated by, actual events or circumstances in the poet's life
(D) provide the attentive reader with a greater degree of illumination concerning his or her own weaknesses and aspirations
(E) can often be read without the reader's being curious about what biographical factors motivated the poet to write them

7. The author indicates which one of the following about biographers' speculation concerning Byron's life?

(A) Such speculation began in earnest with Escarpit's study.
(B) Such speculation continues today.
(C) Such speculation is less important than consideration of Byron's poetry.
(D) Such speculation has not given us a satisfactory sense of Byron's life.
(E) Such speculation has been carried out despite the objections of literary critics.

8. The passage supplies specific information that provides a definitive answer to which one of the following questions?

(A) What does the author consider to be the primary enjoyment derived from reading Byron?
(B) Who among literary critics has primarily studied Byron's poems?
(C) Which moments in Byron's life exerted the greatest pressure on his poetry?
(D) Has Byron ever been considered to be a "great" poet?
(E) Did Byron exert an influence on Europeans in the latter part of the nineteenth century?

SOLUTIONS: Prephrasing the Answer, Part 2

1. Which one of the following titles best expresses the main idea of the passage? *(Synthesis)*

Prephrase: *To study Byron's poetry correctly, one must also study Byron himself.*

(A) An Absence of Method: Why Byron Is Not a "Great" Poet

(B) Byron: The Recurring Presence in Byron's Poetry

(C) Personality and Poetry: The Biographical Dimension of Nineteenth-Century Poetry

(D) Byron's Poetry: Its Influence on the Imagination of Early-Nineteenth-Century Europe

(E) Verbal Shadings: The Fatal Flaw of Twentieth-Century Literary Criticism

Answer (A) is far too negative. Answer (C) is too broad. Answer (D) is odd—influence on imagination?—and misses the point. Answer (E) is too negative!

2. The author's mention of Russell and Praz serves primarily to *(Inference)*

Prephrase: *provide an example of a useful kind of study.*

(A) differentiate them from one another

(B) contrast their conclusions about Byron with those of Escarpit

(C) point out the writers whose studies suggest a new direction for Byron scholarship

(D) provide examples of writers who have written one kind of study of Byron

(E) give credit to the writers who have composed the best studies of Byron

Answer (A) incorrectly suggests that the author is pitting Russell and Praz against each other! Answer (B) incorrectly introduces the idea that the author contrasts the different examples. Answer (C) is out because of "new." Answer (E) is out, too—we have no idea who wrote the best studies, although the author will undoubtedly think the best ones focused on Byron as a person!

3. Which one of the following would the author most likely consider to be a valuable study of Byron? *(Synthesis)*

Prephrase: *Probably something that looks at his poetry by examining his life.*

(A) a study that compared Byron's poetic style with Keats' poetic style

(B) a study that argued that Byron's thought ought not to be analyzed in terms of its importance in the history of ideas

(C) a study that sought to identify the emotions felt by Byron at a particular time in his life

(D) a study in which a literary critic argues that the language of Byron's poetry was more subtle than that of Keats' poetry

(E) a study in which a literary critic drew on experiences from his or her own life

Only (C) includes a focus on Byron's life.

4. Which one of the following statements best describes the organization of the first paragraph of the passage? *(Synthesis)*

Prephrase: *A few ways to study Byron, then a focus on studies of his poetry and why it's important to include his life.*

(A) A generalization is made and then gradually refuted.

(B) A number of theories are discussed and then the author chooses the most convincing one.

(C) Several categories are mentioned and then one category is discussed in some detail.

(D) A historical trend is delineated and then a prediction about the future of the trend is offered.

(E) A classification is made and then a rival classification is substituted in its place.

Answers (A), (D), and (E) don't match at all. Answer (B) is tempting, but the author is not discussing theories or picking the best idea. Answer (C) is a fairly vague restatement of our prephrase. The categories are the different kinds of study of Byron, and the "one category" is studies of Byron's poetry.

5. The author mentions that "Byron's literary craftsmanship is irregular" (lines 27–28) most probably in order to *(Inference)*

Prephrase: *To concede a criticism of Byron before moving ahead and complimenting him.*

(A) contrast Byron's poetic skill with that of Shakespeare

(B) dismiss craftsmanship as a standard by which to judge poets

(C) offer another reason why Byron is not a "great" poet

(D) point out a negative consequence of Byron's belief that the cosmos is incomprehensible

(E) indicate the most-often-cited explanation of why Byron's poetry lacks subtle verbal nuances

Answer (A) is incorrecnt because this portion of the passage doesn't really connect to the part about Shakespeare. Answer (B) is out because the author doesn't say that craftsmanship is unimportant. We're just told that there are other reasons to enjoy Byron. Answer (D) might seem fairly close to the wording in lines 27–32, but just because his lack of method seems to rebuke the cosmos, this doesn't mean that his irregular craftsmanship was caused by his beliefs. For (E), we have no idea if it's the most often cited? No idea.

6. According to the author, Shakespeare's poems differ from Byron's in that Shakespeare's poems *(Identification)*

Prephrase: *We can read Shakespeare's poems without thinking about his life.*

(A) have elicited a wider variety of responses from both literary critics and biographers

(B) are on the whole less susceptible to being read as subtle verbal creations

(C) do not grow out of, or are not motivated by, actual events or circumstances in the poet's life

(D) provide the attentive reader with a greater degree of illumination concerning his or her own weaknesses and aspirations

(E) can often be read without the reader's being curious about what biographical factors motivated the poet to write them

We don't know much about (A)–(D). Answer (C) superficially resembles what we want, but we don't know that Shakespeare's poems weren't connected to his life; the author just focuses on whether we end up "wondering" about that life. If we defer quickly enough on any we're unsure about, we can get to (E), which matches our prephrase very closely, without eating up a lot of time. Notice that we were able to answer this Identification question without digging into the speculative "why" that we tried to explore in our prephrase.

7. The author indicates which one of the following about biographers' speculation concerning Byron's life? *(Identification)*

Prephrase: *It's valuable and it continues.*

(A) Such speculation began in earnest with Escarpit's study.

(B) Such speculation continues today.

(C) Such speculation is less important than consideration of Byron's poetry.

(D) Such speculation has not given us a satisfactory sense of Byron's life.

(E) Such speculation has been carried out despite the objections of literary critics.

Prephrase wins!

8. The passage supplies specific information that provides a definitive answer to which one of the following questions? *(Identification)*

Prephrase: *Straight to the answer choices!*

(A) What does the author consider to be the primary enjoyment derived from reading Byron?

(B) Who among literary critics has primarily studied Byron's poems?

(C) Which moments in Byron's life exerted the greatest pressure on his poetry?

(D) Has Byron ever been considered to be a "great" poet?

(E) Did Byron exert an influence on Europeans in the latter part of the nineteenth century?

Answer (A) is supported by lines 35–37, and none of the other answers are supported. The passage does say that Byron "enthralled early-nineteenth-century Europe" (lines 44–46), but that doesn't mean he exerted an influence on late-nineteenth-century Europe.

As this question set makes clear, prephrasing can often set us up nicely to identify the correct answer when we see it, and to eliminate glaringly wrong choices with a minimum of trouble. The payoff is apparent, and we hope you'll get in the habit of prephrasing wherever possible; just don't expect every answer to fit your prephrases as well as they did here.

Changing How You Work the Questions: Know What You're Looking For

In this chapter, we introduced our general and specific question categories for one purpose—to get you thinking about what each question you encounter is really asking you to do, and how you might go about finding support for the right answer. In the end, it's not so important that you agonize over how to correctly categorize each question; what matters is that you take a moment to figure out what the question wants from you, and that you have developed a strong enough grasp of the passage that you know where to find the answer. A great technique for reviewing a practice set you've completed is to prove (or reprove) every answer you've chosen by identifying the supporting text. You can go back and do this untimed before you even check the answers!

If you're not regularly prephrasing on questions that allow it, definitely focus on adding that to your approach. As we've seen, skillfully working the question and prephrasing an answer doesn't guarantee smooth sailing, but it will make your wrong-to-right process a lot easier. And while you're building up those skills, we should mention that this is a great spot to fit in some cross-training: Logical Reasoning is full of challenging Inference questions that will strengthen your ability to connect statements and catch subtle differences in meaning.

Chapter 6
of
Reading Comprehension

Working Wrong-to-Right

Characteristics of Incorrect Answers

Despite your growing ability to read and analyze passages and to understand questions and right answers, no doubt you've found yourself struggling with some answer choices. Perhaps two answer choices look equally tempting or perhaps none of them do! The LSAT test writers are amazingly skilled at writing tempting wrong answers, so it's worth some time and effort to understand how they do what they do.

If an LSAT question is going to accurately test reading skills, at least some of the answers must require close reading to eliminate. We can imagine that the test writers have taken five correct answers and changed four of them in ways that will go unnoticed by unwary readers. While the test writers put a lot of effort into making those tricky changes, most test-takers don't give a lot of thought to why wrong answers are wrong. They satisfy themselves with a general "Oh yeah, that's wrong" or "The author didn't say that" and move on. True, there are no extra points for accurately categorizing wrong answers, but we need a more nuanced vocabulary about wrong answers to improve our test-taking form. Answers on the LSAT are not wrong in haphazard ways. They are incorrect because of common, concrete flaws. By going from "Oh yeah, that's wrong" to something like "That's wrong because it has too narrow a scope," you will fundamentally improve your ability to sidestep the LSAT's many trap answers.

While the end goal is to improve your ability to spot wrong answers during the test, much of your growth will occur during review of work you've done. That is when you dig in deep and figure out why wrong answers are wrong (even those you didn't pick). It's through slow and patient review that you improve the high-speed performance of your wrong-answer radar.

We can divide the characteristics of incorrect RC answers into three broad categories: interpretation, scope, and degree. Let's jump in.

Interpretation

Most incorrect answers are incorrect because of interpretation issues. These answers generally mistranslate the information in the text in one of two ways:

1. **Contradicted.** The answer choice states the exact opposite of what is written in the text.

2. **Unsupported.** The answer choice presents a logical leap that is unsupported by the text.

We are often tempted by unsupported answers because we read into the text, adding our own knowledge, opinions, or interpretations. Remember, law school rewards literal and precise thinking, not creative interpretations. At other times, we are fooled because we find these choices, like the text, challenging to understand. If we sense that we are missing something, we might feel that the right answer should make a leap in logic, going beyond what we understand. That is rarely the case. As we saw in the previous chapter, all answers can be proved by the text, and they never require a giant leap in logic.

It's easy to imagine the slipups mentioned above—we've all read a bit too much into the text at times. But amazingly, it can be very tempting to pick an answer that is completely contradicted by the text. This can happen if we are uncertain about where opinions fall on the argument scale. Furthermore, just as it's easy to switch directions in our head and mistakenly turn right-left-right when someone told us to turn left-right-left, in the heat of the LSAT, it can be easy to get turned around or perhaps not notice a "not."

Scope

We define scope as the range of subject matter that is discussed. There are two main types of scope issues:

1. Out of scope. The answer choice is outside the scope of the passage (it involves elements that were not mentioned in the passage).

2. Narrow scope. The scope of the answer doesn't match the scope of the question (for example, the question asks about the passage as a whole, but the answer relates to only one paragraph).

Often, the answers to Identification questions are incorrect because they are outside the scope of the passage, and often, the answers to Synthesis questions are incorrect because they are too narrow in scope (or sometimes, too broad).

In **comparative passages** (which we will look at in chapter 8), we will often encounter **half scope** answers. Questions for comparative passages tend to ask about what the two passages have in common, and the wrong answers to these questions often touch on one passage or the other, but not both.

A common subtype of unsupported and out-of-scope answer choices is the **comparison trap**. This trap, which appears in both Reading Comprehension and Logical Reasoning, makes a comparison that we don't have enough information to make. For instance, if we're told that many South Americans favor a certain international treaty, an incorrect answer might state that South Americans support this treaty more than they did in the past or that South Americans view the treaty more favorably than North Americans do. Without further information about past attitudes or the views of North Americans, neither of these statements would be inferable, and thus they would both be considered comparison traps.

Degree

Degree issues show up in two forms:

1. Incorrect degree: opinion. Think of opinions as sitting on a spectrum: disgust, dislike, slight disfavor, objectivity/uncertainty, slight favor, like, and love. An incorrect answer choice of this type will misrepresent the degree of an opinion stated in the passage.

2. Incorrect degree: modifier. Think of a spectrum of modifiers that define number: one, a few, some, many, most, all. LSAT answer choices are often incorrect because a modifier misrepresents the degree of a certain number.

Some test-takers cross out any answer that includes a strong modifier such as "never" or "all." While words like that should raise a red flag, if they're supported by the text, they can be correct. So be vigilant, but flexible.

Incorrect Answer Examples

Take a moment to read the following mini-passage. Then we'll walk through some questions and look at incorrect answers of each type.

Critics of our higher education system point out the often striking difference between the skills students develop in college courses and the skills desired by employers. Students generally enter college with the expectation that it will improve their job prospects, the argument goes, so why not give employers more direct control over the education process? Some commentators have even gone so far as to suggest that traditional college courses be replaced with short, standardized skills-training workshops.

However, the provision of vocational training is not the goal of most university programs. Rather, universities seek to provide students with experience in a particular field of inquiry, as well as exposure to a wide range of disciplines and world views. University students learn to situate themselves not only within the adult world of work and responsibility, but also within the broader streams of historical, social, and physical development that shape and are shaped by their actions and experiences. Before we make any sweeping changes on utilitarian grounds, we ought to consider the utility of the existing order.

1. INTERPRETATION Issues

1. Based on the passage, it can be most reasonably inferred that the author would agree with which one of the following statements?

(A) Universities ought to align their curricula with the specific needs of employers.

(B) University courses provide a better preparation for the world of work than vocational training does.

Contradicted (opposite of what was stated in the text)

Answer choice (A) sounds like the opinion voiced by the critics in the first paragraph. The author goes on to say that vocational training is *not* the goal of most universities, and that we ought to consider the benefits of the current system before making the changes proposed by the critics. The author is on the other end of the scale from the critics, so this choice is contradicted.

Unsupported (makes too big of a leap from the text)

Answer choice (B) makes a couple of unsupported leaps in logic. Although the author seems to defend the value of a university education against those who would like to see students receive only vocational training, this does not mean that the author thinks that universities provide a better preparation for the world of work. (Maybe the author appreciates a traditional university education for broader reasons.) Also, the author hasn't expressed a clear opinion on the value of vocational training, so this choice is a comparison trap.

2. SCOPE Issues

Which one of the following most accurately expresses the main point of the passage?

(A) Job training should be provided by employers rather than by universities.

(B) Standardized skills-training workshops are not sufficient to meet the educational goals of universities.

Out of scope (involves ideas not discussed in the text)

The scale of the passage is about the kind of education universities should provide. Answer (A) is out of scope—there is no mention of how job training should be conducted if it is not provided by universities, so this can't be the author's main point.

Narrow scope (the answer is too limited to provide a complete answer to the question)

After describing a proposal to replace college courses with skills-training workshops, the author states that "the provision of vocational training is not the goal of most university programs." However, this is a point made in support of the larger idea that we should not be too quick to replace existing university programs. Answer (B) is too narrow in scope to be the author's main point.

3. DEGREE Issues

Which one of the following most accurately describes the author's position regarding existing university programs?

(A) unquestioning support

With which one of the following statements would the critics mentioned in line 1 be most likely to agree?

(B) Existing university programs do not provide students with any skills desired by employers.

Incorrect degree: opinion (stronger or weaker than the stated opinion)

While the author does seem to support the status quo at this point, is that support *unquestioning*, as (A) suggests? Notice that the author ends the passage by suggesting that before any changes are made we look more thoroughly at the issue. This is a far cry from supporting one side unquestioningly.

Incorrect degree: modifier (specifies the wrong quantity or proportion)

The critics are concerned about the "striking difference between the skills students develop in college courses and the skills desired by employers." Clearly, they would like to see more overlap between these two groups of skills. But does that mean there is *no* overlap now? We don't know—(B) presents a more extreme version of the information in the passage.

UNSUPPORTED VS. OUT OF SCOPE

As you can probably predict, we're soon going to ask you to categorize a bunch of wrong answers. When that happens, it's likely that you will struggle to distinguish between unsupported and out of scope answers. Our teachers sometimes disagree on how to describe a particular answer choice, so don't be overly concerned if your categorizations don't always match ours. The truth is that we could actually say that ***all*** incorrect answers are unsupported. On a deeply logical level, that is true, but we created these particular wrong answer categories to call your attention to different ways that the test presents incorrect answers. As we use the term here, an unsupported answer presents an interpretation of some portion of the text that may or may not be true. On the other hand, an out-of-scope answer brings up something that just isn't covered by the text at all. Let's look at some examples of unsupported and out of scope statements based on this text:

> Chickens are one of the most widespread and populous of domesticated species. The global chicken population has been estimated to exceed 20 billion individuals across hundreds of different breeds.

Examples of unsupported answers:

> There are more chickens in the world than any other kind of bird.

The passage only compares chickens to domesticated animals. While it might seem reasonable to conclude that chickens outnumber any other species of bird—this is actually true—there is no support for this inference in the passage. In fact, we don't even know from the given statements whether chickens outnumber other domesticated birds.

> Chickens are a highly genetically diverse species.

We know that there are hundreds of breeds, so there must be some genetic diversity. But without knowing more about the genes of these breeds, or how they compare to other species, it's hard to know whether chickens qualify as "highly genetically diverse."

Examples of out of scope answers:

Chicken populations have remained stable over time.

There is absolutely nothing related to this in the text. We only know the current population estimate.

Chickens are able to thrive on a wide variety of diets.

The passage doesn't mention food at all.

Making a distinction between statements that seem connected to the material, but aren't fully supported (basically, bad inferences), and statements that aren't really connected at all will improve your test performance by forcing you to look very precisely at the level of support for each answer choice. After all, the entire LSAT is about figuring out which answers are supported and which aren't.

Wrong-to-Right: Your Secret Weapon

During a test (or practice set), your main strategy for avoiding tempting wrong answers should be to work wrong-to-right. This means that you defer judgment on answers that aren't clearly incorrect, moving on to evaluate the others. There are two reasons to do this. First, you don't have to waste time considering so-so answer choices if a much better choice comes along later. Second, it serves as an accuracy check. In the excitement of finding a "right" answer, it's easy to miss small flaws or differences in wording. However, if you work through all of the answer choices, you may find another answer that looks just as good, forcing you to consider the question more closely. After you've made a full pass, go back and make a careful study of the remaining answers, referring back to the passage as needed.

DRILL IT: Characteristics of Incorrect Answers

Read the following passage and answer the questions to the best of your ability. Do this *untimed*. For every wrong answer, take the time to decide *why* it is wrong: Interpretation (I), Scope (S), or Degree (D). Some answers are wrong for multiple reasons. Be sure to practice working wrong-to-right.

PrepTest 41, Section 4, Passage 1

In a recent court case, a copy-shop owner was accused of violating copyright law when, in the preparation of "course packs"—materials photocopied from books and journals and packaged as readings for (5) particular university courses—he copied materials without obtaining permission from or paying sufficient fees to the publishers. As the owner of five small copy shops serving several educational institutions in the area, he argued, as have others in the photocopy (10) business, that the current process for obtaining permissions is time-consuming, cumbersome, and expensive. He also maintained that course packs, which are ubiquitous in higher education, allow professors to assign important readings in books and journals too (15) costly for students to be expected to purchase individually. While the use of copyrighted material for teaching purposes is typically protected by certain provisions of copyright law, this case was unique in that the copying of course packs was done by a copy (20) shop and at a profit.

Copyright law outlines several factors involved in determining whether the use of copyrighted material is protected, including: whether it is for commercial or nonprofit purposes; the nature of the copyrighted (25) work; the length and importance of the excerpt used in relation to the entire work; and the effect of its use on the work's potential market value. In bringing suit, the publishers held that other copy-shop owners would cease paying permission fees, causing the potential (30) value of the copyrighted works of scholarship to diminish. Nonetheless, the court decided that this reasoning did not demonstrate that course packs would have a sufficiently adverse effect on the current or potential market of the copyrighted works or on the (35) value of the copyrighted works themselves. The court instead ruled that since the copies were for educational purposes, the fact that the copy-shop owner had profited from making the course packs did not prevent him from receiving protection under the law. (40) According to the court, the owner had not exploited copyrighted material because his fee was not based on the content of the works he copied; he charged by the page, regardless of whether the content was copyrighted.

(45) In the court's view, the business of producing and selling course packs is more properly seen as the exploitation of professional copying technologies and a result of the inability of academic parties to reproduce printed materials efficiently, not the exploitation of (50) these copyrighted materials themselves. The court held that copyright laws do not prohibit professors and students, who may make copies for themselves, from using the photoreproduction services of a third party in order to obtain those same copies at a lesser cost.

Remember to do your passage map before you dive into the questions!

(I, S, D, or ✓ for correct)

1. Which one of the following most accurately states the main point of the passage?

___ (A) A court recently ruled that a copy shop that makes course packs does not illegally exploit copyrighted materials but rather it legally exploits the efficiency of professional photocopying technology.
___ (B) A court recently ruled that course packs are protected by copyright law because their price is based solely on the number of pages in each pack.
___ (C) A court recently ruled that the determining factors governing the copyrights of material used in course packs are how the material is to be used, the nature of the material itself, and the length of the copied excerpts.
___ (D) A recent court ruling limits the rights of publishers to seek suit against copy shops that make course packs from copyrighted material.
___ (E) Exceptions to copyright law are made when copyrighted material is used for educational purposes and no party makes a substantial profit from the material.

2. In lines 23–27, the author lists several of the factors used to determine whether copyrighted material is protected by law primarily to

___ (A) demonstrate why the copy-shop owner was exempt from copyright law in this case
___ (B) explain the charges the publishers brought against the copy-shop owner
___ (C) illustrate a major flaw in the publishers' reasoning
___ (D) defend the right to use copyrighted materials for educational purposes
___ (E) provide the legal context for the arguments presented in the case

3. The copy-shop owner as described in the passage would be most likely to agree with which one of the following statements?

___ (A) The potential market value of a copyrighted work should be calculated to include the impact on sales due to the use of the work in course packs.
___ (B) Publishers are always opposed to the preparation and sale of course packs.
___ (C) More copy shops would likely seek permissions from publishers if the process for obtaining permissions were not so cumbersome and expensive.
___ (D) Certain provisions of copyright law need to be rewritten to apply to all possible situations.
___ (E) Copy shops make more of a profit from the preparation and sale of course packs than from other materials.

4. The information in the passage provides the most support for which one of the following statements about copyright law?

___ (A) Copyright law can be one of the most complex areas of any legal system.
___ (B) Courts have been inconsistent in their interpretations of certain provisions of copyright law.
___ (C) The number of the kinds of materials granted protection under copyright law is steadily decreasing.
___ (D) New practices can compel the courts to refine how copyright law is applied.
___ (E) Copyright law is primarily concerned with making published materials available for educational use.

5. Which one of the following describes a role most similar to that of professors in the passage who use copy shops to produce course packs?

___ (A) An artisan generates a legible copy of an old headstone engraving by using charcoal on newsprint and frames and sells high-quality photocopies of it at a crafts market.

___ (B) A choir director tapes a selection of another well-known choir's best pieces and sends it to a recording studio to be reproduced in a sellable package for use by members of her choir.

___ (C) A grocer makes several kinds of sandwiches that sell for less than similar sandwiches from a nearby upscale cafe.

___ (D) A professional graphic artist prints reproductions of several well-known paintings at an exhibit to sell at the museum's gift shop.

___ (E) A souvenir store in the center of a city sells miniature bronze renditions of a famous bronze sculpture that the city is noted for displaying.

6. Which one of the following, if true, would have most strengthened the publishers' position in this case?

___ (A) Course packs for courses that usually have large enrollments had produced a larger profit for the copy-shop owner.

___ (B) The copy-shop owner had actively solicited professors' orders for course packs.

___ (C) The revenue generated by the copy shop's sale of course packs had risen significantly within the past few years.

___ (D) Many area bookstores had reported a marked decrease in the sales of books used for producing course packs.

___ (E) The publishers had enlisted the support of the authors to verify their claims that the copy-shop owner had not obtained permission.

SOLUTIONS: Characteristics of Incorrect Answers

Scale and Passage Map

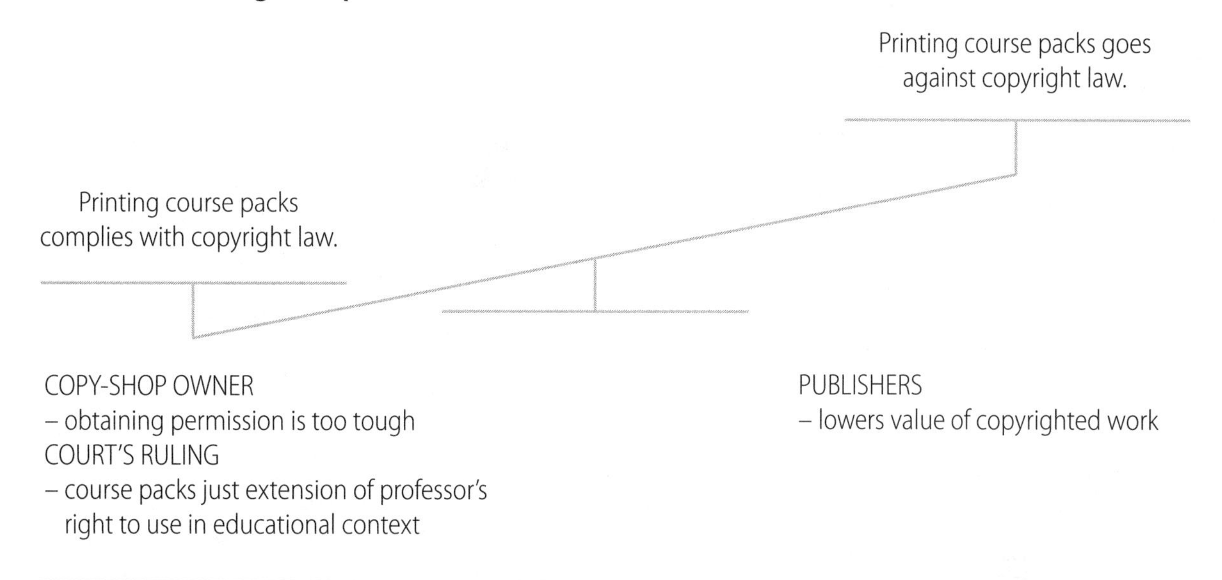

COPY-SHOP OWNER
– obtaining permission is too tough
COURT'S RULING
– course packs just extension of professor's right to use in educational context

PUBLISHERS
– lowers value of copyrighted work

P1: Outline of case and argument for one side. The copy-shop owner argues that obtaining permission is too difficult, and that he is giving students access to more material than would otherwise be affordable.

P2: Relevant law, argument for other side, & court decision. Publishers argue that copying diminishes value of copyrighted works, but court ruled for the copy-shop owner: copies were by-the-page for educational purposes and did not significantly diminish the value of the works.

P3: Explanation of court decision. Course packs are about making professional copying available to professors and students, who are simply using a third party to do what they can legally do themselves.

Because it is presented in the context of a court case, the central argument is relatively clear, and the opinions are arranged on two well-defined sides of the scale. Note that the author remains objective throughout.

1. Which one of the following most accurately states the main point of the passage? *(Synthesis)*

This Synthesis question should directly relate to our scale. The right answer should stress the issue under dispute (the legality of course packs) and include the court's decision.

(A) A court recently ruled that a copy shop that makes course packs does not illegally exploit copyrighted materials but rather it legally exploits the efficiency of professional photocopying technology.

This seems pretty good. Let's see what else we have.

(B) A court recently ruled that course packs are protected by copyright law because their price is based solely on the number of pages in each pack.

SCOPE (narrow). *Price based on pages is mentioned, but this certainly does not capture the* main *point of the passage.*

(C) A court recently ruled that the determining factors governing the copyrights of material used in course packs are how the material is to be used, the nature of the material itself, and the length of the copied excerpts.

INTERPRETATION (unsupported). *These are the factors outlined in copyright law (lines 21–27), not the content of the court's ruling. This is what we call a* ***misquote****—more on that later…*

(D) A recent court ruling limits the rights of publishers to seek suit against copy shops that make course packs from copyrighted material.

INTERPRETATION (unsupported). *The court ruled that the copy-shop owner was entitled to protection under copyright law (lines 31–39), but we don't know anything about limiting the rights of publishers to seek suit.*

(E) Exceptions to copyright law are made when copyrighted material is used for educational purposes and no party makes a substantial profit from the material.

INTERPRETATION (contradicted). *Educational considerations are not "exceptions" to copyright law; they are a part of copyright law (lines 16–18).*

DEGREE (modifier). *The courts found that the course packs would not have a substantial effect on the value of the copyrighted content; however, this does not mean that the copy-shop owner failed to make a substantial profit. On the contrary, "the fact that the copy-shop owner had profited from making the course packs did not prevent him from receiving protection under the law" (lines 37–39).*

Notice that even if answers (C)–(E) were factually correct, all of them would be too narrow in scope to be the main point of the argument. Only (A) gets at the scale—does printing course packs comply with copyright law?—and shows the court's reasoning.

2. In lines 23–27, the author lists several of the factors used to determine whether copyrighted material is protected by law primarily to *(Inference)*

The list of determining factors helps us to understand what immediately follows—the publishers' argument and the court's decision.

(A) demonstrate why the copy-shop owner was exempt from copyright law in this case

INTERPRETATION (unsupported). *The reasons for the copy-shop owner's exemption come later (lines 31–44, 50–54).*

(B) explain the charges the publishers brought against the copy-shop owner

INTERPRETATION (unsupported). *The list does provide criteria for evaluating the publishers' charges, but it does not explain them. That explanation comes next (lines 27–31).*

(C) illustrate a major flaw in the publishers' reasoning

DEGREE (opinion). *Though the publishers lost the case, the author never states that their reasoning had "major flaws." In fact, the author has not even stated her opinion!*

INTERPRETATION (unsupported). *Again, this is not the role these lines play in the argument.*

(D) defend the right to use copyrighted materials for educational purposes

DEGREE (opinion). *This is the same problem as (C), just on the other side of the scale. The author is not supporting a side, and the law by itself does not make it clear which way the decision should go.*

(E) provide the legal context for the arguments presented in the case

These lines serve as background information for the central argument at hand.

3. The copy-shop owner as described in the passage would be most likely to agree with which one of the following statements? *(Inference)*

Hmm, what do we know about the copy-shop owner? Quite a bit, actually, so we may not have a clear prephrase to this rather open-ended question. We just want to go into the answer choices with a strong sense of his position—he's providing a valuable service and obtaining the necessary permissions for all that material would be too difficult.

(A) The potential market value of a copyrighted work should be calculated to include the impact on sales due to the use of the work in course packs.

INTERPRETATION (unsupported). *This is an interesting idea, and the copy-shop owner certainly might agree with this statement if it were presented to him, but we simply don't have the information to determine what he thinks about the calculation of market value. All of the owner's opinions are clearly stated in lines 9–16, and there is nothing relevant to this answer.*

(B) Publishers are always opposed to the preparation and sale of course packs.

SCOPE (out of scope). *Remember that this question is about what the* copy-shop owner *thinks, so this choice is telling us what he thinks about what the publishers think. That's rather complicated, and we know nothing about it.*

DEGREE (modifier). *Furthermore, it is highly unlikely that* all *publishers will* always *feel the same way about something. There must be some rebellious publishers out there who don't have a problem with course packs!*

(C) More copy shops would likely seek permissions from publishers if the process for obtaining permissions were not so cumbersome and expensive.

This can be directly inferred from the text. Although the copy-shop owner doesn't say anything specific about other copy shops, we know that he is making an argument that others have made—the permission process is too difficult to be practical.

(D) Certain provisions of copyright law need to be rewritten to apply to all possible situations.

SCOPE (out of scope). *This is far removed from any opinions of the copy-shop owner that we've been provided with.*

DEGREE (modifier). *Furthermore, even if this were within the scope of the passage, it would be highly unlikely that anyone would think these provisions should cover* all *possible situations.*

(E) Copy shops make more of a profit from the preparation and sale of course packs than from other materials.

SCOPE (out of scope). *The passage never discusses profits made from the sale of other materials. This is a comparison trap.*

4. The information in the passage provides the most support for which one of the following statements about copyright law? *(Synthesis)*

Another open-ended Inference question—no prephrase here.

(A) Copyright law can be one of the most complex areas of any legal system.

SCOPE (out of scope). *The complexity of other areas of law is not discussed. This is a comparison trap.*

(B) Courts have been inconsistent in their interpretations of certain provisions of copyright law.

INTERPRETATION (unsupported). *The courts disagree with the publishers' argument (lines 35–39), and it seems that different circumstances can yield different results (lines 16–27). However, there is no evidence given that courts are inconsistent in their interpretations.*

(C) The number of the kinds of materials granted protection under copyright law is steadily decreasing.

SCOPE (out of scope). *This is not mentioned in the passage.*

(D) New practices can compel the courts to refine how copyright law is applied.

The role of copy shops in today's world has compelled the courts to refine their interpretation of the law (lines 18–20, 45–50).

(E) Copyright law is primarily concerned with making published materials available for educational use.

DEGREE (modifier). *Though this specific passage is about copyright law relative to educational use, we cannot infer from this one case that copyright law itself is* primarily *concerned with educational use. We don't know much about other applications of copyright law—this is a comparison trap.*

5. Which one of the following describes a role most similar to that of professors in the passage who use copy shops to produce course packs? *(Inference)*

What do we know about these professors? According to the passage, the professors are hiring a third party to do something that they are legally allowed to do themselves. The third party is simply able to do it more efficiently and cost-effectively (lines 45–54).

(A) An artisan generates a legible copy of an old headstone engraving by using charcoal on newsprint and frames and sells high-quality photocopies of it at a crafts market.

INTERPRETATION (unsupported). *This doesn't bring in a third party. The artisan is creating and selling artistic reproductions. This would be like the copy-shop owner independently printing fancy editions of old works.*

(B) A choir director tapes a selection of another well-known choir's best pieces and sends it to a recording studio to be reproduced in a sellable package for use by members of her choir.

This is very similar to a professor who picks parts of books and journals and then sends them out for reproduction and eventual sale to her students.

(C) A grocer makes several kinds of sandwiches that sell for less than similar sandwiches from a nearby upscale cafe.

INTERPRETATION (unsupported). *Again, there is no third party here. The grocer is simply competing on price with the cafe, and is not necessarily copying that cafe's ideas. This would be like a professor writing her own low-priced alternatives to the available texts.*

(D) A professional graphic artist prints reproductions of several well-known paintings at an exhibit to sell at the museum's gift shop.

INTERPRETATION (unsupported). *Still no third party here. This would be like the professor copying the books herself to make money.*

(E) A souvenir store in the center of a city sells miniature bronze renditions of a famous bronze sculpture that the city is noted for displaying.

INTERPRETATION (unsupported). *This is just like (D). Someone is selling copies for a profit, with no third party or educational motive. While topic shifts for analogy questions are the norm, in this case, the use of the material for educational purposes is a central issue. Looking back, we can see that (B) is the only choice in which someone is using a third party to make selected information available to others.*

6. Which one of the following, if true, would have most strengthened the publishers' position in this case? *(Inference)*

The publishers' position is that the sale of course packs without permission fees reduces the value of the copyrighted works (lines 27–31), so we're looking for something that makes this seem likely.

(A) Course packs for courses that usually have large enrollments had produced a larger profit for the copy-shop owner.

SCOPE (out of scope). *Knowing the type of course that produces the most profit for the copy-shop owner does not help us to determine whether the publishers' sales were impacted. What is this out-of-the-blue contrast between smaller and larger classes? A comparison trap!*

(B) The copy-shop owner had actively solicited professors' orders for course packs.

SCOPE (out of scope). *Whether the copy-shop owner solicited professors is not directly or indirectly related to the issue of whether the sales of these packs hurt the publishers.*

(C) The revenue generated by the copy shop's sale of course packs had risen significantly within the past few years.

SCOPE (out of scope). *Comparison trap! This answer compares current profits with past profits, but doesn't tell us whether those profits were significant enough to reduce the value of the copyrighted works.*

(D) Many area bookstores had reported a marked decrease in the sales of books used for producing course packs.

If this were the case, it would seem that publishers' sales were significantly impacted.

(E) The publishers had enlisted the support of the authors to verify their claims that the copy-shop owner had not obtained permission.

SCOPE (out of scope). *Whether the copy-shop owner obtained permission is not in question. We already know he didn't (lines 5–12).*

Fine-Tuning

Language Matches: Paraphrases and Misquotes

The LSAT has a nasty trick up its sleeve to make the answers harder to find, especially on Identification questions. The right answer might say something that matches the passage very closely, but in completely different language—this is a **paraphrase**. Meanwhile, one or more wrong answers will take their language directly from the passage, but will misuse it or add something incorrect—this is a **misquote**. Let's look at an example:

PrepTest 31, Section 4, Passage 1 *(paragraph 3 only)*

Materials in an ideal industrial ecosystem would
(30) not be depleted any more than are materials in a
biological ecosystem, in which plants synthesize
nutrients that feed herbivores, some of which in turn
feed a chain of carnivores whose waste products and
remains eventually feed further generations of plants.
(35) A chunk of steel could potentially show up one year in
a tin can, the next year in an automobile, and 10 years
later in the skeleton of a building. Some manufacturers
are already making use of "designed offal" in the
manufacture of metals and some plastics: tailoring the
(40) production of waste from a manufacturing process so
that the waste can be fed directly back into that process
or a related one. Such recycling still requires the
expenditure of energy and the unavoidable generation
of some wastes and harmful by-products, but at much
(45) lower levels than are typical today.

6

3. The author of the passage would most probably agree with which one of the following statements about the use of "designed offal" (line 38)?

(A) It is a harmful step that requires the consumption of critical natural resources and results in the generation of waste and harmful by-products.

(B) It is not an entirely helpful step because it draws attention away from the central problems that still need to be solved.

(C) It is a temporary solution that will not contribute to the establishment of an industrial ecosystem.

(D) It is a promising step in the right direction, but it does not solve all of the problems that need to be addressed.

(E) It is the most practical solution to the environmental problems facing the world.

How would we prephrase an answer to this question? The author seems to like the idea of designed offal because the reuse of materials reduces waste. However, the process still does generate waste and by-products, and it requires energy. So our prephrase might be that the use of designed offal is better than the status quo, but still problematic. Scanning the answer choices, we can eliminate (E), which is purely positive. The fact that (A) is purely negative makes it look like a bad choice, too, but hold on. It says exactly what the passage said, right? The use of designed offal generates waste and harmful by-products! Should we hold on to this answer because the language matches so closely? Absolutely not. The first part of this answer ignores the author's point that these harmful products are generated at lower levels than is typical today. This is a misquote!

That leaves us with the three more moderate choices in the middle. We can probably agree with (B) that designed offal would not be an entirely helpful step, but does it draw attention away from the central problems? Do we even know what these central problems are? If there's support for this idea, it's nowhere in paragraph three. Let's cut it.

Answer (C) both acknowledges the use of designed offal as some kind of solution and points out a limitation. This draws language from the passage and looks good! Let's see if we can eliminate (D).

Is it safe to call the designed offal a "promising step"? Yes—it reduces waste. Does it solve all of the problems that need to be addressed? No—we still end up with pollution. Answer (D) seems good; let's look back and see if there's any concrete way to eliminate (C).

Looking back at (C), we could try to pick at the word "temporary." After all, do we know we can't keep on using designed offal indefinitely? That looks fishy, but what about the second part? It says that designed offal will *not* lead to an industrial ecosystem. This goes in the opposite direction from (D), which says it's a step in the right direction. It looks like this is the issue we need to resolve: could the use of designed offal lead to the development of an industrial ecosystem? Looking back, we see that the author describes an "ideal" system in which all materials are reused, and then immediately goes on to say that "some manufacturers are already making use of 'designed offal.'" The word "already" indicates that the author believes these manufacturers are doing something that others will do in the future we've just envisioned. This sounds like it *could* help to bring about an industrial ecosystem (though perhaps not immediately the *ideal* one), so we can safely say it's a step in the right direction. ***Answer (D) wins!***

Notice that (D) doesn't match the language of the passage at all. It doesn't mention reuse, waste, by-products, or industrial ecosystems. Likewise, the passage doesn't mention steps or problems. However, we can see the conceptual match when we look at what the author is trying to say—(D) is a paraphrase. Meanwhile, the answers that *did* draw language from the passage did not use that language correctly: they were misquotes. This is by design—the LSAT is supposed to test more than our ability to scan for text. Now we don't want to let this spook us into eliminating any answer choice that reuses language from the passage. After all, there are plenty of good answers that are tough enough without the LSAT using this trick. However, we also don't want to carelessly choose an answer choice because some of the words in it sound like something the author said. If we lean on our scale and passage map, and go back for support as needed, we can knock out problem answers and find a choice that provides what the question is really asking for.

What if all the answers look bad?

We've all been there. We confidently cross out the first four choices only to find that answer choice (E) looks at least as bad as the rest. Now what? Do we start over from the beginning? Guess and move on? Try to find the least objectionable of the bunch? Depending on the situation, each of these can be a viable strategy. Here are a few factors that might lead you to eliminate all the answers. Each is followed by advice for handling the situation or—better yet—avoiding it in the first place!

1. You misread the question.

Any time you call tech support because your computer isn't working, they're going to want to make sure it's plugged in first. This is the same idea: make sure you're answering the right question. Maybe the question asked about the opinion of someone in the passage and you assumed it was about the author's opinion. Maybe the question asked about the traits of prokaryotes, not eukaryotes. Maybe you're dealing with a Synthesis question and you've only found one part of the answer. Maybe it was really an EXCEPT question (okay, then we'd expect most of the answers to look right, nor wrong). These things happen, but you want to catch that mistake earlier rather than later. Get in the practice of carefully reading the question stem—perhaps even underlining key words in it—and producing a prephrase whenever possible.

2. You need to look elsewhere.

A good passage map will keep you looking in the right place most of the time, but if you can't seem to find support for any of the answer choices, maybe you're looking in the wrong place. Were you able to come up with a good prephrase in the first place? Is there any other part of the passage that might be relevant to the question? Do a quick scan. Maybe paragraph four gets deep into a certain idea, but paragraph one introduces it with a spin that isn't repeated in the later portion.

3. You are stuck on one idea.

Maybe you had a really clever prephrase that you were just *sure* was going to show up in the answer. Or, maybe you've decided that the author is interested in proving Theory X wrong and nothing else. You may need to cast a wider net: is there another way to answer the question? Did you cross out the answer choices because they weren't supported by the passage or because they didn't fit your expectations? Try going back through and eliminating the answers that *must* be wrong due to issues of interpretation, scope, or degree, deferring judgment on any that aren't clearly incorrect. Then, consider the remaining choices afresh, without worrying about your initial idea. You might realize that one of them works better than you thought.

4. The answers are really abstract.

Maybe the right answer matches your prephrase quite well, but it's in really abstract language. Instead of saying "global warming was slowed down by Arctic ice, which is now melting," the correct answer says "a certain set of circumstances is leading to the elimination of certain factors that had previously mitigated the development of those circumstances." Don't be too quick to knock an answer choice out just because it gives you a headache! Defer, and then deal with the headache later if you need to.

Pay attention to the situations in which you end up eliminating all the answers or getting stuck between two—this is often caused by one of the above as well. See if you can identify what leads you to that situation so that you can practice your countermove!

DRILL IT: Similar Answers

Take a few minutes to read this passage and work up the scale and passage map before trying the questions. We've "twisted" the original questions into an extra-tough batch by making all the answer choices similar to one another, although the correct answers are still straight from the real LSAT. Your job is to carefully work wrong-to-right, eliminating all the answers that are incorrect due to issues of interpretation, scope, or degree. What small differences between the choices make one choice right and another wrong? As in the last drill, mark each wrong answer choice with an I, S, D, or ✓ (Interpretation, Scope, Degree, or correct). You may also want to underline the offending words in each wrong choice.

PrepTest 17, Section 4, Passage 4

Some meteorologists have insisted that the severity of the drought in sub-Saharan West Africa and its long duration (nearly 40 years to date) must be a sign of a long-term alteration in climate. (5) Among the theories proposed to explain this change, one hypothesis that has gained widespread attention attributes the drought to a cooling of the Northern Hemisphere. This hypothesis is based on the fact that, between 1945 and the early 1970s, the (10) average annual air temperatures over the landmasses of the Northern Hemisphere decreased by about half a degree Fahrenheit (approximately one quarter of a degree Celsius—a small but significant amount). Several meteorologists have (15) suggested that this cooling was caused by an increase in atmospheric dust emanating from volcanic eruptions and from urban and industrial pollution; the dust reflected incoming sunlight, causing the ground to receive less solar radiation (20) and to transfer less heat to the atmosphere. The cooling seemed to be more pronounced in the middle and high latitudes than in the tropics, an observation that is consistent with the fact that the Sun's rays enter the atmosphere at a greater angle (25) farther north, and so have to pass through more dust-laden atmosphere on the way to the Earth.

Since winds are set in motion by differences in air pressure caused by unequal heating of the atmosphere, supporters of the cooling hypothesis (30) have argued that a growing temperature differential between the unusually cool middle and high latitudes and the warm tropical latitudes is causing a southward expansion of the circumpolar vortex—the high-altitude westerly winds that circle (35) the Northern Hemisphere at middle latitudes. According to this hypothesis, as the circumpolar vortex expands, it forces south other components of large-scale atmospheric circulation and, in effect, displaces the northward-moving monsoon that (40) ordinarily brings sub-Saharan rain. Proponents have further argued that this change in atmospheric circulation might be long-term since cooling in the Northern Hemisphere could be perpetuated by increases in ice and snow coverage there, which (45) would lead to reflection of more sunlight away from the Earth, to further cooling, and, indirectly, to further drought in sub-Saharan West Africa.

Despite these dire predictions, and even though the current African drought has lasted longer than (50) any other in this century, the notion that the drought is caused by cooling of the Northern Hemisphere is, in fact, not well supported. Contrary to the predictions of the cooling hypothesis, during one period of rapid Northern Hemisphere cooling (55) in the early 1950s, the sub-Sahara was unusually rainy. Moreover, in the early 1980s, when the drought was particularly severe, Northern Hemisphere lands actually warmed slightly. And further doubt has been cast on the hypothesis by (60) recent analyses suggesting that, when surface temperatures of water as well as land are taken into account, the Northern Hemisphere may not have cooled at all.

(I, S, D, or ✓ for correct)

MLSAT-Twisted 1. The author's attitude toward the cooling hypothesis is best described as one of *(Synthesis)*

____ (A) vehement opposition
____ (B) cautious skepticism
____ (C) growing disbelief
____ (D) reasoned ambivalence
____ (E) confident dismissal

MLSAT-Twisted 2. Which one of the following best expresses the main idea of the passage? *(Synthesis)*

____ (A) The severity of the drought in sub-Saharan West Africa has not been affected by cooling in the Northern Hemisphere.
____ (B) Northern Hemisphere cooling is not the primary cause of drought in sub-Saharan West Africa.
____ (C) The suggestion that Northern Hemisphere cooling is contributing to a decline of rainfall in sub-Saharan West Africa is open to question.
____ (D) There are cases in which Northern Hemisphere cooling is not associated with a decline in rainfall in sub-Saharan West Africa.
____ (E) The suggestion by some meteorologists that Northern Hemisphere cooling is a product of diminished rainfall in sub-Saharan West Africa is not well supported.

MLSAT-Twisted 3. According to the passage, proponents of the cooling hypothesis suggested that the circumpolar vortex is likely to expand when which one of the following occurs? *(Identification)*

____ (A) There is a growing temperature differential between the middle and tropical latitudes.
____ (B) There is a growing temperature differential between southward and westward winds.
____ (C) The tropical latitudes become unusually cool.
____ (D) There is a significant increase in the difference between the average annual atmospheric temperature of the tropics and that of the more northern latitudes.
(E) There is a significant increase in the difference between the average annual atmospheric temperatures of the middle and the high latitudes in the Northern Hemisphere.

MLSAT-Twisted 4. Which one of the following best describes the organization of the passage? *(Synthesis)*

____ (A) Opposing points of view are presented, evidence supporting each point of view is discussed, and then one point of view is questioned.
____ (B) Opposing points of view are presented, evidence supporting one point of view is discussed, and then one point of view is questioned.
____ (C) A theory explaining a phenomenon is proposed, supporting evidence is considered, and then the theory is adjusted in response to new research.
____ (D) A theory explaining a phenomenon is proposed, supporting evidence is considered, and then the theory is disputed.
____ (E) A theory is explained in detail and its plausibility is demonstrated, but most of its predictions are contradicted.

SOLUTIONS: Similar Answers

Scale and Passage Map

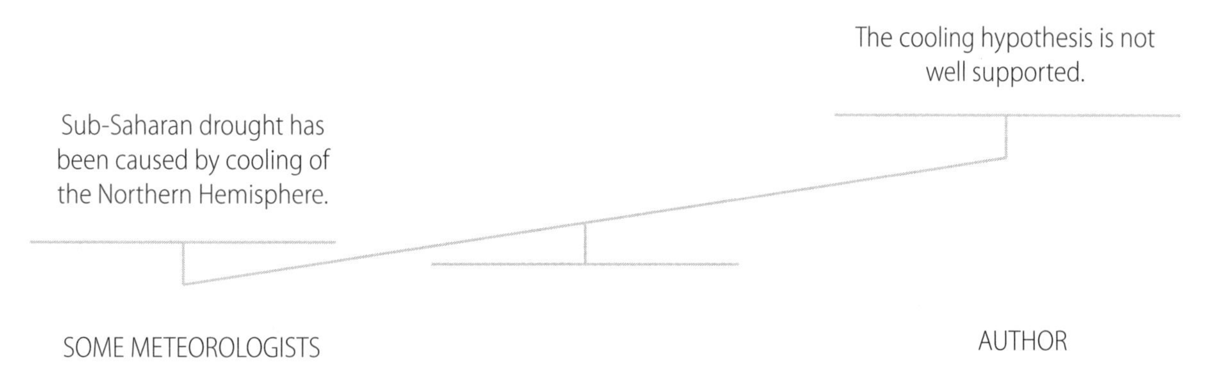

P1: Introduction of one explanation for a phenomenon. A well-known hypothesis is that the drought in sub-Saharan Africa was caused by long-term climate change brought about by cooling of the Northern hemisphere due to the reflection of sunlight by atmospheric dust.

P2: More detailed explanation. According to this "cooling hypothesis," temperature differences between the north and south cause an expansion of the circumpolar vortex, driving away rain-carrying monsoons.

P3: Refutation of the explanation. A cooling Northern Hemisphere and sub-Saharan drought don't seem to match up. Also, the Northern Hemisphere may not actually have cooled.

MLSAT-Twisted 1. The author's attitude toward the cooling hypothesis is best described as one of

We can definitely prephrase this one. The author ends the passage with a full paragraph putting down the cooling hypothesis. Clearly, the author's attitude toward the hypothesis is negative. So what do we do when we scan down the answer choices and see that all of them look fairly negative? We fine-tune. What exactly does the author think? Apparently there isn't much support for the cooling hypothesis—its predictions don't hold up, and the Northern Hemisphere may not actually be cooling. However, the author doesn't say anything terribly mean about the idea or say that it is definitively false.

(A) vehement opposition

The author doesn't support the idea, but doesn't get vehement about it. ***DEGREE (opinion).***

(B) cautious skepticism

This sounds good, if a little weak.

(C) growing disbelief

This one is tricky. The author certainly doesn't seem to believe in this hypothesis, but is this disbelief growing? We don't know anything about the author's earlier level of belief—this is a comparison trap. ***INTERPRETATION (unsupported).***

(D) reasoned ambivalence

Ambivalence would indicate that the author is pulled in two different directions, and we have no indication of a pull in the other direction. ***INTERPRETATION (unsupported).***

(E) confident dismissal

This one also looks good. The author seems fairly confident in dismissing the hypothesis. We're told flat out that the theory is "not well supported" (lines 50–52).

So how do we choose between (B) and (E)? Since (B) seems a bit weak, we might be tempted to drop it in favor of (E). However, this would be a mistake. Generally, when we are faced with two similar answers, one of which is milder than the other, we are better off with the mild choice! In this case, we can see that the author is not absolutely certain. The predictions of the cooling hypothesis don't seem to hold up (lines 53–58), and the Northern Hemisphere *may* have cooled, but the author doesn't know for sure. Despite the author's criticism, we've also seen some evidence for the hypothesis, such as the apparent increase in cooling at higher latitudes (lines 21–26). **We're better off with (B)**—cautious skepticism.

MLSAT-Twisted 2. Which one of the following best expresses the main idea of the passage?

This is similar to the last one. We want the author's side of the scale: the cooling hypothesis is not well supported.

(A) The severity of the drought in sub-Saharan West Africa has not been affected by cooling in the Northern Hemisphere.

This is a bit too much. The author isn't a fan of the cooling hypothesis, but we never get a complete dismissal of the idea. ***DEGREE (opinion).***

(B) Northern Hemisphere cooling is not the primary cause of drought in sub-Saharan West Africa.

This is a bit milder than (A), because it leaves open the possibility that cooling is a cause, just not the primary one. However, this is still an absolute statement, rather than a statement of doubt. Also, there is no discussion of whether any one factor is the primary *cause.* ***DEGREE (opinion/modifier).***

(C) The suggestion that Northern Hemisphere cooling is contributing to a decline of rainfall in sub-Saharan West Africa is open to question.

This should work. It only says that the issue is open to question; that seems similar to "not well supported."

(D) There are cases in which Northern Hemisphere cooling is not associated with a decline in rainfall in sub-Saharan West Africa.

The author cites such a case (lines 53–56), but that's not the overall point. ***SCOPE (narrow).***

(E) The suggestion by some meteorologists that Northern Hemisphere cooling is a product of diminished rainfall in sub-Saharan West Africa is not well supported.

This looks a lot like (C). Aside from some slight differences in wording ("open to question" vs. "not well supported," "a decline in rainfall vs. "diminished rainfall"), they seem to be saying the same thing. But wait! Can you spot the big difference? Choice (C) is talking about the idea that cooling causes drought, while (E) says that some people think cooling is caused by *drought! There's nothing about that in the passage. Answer* ***(C) wins.***

MLSAT-Twisted 3. According to the passage, proponents of the cooling hypothesis suggested that the circumpolar vortex is likely to expand when which one of the following occurs?

Lines 29–34 tell us that according to the cooling hypothesis, a growing difference in temperature between the warm tropical latitudes on the one hand and the cooling middle and northern latitudes on the other is causing the circumpolar vortex to expand south. We can expect a comparison trap—one or more wrong answers will try to compare the middle and northern latitudes, while the passage lumps them together!

(A) There is a growing temperature differential between the middle and tropical latitudes.

Although it doesn't mention northern latitudes, a difference between the middle and tropical latitudes would still fit the description. Let's defer judgment.

(B) There is a growing temperature differential between southward and westward winds.

This isn't the comparison trap we were expecting, but it does make a comparison that we can't support. The passage mentions that the circumpolar vortex, which consists of westerly winds, is expanding southward, but there is no comparison of southward and westward winds. ***INTERPRETATION (unsupported).***

(C) The tropical latitudes become unusually cool.

If the tropical latitudes become cooler, this will make them closer in temperature to the northern latitudes. We want to see an increase *in the difference!* ***INTERPRETATION (contradicted).***

(D) There is a significant increase in the difference between the average annual atmospheric temperature of the tropics and that of the more northern latitudes.

This looks fairly similar to (A). Let's defer on this.

(E) There is a significant increase in the difference between the average annual atmospheric temperatures of the middle and the high latitudes in the Northern Hemisphere.

Here's the comparison trap we predicted. We aren't looking for a difference between middle and high. ***INTERPRETATION (unsupported).***

Coming back to (A) and (D), we see that they both look like the description in lines 30–34: "a growing temperature differential between the unusually cool middle and high latitudes and the warm tropical latitudes is causing a southward expansion of the circumpolar vortex." So what's the difference between them? First, (A) uses the same language as the passage—"temperature differential"—while (D) refers to the difference between average temperatures. Is this a problem for (D)? Absolutely not—this is a paraphrase. So what else is different? Answer (A) refers only to the differential between the middle and tropical latitudes, while (D) compares the tropical latitudes and all the more northern latitudes (this would include both the middle and high latitudes). Could the expansion be driven by a difference between middle and tropical latitudes, without anything changing up north? It might, but we don't know for sure. Answer ***(D) is correct*** *because it better matches the text, without leaving any of the different latitudes out.*

MLSAT-Twisted 4. Which one of the following best describes the organization of the passage?

Structural questions like this one are all about the passage map, so we can prephrase straight from there. The author introduces the cooling hypothesis and explains it in detail before letting us know it doesn't look good.

(A) Opposing points of view are presented, evidence supporting each point of view is discussed, and then one point of view is questioned.

(B) Opposing points of view are presented, evidence supporting one point of view is discussed, and then one point of view is questioned.

These two look really similar! The only difference is whether we see support for one point of view or for both. Skimming back over the passage, we see a lot of discussion of the cooling hypothesis, and maybe a little support for it (lines 8–12, 20–26), but is there any support for the other point of view? Wait, what other point of view? The author puts down the cooling hypothesis at the end, but we aren't presented with any competing hypothesis. Answer choices (A) and (B) are both out. ***SCOPE (out of scope).***

(C) A theory explaining a phenomenon is proposed, supporting evidence is considered, and then the theory is adjusted in response to new research.

(D) A theory explaining a phenomenon is proposed, supporting evidence is considered, and then the theory is disputed.

Another closely matched pair. The only difference is the ending. The first two parts look okay—we have the cooling hypothesis and some support for it—but what about the end? We see some new research ("recent analyses" in line 60), but does the theory get adjusted? No, the author just says it's not well supported (lines 50–52). Answer (C) is out. Let's hang on to (D).

(E) A theory is explained in detail and its plausibility is demonstrated, but most of its predictions are contradicted.

This looks fairly reasonable. We have a very detailed description, and the second paragraph explains how cooling could cause a drought in Africa—that sounds like a demonstration of plausibility. Then, at the end, we see its predictions get slammed down, right? Okay, but can you spot the dangerous word here? This answer choice says that most *of the predictions are contradicted, but we don't know how many predictions the hypothesis has produced. We have a few data points that don't fit the hypothesis (lines 53–58). After that, the passage attacks the underlying* cause*—cooling in the Northern Hemisphere—rather than any additional predictions. Additionally, the author acknowledges that the continued African drought is consistent with the hypothesis (lines 48–50).* ***DEGREE (modifier).***

Furthermore, the fact that some of the predictions have not come true is used to argue that the underlying theory is questionable. Thus, this answer is missing the larger picture. ***SCOPE (narrow).***

All we're left with now is the real answer, (D). *In some ways, we like our made-up answer (E) better. After all, the author doesn't mention much support for the cooling hypothesis—we're mostly told how it might work—but if we have to choose between an imperfect-seeming answer and one that has a single* wrong *word in it, we need to eliminate the wrong answer, no matter how unsatisfying the right answer may be.*

It's important to keep in mind that the right answer will often be written in an off-putting manner to make it harder to spot, while the wrong answers will be candy-coated to go down smooth! This is where a calm, cool, wrong-to-right process serves us very well! Get in the habit of making the easy eliminations first, and then digging deep only if there are several plausible answers. Then go back later when the time pressure is gone and review your work. The long-term goal is to be able to get better and faster at spotting wrong answers, even when the pressure is on! If you found that this drill strengthened your wrong-to-right muscles, make a note on your calendar to come back to it in a week or two when you've forgotten the answers. In the meantime, you can see more of these in your online resources.

 For more practice, log in to your Student Center!

Changing How You Work the Questions: Deeply Review Tempting Answers

Deep review is the key to honing your wrong-answer radar. Consider this answer sheet:

~~(A)~~

(B)
~~(C)~~
~~(D)~~
(E)

What do you think is the minimum review you should do?

Regardless of whether (B) turns out to be right or wrong, you should look for specific textual support for your choice if you didn't earlier. You should also identify *exactly* what's wrong with (E), the answer you couldn't easily eliminate but didn't pick. It's crucial that you slay any tempting answers that you have faced. Ideally, you would do this review without knowing whether you answered the question correctly, and definitely without knowing which answer is correct if you got it wrong. (We recommend that you put a star next to tough questions as you do a practice set and review all of those before checking your answers, and then, when you mark up your answer sheet, just mark right or wrong instead of writing in which answer is correct.)

The LSAT test writers put a lot of time and thought into writing tempting wrong answers. In order to sidestep their traps, you need to match their effort.

Chapter 6¾ of Reading Comprehension

Part 3: Apply Your Knowledge

Progress Check

Grade Yourself

We've done a lot so far—it's almost time to crack open an RC cola and celebrate finishing all the foundational work in this book. We'll actually go ahead and tell you what's in the rest of the book: some advice on improving your timing, a reminder to do everything we've told you even when the passages are difficult or strange, a bunch of practice, and some final thoughts. Valuable stuff, but at this point it's all about putting what you've learned into practice. The essential question, therefore, is how much of a 170+ approach you've started putting into place. It's fine if you gave some of the recommended strategies a test drive and found that something else works better for you, but if you're simply reading and studying the same way you've always done out of force of habit, it's time to break out.

To that end, here's a chart to help you identify weaknesses in your overall RC approach. Mark where you fall on each of the spectrums. When you're done, we'll have you do a special four-passage practice set to start addressing any shortcomings.

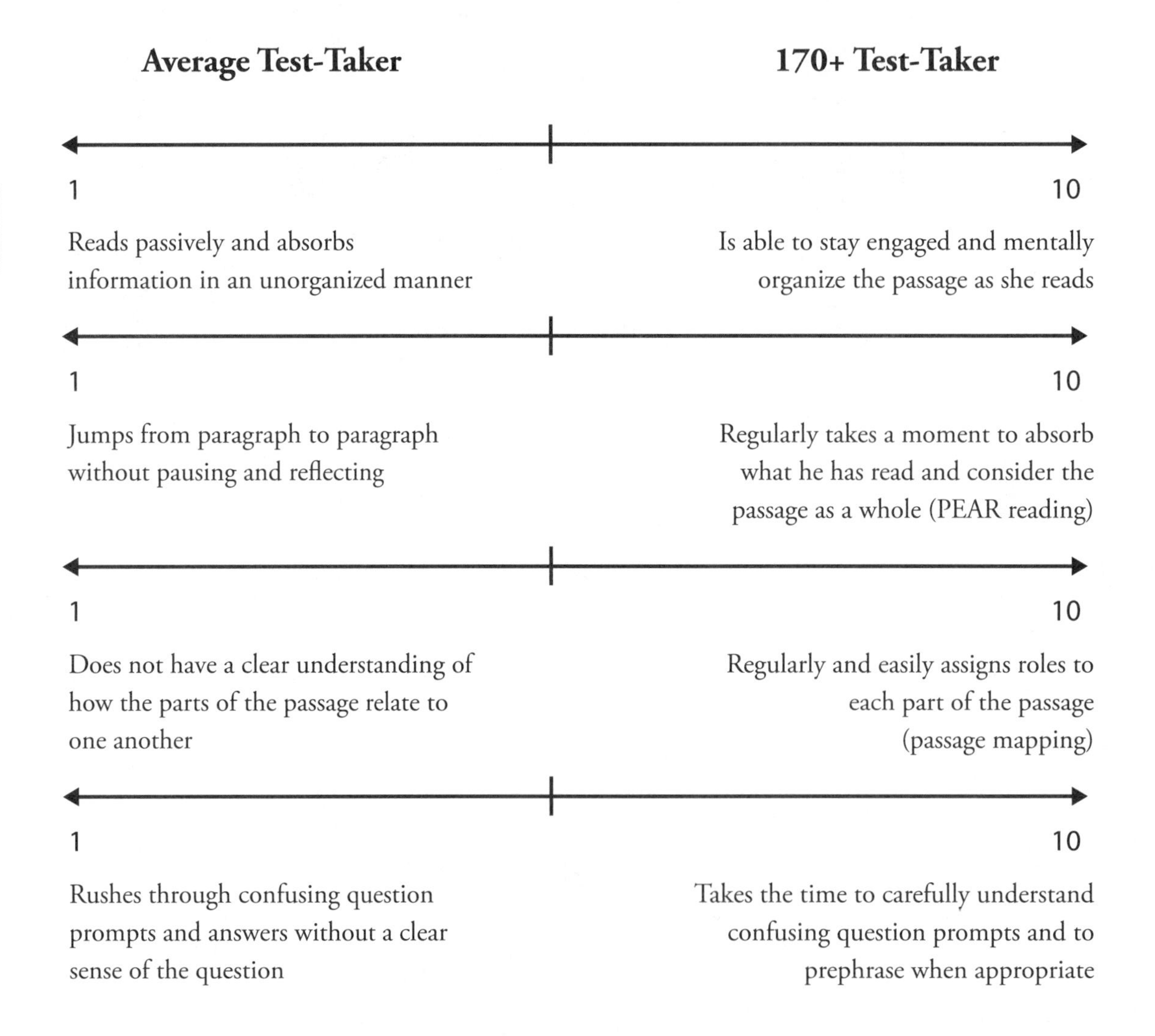

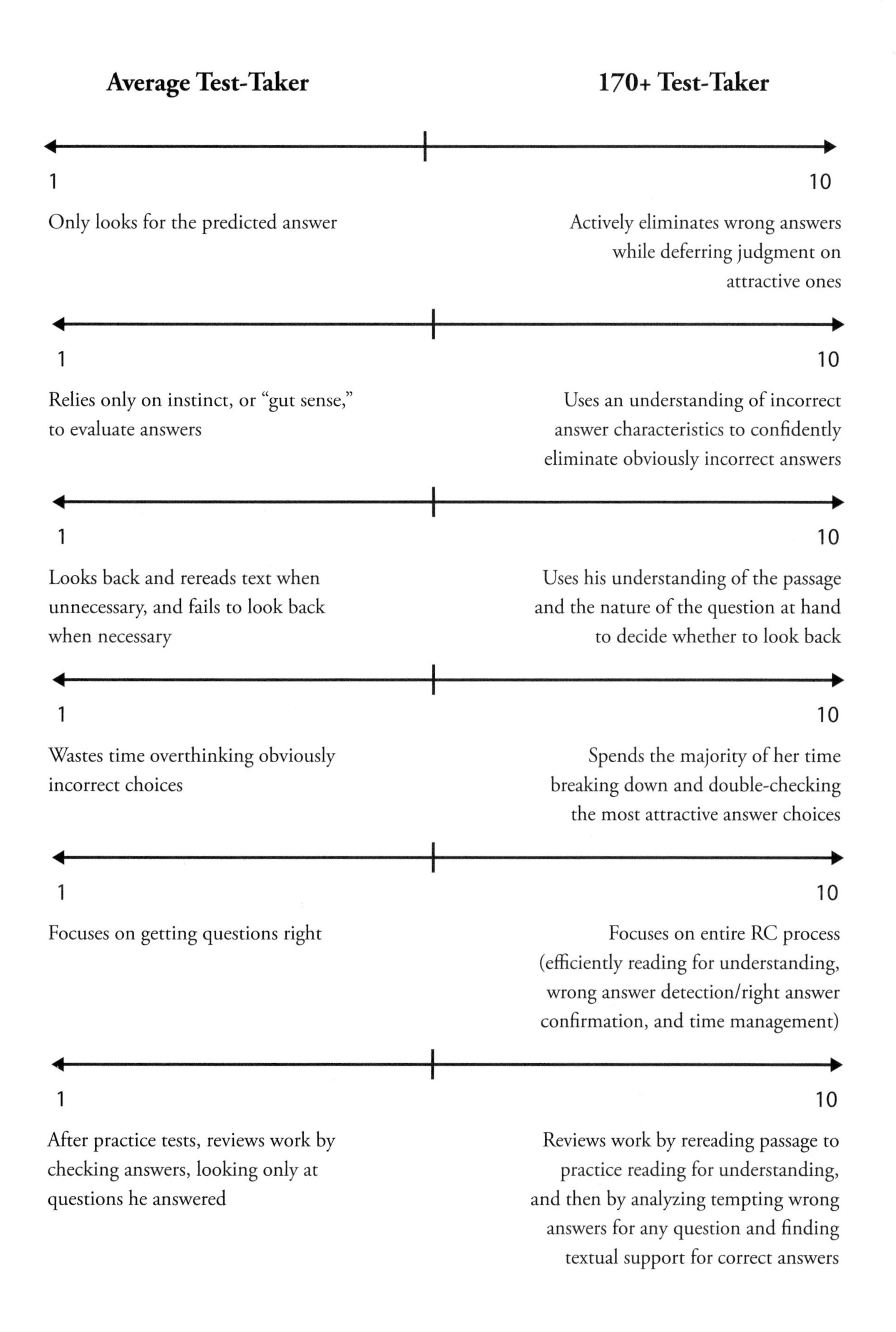
Average Test-Taker
170+ Test-Taker
1
10
Only looks for the predicted answer
Actively eliminates wrong answers while deferring judgment on attractive ones
1
10
Relies only on instinct, or "gut sense," to evaluate answers
Uses an understanding of incorrect answer characteristics to confidently eliminate obviously incorrect answers
1
10
Looks back and rereads text when unnecessary, and fails to look back when necessary
Uses his understanding of the passage and the nature of the question at hand to decide whether to look back
1
10
Wastes time overthinking obviously incorrect choices
Spends the majority of her time breaking down and double-checking the most attractive answer choices
1
10
Focuses on getting questions right
Focuses on entire RC process (efficiently reading for understanding, wrong answer detection/right answer confirmation, and time management)
1
10
After practice tests, reviews work by checking answers, looking only at questions he answered
Reviews work by rereading passage to practice reading for understanding, and then by analyzing tempting wrong answers for any question and finding textual support for correct answers

Now that you've graded yourself, hide your report card from your parents and do something about those weaknesses! For most of the above, the fix is to do some practice sets in which you pay particular attention to one step in the process. The upcoming practice set is a great place to start. Focus on prephrasing, using PEAR, or whatever the goal is, and forgive yourself if you temporarily fall short in other areas. If you often get down to two answers and feel unable to decide confidently (regardless of whether you eventually choose right or wrong), strengthen your review process, intensifying your focus both on identifying textual support for correct answers and on wrong-answer analysis. For each tempting wrong answer, verbalize a clear explanation for why it's wrong and then use our explanations to check your thinking.

Still Lost?

If you're still finding yourself lost on at least two passages per set, you should continue to focus on reading for the scale and PEAR, but you may also need to spend some time developing the fundamental skill of comprehending what you read. We've discussed most of the following ideas before, but in the excitement of the first few chapters, you may have missed them. This pause in the book, before we start focusing on more difficult and unusual passages, is a great time to try incorporating some of these new techniques:

1. If you're finding the passage content simply leaving your brain the moment it enters, practice visualizing what you're reading. You can read more about this on page 51.
2. Take more notes the more difficult a passage gets. You can read more about this on page 58.
3. Quickly skim the passage to identify the passage's general topic before you dive in. Here, when we say "quickly," we mean *quickly*—perhaps just four seconds. In life, it's rare that you're handed a random piece of text with no context or introduction and expected to read and comprehend quickly. A quick skim can at least tell you that a passage is about medieval art, European legal doctrine, etc., and give you a head start on getting to the scale.
4. Force yourself to spend a little time mentally building a passage map. It can be hard to keep your cool and not dive into the questions, but a quick review of what you've read can increase your grasp and save you time during the questions. You can review the process in chapter 4.
5. Note-taking and visualization can help you to better remember what you read, but it is also possible to increase your working memory—your brain's short-term capacity to hold information—by summarizing passages aloud after reading them. (This is obviously not a technique to use on test day!) You can practice this on non-LSAT passages from academic texts. If you have a friend to study with, this is a great partner exercise. Speaking of academic texts…
6. If you have a particular topic weakness—science or humanities, for example—let that topic take over your leisure reading for a while. Focus on reading with comprehension and try to enjoy learning about a new topic. You can find a list of suggested reading in your Student Center.

There's one more issue that you may be facing: timing. We have lots to say about time management in the next chapter, but before we get into that, go ahead and do the following set of passages with a focus on improving the weaknesses you identified above.

DRILL IT: Coached Practice Set

Now that you have a sense of what to work on, let's put it all together and see if you can move yourself a few notches closer to a 170+ technique. In order to prevent you from slipping back into your old RC habits, we're going to sit in and remind you what to do at each step along the way. You should only give yourself 30 minutes for this set, as we've cherry-picked the questions to focus on important parts of the process. See you in 30 minutes!

Passage 1: PT42, S3, P3

Because the market system enables entrepreneurs and investors who develop new technology to reap financial rewards from their risk of capital, it may seem that the primary result of this activity is that some (5) people who have spare capital accumulate more. But in spite of the fact that the profits derived from various technological developments have accrued to relatively few people, the developments themselves have served overall as a remarkable democratizing force. In fact, (10) under the regime of the market, the gap in benefits accruing to different groups of people has been narrowed in the long term.

Did you notice the pivot to the author's position? What do you think the rest of this passage will be about?

This tendency can be seen in various well-known technological developments. For example, before the (15) printing press was introduced centuries ago, few people had access to written materials, much less to scribes and private secretaries to produce and transcribe documents. Since printed materials have become widely available, however, people without special (20) position or resources—and in numbers once thought impossible—can take literacy and the use of printed texts for granted. With the distribution of books and periodicals in public libraries, this process has been extended to the point where people in general can have (25) essentially equal access to a vast range of texts that would once have been available only to a very few. A more recent technological development extends this process beyond printed documents. A child in school with access to a personal computer and modem— (30) which is becoming fairly common in technologically advanced societies—has computing power and database access equal to that of the best-connected scientists and engineers at top-level labs of just fifteen years ago, a time when relatively few people had (35) personal access to any computing power. Or consider the uses of technology for leisure. In previous centuries only a few people with abundant resources had the ability and time to hire professional entertainment, and to have contact through travel and written (40) communication—both of which were prohibitively expensive—with distant people. But now broadcast technology is widely available, and so almost anyone can have an entertainment cornucopia unimagined in earlier times. Similarly, the development of (45) inexpensive mail distribution and telephone connection and, more recently, the establishment of the even more efficient medium of electronic mail have greatly extended the power of distant communication.

What were those examples of? Put a mark next to each example.

This kind of gradual diffusion of benefits across (50) society is not an accident of these particular technological developments, but rather the result of a general tendency of the market system. Entrepreneurs and investors often are unable to maximize financial success without expanding their market, and this (55) involves structuring their prices to the consumers so as to make their technologies genuinely accessible to an ever-larger share of the population. In other words, because market competition drives prices down, it tends to diffuse access to new technology across (60) society as a result.

How did that relate to what the author said in the first paragraph? What's the author's goal in this last paragraph?

Don't forget to do your passage map!

16. Which one of the following does the passage identify as being a result of technological development?

Be sure to confirm your answer using the text.

(A) burgeoning scientific research
(B) educational uses of broadcasting
(C) widespread exchange of political ideas
(D) faster means of travel
(E) increased access to databases

18. Which one of the following most accurately represents the primary function of the reference to maximization of financial success (lines 52–54)?

Prephrase this, then work wrong-to-right.

(A) It forms part of the author's summary of the benefits that have resulted from the technological developments described in the preceding paragraph.
(B) It serves as the author's logical conclusion from data presented in the preceding paragraph regarding the social consequences of technological development.
(C) It forms part of a speculative hypothesis that the author presents for its interest in relation to the main topic rather than as part of an argument.
(D) It serves as part of a causal explanation that reinforces the thesis in the first paragraph regarding the benefits of technological development.
(E) It forms part of the author's concession that certain factors complicate the argument presented in the first two paragraphs.

19. It can be most reasonably inferred from the passage that the author would agree with which one of the following statements?

Can you eliminate any answers because they are clearly contradicted by the author's position? Any that are too extreme or out of scope? When you're down to two or three, use your passage map to find the relevant text for each remaining answer choice and pick the one that is closest to the text.

(A) The profits derived from computer technology have accrued to fewer people than have the profits derived from any other technological development.
(B) Often the desire of some people for profits motivates changes that are beneficial for large numbers of other people.
(C) National boundaries are rarely barriers to the democratizing spread of technology.
(D) Typically, investment in technology is riskier than many other sorts of investment.
(E) Greater geographical mobility of populations has contributed to the profits of entrepreneurs and investors in technology.

20. From the passage it can be most reasonably inferred that the author would agree with which one of the following statements?

Same approach as for the last question. It's not possible to predict this answer; instead, work your way through all the answers before deciding.

(A) The democratizing influence of technology generally contributes to technological obsolescence.
(B) Wholly unregulated economies are probably the fastest in producing an equalization of social status.
(C) Expanded access to printed texts across a population has historically led to an increase in literacy in that population.
(D) The invention of the telephone has had a greater democratizing influence on society than has the invention of the printing press.
(E) Near equality of financial assets among people is a realistic goal for market economies.

Passage 2: PT42, S3, P4

Neurobiologists once believed that the workings of the brain were guided exclusively by electrical signals; according to this theory, communication between neurons (brain cells) is possible because electrical (5) impulses travel from one neuron to the next by literally leaping across synapses (gaps between neurons). But many neurobiologists puzzled over how this leaping across synapses might be achieved, and as early as 1904 some speculated that electrical impulses (10) are transmitted between neurons chemically rather than electrically.

Predict what's going to be said in the rest of this paragraph and passage.

According to this alternative theory, the excited neuron secretes a chemical called a neurotransmitter that binds with its corresponding receptor molecule in the receiving neuron. This binding (15) of the neurotransmitter renders the neuron permeable to ions, and as the ions move into the receiving neuron they generate an electrical impulse that runs through the cell; the electrical impulse is thereby transmitted to the receiving neuron.

The details are less important than the big picture. What was that an example of?

(20) This theory has gradually won acceptance in the scientific community, but for a long time little was known about the mechanism by which neurotransmitters manage to render the receiving neuron permeable to ions. In fact, some scientists (25) remained skeptical of the theory because they had trouble imagining how the binding of a chemical to a receptor at the cell surface could influence the flow of ions through the cell membrane. Recently, however, researchers have gathered enough evidence for a (30) convincing explanation: that the structure of receptors plays the pivotal role in mediating the conversion of chemical signals into electrical activity.

How does this relate to the question raised in the first paragraph?

The new evidence shows that receptors for neurotransmitters contain both a neurotransmitter (35) binding site and a separate region that functions as a channel for ions; attachment of the neurotransmitter to the binding site causes the receptor to change shape and so results in the opening of its channel component. Several types of receptors have been isolated that (40) conform to this structure, among them the receptors for acetylcholine, gamma-aminobutyric acid (GABA), glycine, and serotonin. These receptors display enough similarities to constitute a family, known collectively as neurotransmitter-gated ion channels.

Again, don't worry about knowing every detail. In general, what was that last paragraph?

(45) It has also been discovered that each of the receptors in this family comes in several varieties so that, for example, a GABA receptor in one part of the brain has slightly different properties than a GABA receptor in another part of the brain. This discovery is (50) medically significant because it raises the possibility of the highly selective treatment of certain brain disorders. As the precise effect on behavior of every variety of each neurotransmitter-gated ion channel is deciphered, pharmacologists may be able to design (55) drugs targeted to specific receptors on defined categories of neurons that will selectively impede or enhance these effects. Such drugs could potentially help ameliorate any number of debilitating conditions, including mood disorders, tissue damage associated (60) with stroke, or Alzheimer's disease.

How did this relate to the general discussion?

Do that passage map!

21. Which one of the following most completely and accurately states the main point of the passage?

Prephrase and then work wrong-to-right! Be careful of answers that are too narrow, referencing something in the passage that is not the main idea.

(A) Evidence shows that the workings of the brain are guided, not by electrical signals, but by chemicals, and that subtle differences among the receptors for these chemicals may permit the selective treatment of certain brain disorders.
(B) Evidence shows that the workings of the brain are guided, not by electrical signals, but by chemicals, and that enough similarities exist among these chemicals to allow scientists to classify them as a family.
(C) Evidence shows that electrical impulses are transmitted between neurons chemically rather than electrically, and that enough similarities exist among these chemicals to allow scientists to classify them as a family.
(D) Evidence shows that electrical impulses are transmitted between neurons chemically rather than electrically, and that subtle differences among the receptors for these chemicals may permit the selective treatment of certain brain disorders.
(E) Evidence shows that receptor molecules in the brain differ subtly from one another, and that these differences can be exploited to treat certain brain disorders through the use of drugs that selectively affect particular parts of the brain.

23. Each of the following statements is affirmed by the passage EXCEPT:

Keep an eye on that EXCEPT. One way to do that is to draw a line around "EXCEPT" and down through the answer choices as a reminder.

(A) The secretion of certain chemicals plays a role in neuron communication.
(B) The flow of ions through neurons plays a role in neuron communication.
(C) The binding of neurotransmitters to receptors plays a role in neuron communication.
(D) The structure of receptors on neuron surfaces plays a role in neuron communication.
(E) The size of neurotransmitter binding sites on receptors plays a role in neuron communication.

24. The author most likely uses the phrase "defined categories of neurons" in lines 55–56 in order to refer to neurons that

Prephrase and look out for answers that are factually true but don't describe why the author used the phrase.

(A) possess channels for ions
(B) respond to drug treatment
(C) contain receptor molecules
(D) influence particular brain functions
(E) react to binding by neurotransmitters

25. Which one of the following most accurately describes the organization of the passage?

Prephrase and keep in mind that the wrong answers will often have one or more accurate elements.

(A) explanation of a theory; presentation of evidence in support of the theory; presentation of evidence in opposition to the theory; argument in favor of rejecting the theory; discussion of the implication of rejecting the theory
(B) explanation of a theory; presentation of evidence in support of the theory; explanation of an alternative theory; presentation of information to support the alternative theory; discussion of an experiment that can help determine which theory is correct
(C) explanation of a theory; description of an obstacle to the theory's general acceptance; presentation of an explanation that helps the theory overcome the obstacle; discussion of a further implication of the theory
(D) explanation of a theory; description of an obstacle to the theory's general acceptance; argument that the obstacle is insurmountable and that the theory should be rejected; discussion of the implications of rejecting the theory
(E) explanation of a theory; description of how the theory came to win scientific acceptance; presentation of new information that challenges the theory; modification of the theory to accommodate the new information; discussion of an implication of the modification.

Passage 3: PT41, S4, P2

Countee Cullen (Countee Leroy Porter, 1903–1946) was one of the foremost poets of the Harlem Renaissance, the movement of African American writers, musicians, and artists centered in the (5) Harlem section of New York City during the 1920's. Beginning with his university years, Cullen strove to establish himself as an author of romantic poetry on abstract, universal topics such as love and death. Believing poetry should consist of "lofty thoughts (10) beautifully expressed," Cullen preferred controlled poetic forms. He used European forms such as sonnets and devices such as quatrains, couplets, and conventional rhyme, and he frequently employed classical allusions and Christian religious imagery, (15) which were most likely the product both of his university education and of his upbringing as the adopted son of a Methodist Episcopal reverend.

 *Where do you think this is going?*

Some literary critics have praised Cullen's skill at writing European-style verse, finding, for example, in (20) "The Ballad of the Brown Girl" an artful use of diction and a rhythm and sonority that allow him to capture the atmosphere typical of the English ballad form of past centuries. Others have found Cullen's use of European verse forms and techniques unsuited to treating (25) political or racial themes, such as the themes in "Uncle Jim," in which a young man is told by his uncle of the different experiences of African Americans and whites in United States society, or "Incident," which relates the experience of an eight-year-old child who hears a (30) racial slur. One such critic complained that Cullen's persona as expressed in his work sometimes seems to vacillate between aesthete and spokesperson for racial issues. But Cullen himself rejected this dichotomy, maintaining that his interest in romantic (35) poetry was quite compatible with his concern over racial issues. He drew a distinction between poetry of solely political intent and his own work, which he believed reflected his identify as an African American. As the heartfelt expression of his personality (40) accomplished by means of careful attention to his chosen craft, his work could not help but do so.

 *Many sides of an issue were described above. Make sure you have a clear sense of the issue before moving on. Did you notice the author?*

Explicit references to racial matters do in fact decline in Cullen's later work, but not because he felt any less passionately about these matters. Rather, (45) Cullen increasingly focused on the religious dimension of his poetry. In "The Black Christ," in which the poet imagines the death and resurrection of a rural African American, and "Heritage," which expresses the tension between the poet's identification with Christian (50) traditions and his desire to stay close to his African heritage, Cullen's thoughts on race were subsumed within what he conceived of as broader and more urgent questions about the suffering and redemption of the soul. Nonetheless, Cullen never abandoned his (55) commitment to the importance of racial issues, reflecting on one occasion that he felt "actuated by a strong sense of race consciousness" that "grows upon me, I find, as I grow older."

 *How does this last paragraph relate to the issue discussed in depth in the second paragraph?*

 *Passage map!*

7. Which one of the following most accurately states the main point of the passage?

 *Prephrase and work wrong-to-right.*

(A) While much of Cullen's poetry deals with racial issues, in his later work he became less concerned with racial matters and increasingly interested in writing poetry with a religious dimension.
(B) While Cullen used European verse forms and his later poems increasingly addressed religious themes, his poetry never abandoned a concern for racial issues.
(C) Though Cullen used European verse forms, he acknowledged that these forms were not very well suited to treating political or racial themes.
(D) Despite the success of Cullen's poetry at dealing with racial issues, Cullen's primary goal was to re-create the atmosphere that characterized the English ballad.
(E) The religious dimension throughout Cullen's poetry complemented his focus on racial issues by providing the context within which these issues could be understood.

8. Given the information in the passage, which one of the following most closely exemplifies Cullen's conception of poetry?

Quickly remind yourself of his conception of poetry. Eliminate obvious wrong answers and then drill down into the details during your second pass.

(A) a sonnet written with careful attention to the conventions of the form to re-create the atmosphere of sixteenth-century English poetry
(B) a sonnet written with deliberate disregard for the conventions of the form to illustrate the perils of political change
(C) a sonnet written to explore the aesthetic impact of radical innovations in diction, rhythm, and sonority
(D) a sonnet written with great stylistic freedom to express the emotional upheaval associated with romantic love
(E) a sonnet written with careful attention to the conventions of the form expressing feelings about the inevitability of death

9. Which one of the following is NOT identified by the author of the passage as characteristic of Cullen's poetry?

Eliminate characteristics that you clearly remember, then use the text to make final eliminations.

(A) It often deals with abstract, universal subject matter.
(B) It often employs rhyme, classical allusions, and religious imagery.
(C) It avoids traditional poetic forms in favor of formal experimentation.
(D) It sometimes deals explicitly with racial issues.
(E) It eventually subsumed racial issues into a discussion of religious issues.

10. The passage suggests which one of the following about Cullen's use of controlled poetic forms?

Eliminate obvious wrong answers, then go back to the text.

(A) Cullen used controlled poetic forms because he believed they provided the best means to beautiful poetic expression.
(B) Cullen's interest in religious themes naturally led him to use controlled poetic forms.
(C) Only the most controlled poetic forms allowed Cullen to address racial issues in his poems.
(D) Cullen had rejected the less controlled poetic forms he was exposed to prior to his university years.
(E) Less controlled poetic forms are better suited to poetry that addresses racial or political issues.

Passage 4: PT41, S4, P4

Although philanthropy—the volunteering of private resources for humanitarian purposes—reached its apex in England in the late nineteenth century, modern commentators have articulated two major (5) criticisms of the philanthropy that was a mainstay of England's middle-class Victorian society. The earlier criticism is that such philanthropy was even by the later nineteenth century obsolete, since industrialism had already created social problems that were beyond the (10) scope of small, private voluntary efforts. Indeed, these problems required substantial legislative action by the state. Unemployment, for example, was not the result of a failure of diligence on the part of workers or a failure of compassion on the part of employers, nor (15) could it be solved by well-wishing philanthropists.

Summarize that first criticism and get ready for the second...

The more recent charge holds that Victorian philanthropy was by its very nature a self-serving exercise carried out by philanthropists at the expense of those whom they were ostensibly serving. In this view, (20) philanthropy was a means of flaunting one's power and position in a society that placed great emphasis on status, or even a means of cultivating social connections that could lead to economic rewards. Further, if philanthropy is seen as serving the interests (25) of individual philanthropists, so it may be seen as serving the interests of their class. According to this "social control" thesis, philanthropists, in professing to help the poor, were encouraging in them such values as prudence, thrift, and temperance, values perhaps (30) worthy in themselves but also designed to create more productive members of the labor force. Philanthropy, in short, was a means of controlling the labor force and ensuring the continued dominance of the management class.

Summarize the second criticism. Anticipate what's coming next.

(35) Modern critics of Victorian philanthropy often use the words "amateurish" or "inadequate" to describe Victorian philanthropy, as though Victorian charity can only be understood as an antecedent to the era of state-sponsored, professionally administered charity. This (40) assumption is typical of the "Whig fallacy": the tendency to read the past as an inferior prelude to an enlightened present. If most Victorians resisted state control and expended their resources on private, voluntary philanthropies, it could only be, the argument (45) goes, because of their commitment to a vested interest, or because the administrative apparatus of the state was incapable of coping with the economic and social needs of the time.

Feel the author? Which of the viewpoints is she discussing?

This version of history patronizes the Victorians, (50) who were in fact well aware of their vulnerability to charges of condescension and complacency, but were equally well aware of the potential dangers of state-managed charity. They were perhaps condescending to the poor, but—to use an un-Victorian metaphor—they (55) put their money where their mouths were, and gave of their careers and lives as well.

Passage map!

21. Which one of the following best summarizes the main idea of the passage?

Prephrase and watch out for answers with a narrow scope.

(A) While the motives of individual practitioners have been questioned by modern commentators, Victorian philanthropy successfully dealt with the social ills of nineteenth-century England.
(B) Philanthropy, inadequate to deal with the massive social and economic problems of the twentieth century, has slowly been replaced by state-sponsored charity.
(C) The practice of reading the past as a prelude to an enlightened present has fostered revisionist views of many institutions, among them Victorian philanthropy.
(D) Although modern commentators have perceived Victorian philanthropy as either inadequate or self-serving, the theoretical bias behind these criticisms leads to an incorrect interpretation of history.
(E) Victorian philanthropists, aware of public resentment of their self-congratulatory attitude, used devious methods to camouflage their self-serving motives.

22. According to the passage, which one of the following is true of both modern criticisms made about Victorian philanthropy?

Remind yourself of the two criticisms, then eliminate obvious wrong answers before confirming the correct one with the text.

(A) Both criticisms attribute dishonorable motives to those privileged individuals who engaged in private philanthropy.
(B) Both criticisms presuppose that the social rewards of charitable activity outweighed the economic benefits.
(C) Both criticisms underemphasize the complacency and condescension demonstrated by the Victorians.
(D) Both criticisms suggest that government involvement was necessary to cure social ills.
(E) Both criticisms take for granted the futility of efforts by private individuals to enhance their social status by means of philanthropy.

25. It can be inferred from the passage that a social control theorist would be most likely to agree with which one of the following statements concerning the motives of Victorian philanthropists?

Remind yourself of the definition of a social control theorist, and be on the lookout for logical but unsupported answers.

(A) Victorian philanthropists were driven more by the desire for high social status than by the hope of economic gain.
(B) Victorian philanthropists encouraged such values as thrift and temperance in order to instill in the working class the same acquisitiveness that characterized the management class.
(C) Though basically well-intentioned, Victorian philanthropists faced problems that were far beyond the scope of private charitable organizations.
(D) By raising the living standards of the poor, Victorian philanthropists also sought to improve the intellectual status of the poor.
(E) Victorian philanthropists see philanthropy as a means to an end rather than as an end in itself.

26. Which of the following best describes the organization of the passage?

Prephrase and wrong-to-right!

(A) Two related positions are discussed, then both are subjected to the same criticism.
(B) Two opposing theories are outlined, then a synthesis between the two is proposed.
(C) A position is stated, and two differing evaluations of it are given.
(D) Three examples of the same logical inconsistency are given.
(E) A theory is outlined, and two supporting examples are given.

SOLUTIONS: Coached Practice Set

Scale and Passage Map

Passage 1: PT42, S3, P3

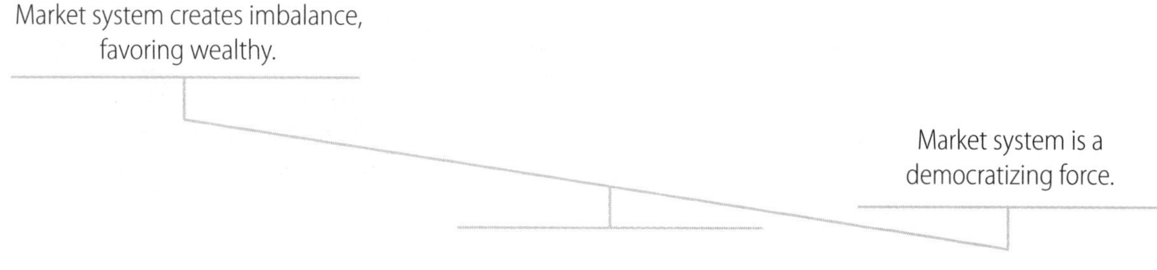

AUTHOR

– printing press
– personal computer
– broadcast technology
– mail/phone/email
– prices down, access up

P1: Introduction of argument and author's position. New technology reduces benefit gap.

P2: Support for author's position. Three examples of new technology becoming inexpensive and accessible.

P3: Explanation of phenomenon. How market forces cause technology to become inexpensive.

16. Which one of the following does the passage identify as being a result of technological development? *(Identification)*

Tough to prephrase this question, as the answer may relate to one of several benefits.

(A) burgeoning scientific research

Seems logical, but there is no support for this in the text.

(B) educational uses of broadcasting

Education was mentioned, as was broadcasting, but not together!

(C) widespread exchange of political ideas

Out of scope.

(D) faster means of travel

Travel is mentioned (lines 36–41). However, the passage discusses price, not speed.

(E) increased access to databases

Bingo! Lines 28–35 directly support this.

18. Which one of the following most accurately represents the primary function of the reference to maximization of financial success (lines 52–54)? *(Synthesis)*

This is an explanation of how, over time, technology becomes more accessible and benefits a wider group of people.

(A) It forms part of the author's summary of the benefits that have resulted from the technological developments described in the preceding paragraph.

No—this isn't a summary of benefits but an explanation of how the benefits came about.

(B) It serves as the author's logical conclusion from data presented in the preceding paragraph regarding the social consequences of technological development.

Conclusion? No, this is support.

(C) It forms part of a speculative hypothesis that the author presents for its interest in relation to the main topic rather than as part of an argument.

Tricky wording here! Without getting too deep into this answer choice, we can see that it is wrong from the words "speculative hypothesis" alone. This is not presented as speculation.

(D) It serves as part of a causal explanation that reinforces the thesis in the first paragraph regarding the benefits of technological development.

Somewhat tricky wording again, but this seems right—it's an explanation for the main point, which was made in the first paragraph.

(E) It forms part of the author's concession that certain factors complicate the argument presented in the first two paragraphs.

Concession? Complications? No—maximization of financial success is an explanation.

19. It can be most reasonably inferred from the passage that the author would agree with which one of the following statements? *(Inference)*

It's not worth prephrasing a question like this—the correct answer might draw an inference from a large point or from a small detail.

(A) The profits derived from computer technology have accrued to fewer people than have the profits derived from any other technological development.

This is a comparison trap. The passage doesn't compare benefits.

(B) Often the desire of some people for profits motivates changes that are beneficial for large numbers of other people.

This inference requires no further assumptions or extrapolations on our part. Lines 5–12 and 52–60 combine to make this point clearly. Also, did you notice that (B) is essentially the right side of our scale?

(C) National boundaries are rarely barriers to the democratizing spread of technology.

National boundaries? Out of scope.

(D) Typically, investment in technology is riskier than many other sorts of investment.

Another comparison trap!

(E) Greater geographical mobility of populations has contributed to the profits of entrepreneurs and investors in technology.

While the passage does suggest that travel has become less expensive (lines 35–41), geographical mobility is out of scope.

20. From the passage it can be most reasonably inferred that the author would agree with which one of the following statements? *(Inference)*

Another Inference question for which we can't prephrase.

(A) The democratizing influence of technology generally contributes to technological obsolescence.

The passage mentions some technologies becoming more powerful or efficient (lines 27–34 and 46-48), but never mentions obsolescence.

(B) Wholly unregulated economies are probably the fastest in producing an equalization of social status.

Unregulated economies? Fastest? Out of scope–mania!

(C) Expanded access to printed texts across a population has historically led to an increase in literacy in that population.

Again, the text—lines 18–23—basically proves answer (C). If the expanded access has allowed us to take literacy for granted, we can infer that that access has led to an increase in literacy.

(D) The invention of the telephone has had a greater democratizing influence on society than has the invention of the printing press.

Comparison trap!

(E) Near equality of financial assets among people is a realistic goal for market economies.

Inferences are baby steps from the text, not large jumps or predictions.

Scale and Passage Map

Passage 2: PT42, S3, P4

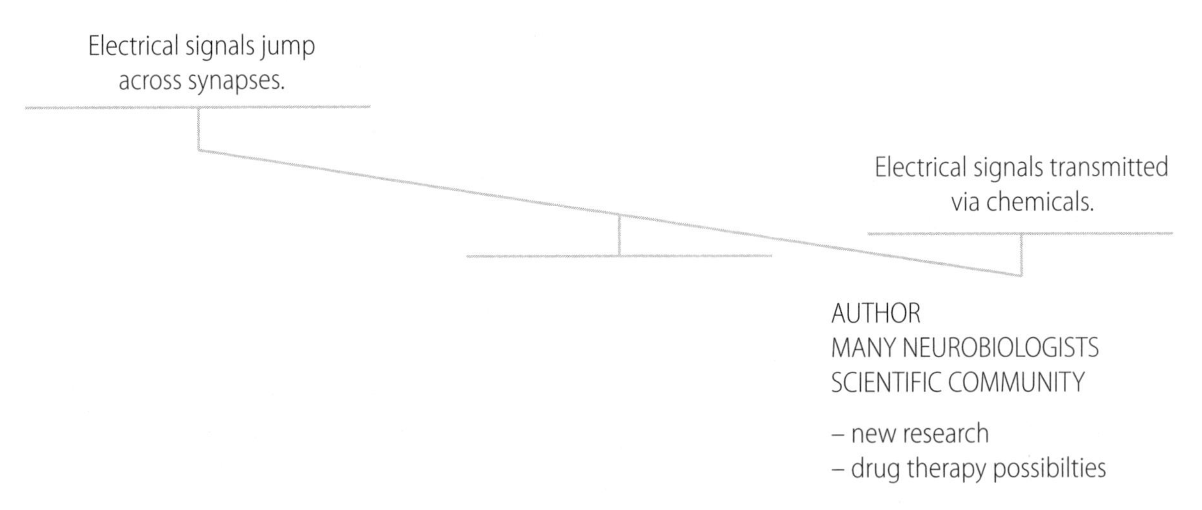

Note that we've placed the author under the right side of the scale. The author's opinion is subtle, but lines 28–32 give us an indication that the author has been "convinced."

This passage ends with a "curved tail," in which the central argument is used as a springboard into the implications for drug therapy and treatments for diseases.

P1: Introduction of question about earlier theory, followed by alternative theory. If brain signals are electric, how do they leap across synapses? A newer theory says the electrical impulse is transmitted chemically.

P2: Objections to the theory; new explanation that addresses the objections. It was unclear how chemical communication could work until recent evidence allowed for a convincing explanation.

P3: Details of the new explanation. Neurotransmitters cause the receptors to change shape and open their ion channels.

P4: New findings and applications of theory. A variety of receptors exist and this may make it possible to develop targeted treatments for brain disorders.

21. Which one of the following most completely and accurately states the main point of the passage? *(Synthesis)*

The main point seems to be that brain signals are sent chemically, but that's established really early. The second half gets into different kinds of receptors and medical applications.

(A) Evidence shows that the workings of the brain are guided, not by electrical signals, but by chemicals, and that subtle differences among the receptors for these chemicals may permit the selective treatment of certain brain disorders.

Looks good!

(B) Evidence shows that the workings of the brain are guided, not by electrical signals, but by chemicals, and that enough similarities exist among these chemicals to allow scientists to classify them as a family.

This is similar to (A), but the second part here is not quite right. It's grouping the neurotransmitters instead of the receptors. Also, this grouping doesn't seem big enough to be the main point. The application mentioned in (A) seems more important.

(C) Evidence shows that electrical impulses are transmitted between neurons chemically rather than electrically, and that enough similarities exist among these chemicals to allow scientists to classify them as a family.

What is this, another Similar Answers Drill? This looks a whole lot like (B). Eliminate.

(D) Evidence shows that electrical impulses are transmitted between neurons chemically rather than electrically, and that subtle differences among the receptors for these chemicals may permit the selective treatment of certain brain disorders.

Okay, this looks just like (A). Defer.

(E) Evidence shows that receptor molecules in the brain differ subtly from one another, and that these differences can be exploited to treat certain brain disorders through the use of drugs that selectively affect particular parts of the brain.

Finally, a quick elimination! This one is focused only on the last paragraph and doesn't even mention the chemical vs. electrical issue.

So how do we settle the (A) vs. (D) issue? Looking back, we can see that the only difference is the first part. So what is the difference between those statements? Answer (A) says that the brain doesn't use electrical signals and (D) says that electrical impulses are transmitted chemically. So (A) is saying that the signals aren't electrical at all—that's not right! The impulses are electrical, but they travel across synapses via chemicals (neurotransmitters) (lines 9–19). Subtle! Answer (D) wins.

23. Each of the following statements is affirmed by the passage EXCEPT: *(Identification)*

No prephrase possible here, and we'll need to remember that "EXCEPT"!

(A) The secretion of certain chemicals plays a role in neuron communication.

(B) The flow of ions through neurons plays a role in neuron communication.

(C) The binding of neurotransmitters to receptors plays a role in neuron communication.

All of those were discussed in lines 11–19, so they're out.

(D) The structure of receptors on neuron surfaces plays a role in neuron communication.

This shows up in lines 30–32. Eliminate.

(E) The size of neurotransmitter binding sites on receptors plays a role in neuron communication.

Size? That doesn't sound familiar, and since we've found support for the other four choices, we can go with this one without spending a lot of time searching.

24. The author most likely uses the phrase "defined categories of neurons" in lines 55–56 in order to refer to neurons that

This phrase is used in the middle of a sentence about finding out what different parts of the brain do to our behavior and then creating drugs to affect that behavior, so these "defined categories of neurons" must be those that have certain effects that we'd be interested in changing.

(A) possess channels for ions

It seems that all neurons have ion channels (lines 33–36), but that's not what the author is talking about in this portion.

(B) respond to drug treatment

Very tempting answer! Looking back at the text, we never learned that the neurons definitely do respond, just that this discovery raises the possibility of treatment (lines 49–52).

(C) contain receptor molecules

Another broad generalization about neurons that doesn't get at the specific meaning here.

(D) influence particular brain functions

There we go. We want to look at neurons that have particular effects that we can influence.

(E) react to binding by neurotransmitters

The same problem as (A) and (C).

25. Which one of the following most accurately describes the organization of the passage? *(Synthesis)*

Passage map to the rescue: alternative theory, objections, new explanation, application.

(A) explanation of a theory; presentation of evidence in support of the theory; presentation of evidence in opposition to the theory; argument in favor of rejecting the theory; discussion of the implication of rejecting the theory

The last two bits about rejecting the theory make this a quick elimination.

(B) explanation of a theory; presentation of evidence in support of the theory; explanation of an alternative theory; presentation of information to support the alternative theory; discussion of an experiment that can help determine which theory is correct

This is making the whole passage into a war between two theories. We never really see any support for the purely electrical theory—the chemical theory is a clear winner.

(C) explanation of a theory; description of an obstacle to the theory's general acceptance; presentation of an explanation that helps the theory overcome the obstacle; discussion of a further implication of the theory

Strong match with our prephrase!

(D) explanation of a theory; description of an obstacle to the theory's general acceptance; argument that the obstacle is insurmountable and that the theory should be rejected; discussion of the implications of rejecting the theory

Rejection again? Out!

(E) explanation of a theory; description of how the theory came to win scientific acceptance; presentation of new information that challenges the theory; modification of the theory to accommodate the new information; discussion of an implication of the modification.

Modification of the theory? Out of scope. Also, the only new information that came in was support for the theory (lines 28–30).

Scale and Passage Map

Passage 3: PT41, S4, P2

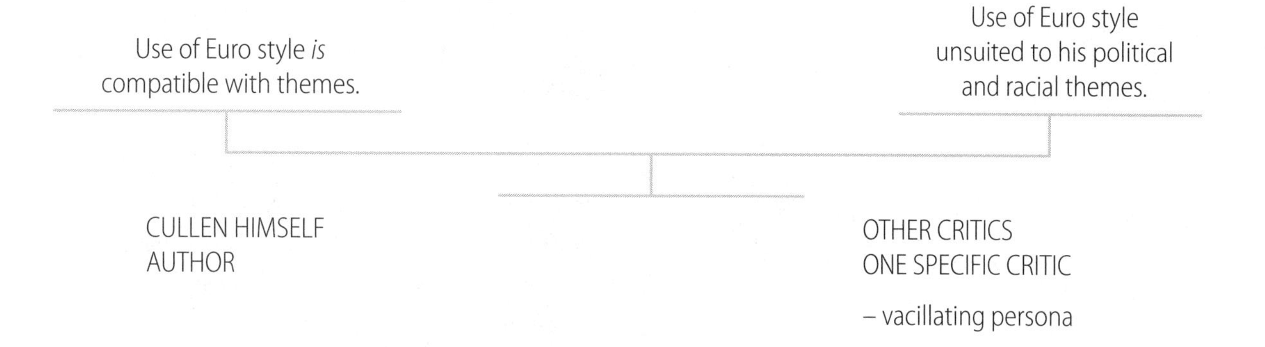

Note the very subtle indication of the author's opinion in lines 40–43. Also note the "curved tail" in the last paragraph, in which the author moves beyond the central argument to discuss trends in Cullen's later work.

P1: Introduction of subject. Cullen was a Harlem Renaissance poet who used controlled forms to write about universal subjects.

P2: Introduction of central argument and author's opinion. Some critics argue that Cullen's form is incompatible with his poems' political and racial themes; the author supports Cullen in disagreeing.

P3: Shift of focus. Cullen's poetry became more religious, but he remained committed to racial themes.

7. Which one of the following most accurately states the main point of the passage? *(Synthesis)*

The passage was mainly about Cullen's poetic form being compatible with his themes, but perhaps the answer will reference the curved tail in the last paragraph.

(A) While much of Cullen's poetry deals with racial issues, in his later work he became less concerned with racial matters and increasingly interested in writing poetry with a religious dimension.

Cullen (and the author) disagree with this in the last two sentences of the passage. Racial matters were subsumed but never abandoned. Also, there's no mention of form in this answer.

(B) While Cullen used European verse forms and his later poems increasingly addressed religious themes, his poetry never abandoned a concern for racial issues.

The emphasis on the last paragraph is suspect—where are the critics?—but this ends up being the best available answer. It gets to forms, racial issues, and religion.

(C) Though Cullen used European verse forms, he acknowledged that these forms were not very well suited to treating political or racial themes.

This is contradicted by our scale!

(D) Despite the success of Cullen's poetry at dealing with racial issues, Cullen's primary goal was to re-create the atmosphere that characterized the English ballad.

His primary goal was re-creating an atmosphere? Unsupported. We can't say this was his primary goal (or even a goal at all) just because some critics say that he did this (lines 18–23).

(E) The religious dimension throughout Cullen's poetry complemented his focus on racial issues by providing the context within which these issues could be understood.

At best, this is too narrow, focusing only on the last paragraph, but there is also no support for this particular assertion about context.

8. Given the information in the passage, which one of the following most closely exemplifies Cullen's conception of poetry? *(Inference)*

We see his conception spelled out clearly in lines 6–14: he wanted to write "lofty thoughts beautifully expressed," using controlled forms and conventional devices to write about "universal topics such as love and death."

(A) a sonnet written with careful attention to the conventions of the form to re-create the atmosphere of sixteenth-century English poetry

The goal is to re-create an atmosphere? This is the same trap as 7(D). Unsupported.

(B) a sonnet written with deliberate disregard for the conventions of the form to illustrate the perils of political change

(C) a sonnet written to explore the aesthetic impact of radical innovations in diction, rhythm, and sonority

(D) a sonnet written with great stylistic freedom to express the emotional upheaval associated with romantic love

Disregard for conventions? Radical innovations? Stylistic freedom? He liked "controlled poetic forms" and "conventional rhyme." Contradicted!

(E) a sonnet written with careful attention to the conventions of the form expressing feelings about the inevitability of death

This sounds a lot like what the text was describing. Death was one of the topics specifically mentioned, and we know that he liked controlled forms.

9. Which one of the following is NOT identified by the author of the passage as characteristic of Cullen's poetry? *(Identification)*

This works like an "EXCEPT" question.

(A) It often deals with abstract, universal subject matter.

Lines 6–8.

(B) It often employs rhyme, classical allusions, and religious imagery.

Lines 11–14.

(C) It avoids traditional poetic forms in favor of formal experimentation.

This answer jumps out as incongruous. Because we spent some time reviewing the first paragraph for the last question, we might quickly see that this assertion is contradicted—Cullen used traditional forms! However, if we were uncertain about (C), we could also get to the right answer by finding textual support for the other four answers, as we've done here.

(D) It sometimes deals explicitly with racial issues.

Lines 25–30.

(E) It eventually subsumed racial issues into a discussion of religious issues.

Lines 51–54.

10. The passage suggests which one of the following about Cullen's use of controlled poetic forms? *(Inference)*

Wow, the test writers seem to be very fond of the first paragraph! We won't complain—we've mastered that content by now! However, it's not clear from the question what we're looking for. We know Cullen liked those forms, but what are we supposed to say about them?

(A) Cullen used controlled poetic forms because he believed they provided the best means to beautiful poetic expression.

This is practically a rephrase of the sentence starting on line 9. The author is telling us, "Believing X, Cullen did Y." The only thing we are inferring is that this means he did Y because he believed X. This seems pretty safe, especially once we run through (B)–(E).

(B) Cullen's interest in religious themes naturally led him to use controlled poetic forms.

(C) Only the most controlled poetic forms allowed Cullen to address racial issues in his poems.

These are unsupported. We don't know that he needed these forms to explore religious or racial issues. We just know that he liked them because he liked beautiful expression.

(D) Cullen had rejected the less controlled poetic forms he was exposed to prior to his university years.

Contradicted.

(E) Less controlled poetic forms are better suited to poetry that addresses racial or political issues.

This is the opinion of the critics cited in lines 23–25, but the author never sides with these critics. Unsupported.

Scale and Passage Map

Passage 4: PT41, S4, P4

Victorian philanthropy was inferior prelude to an enlightened present.

Good for Victorian philanthropists! At least they tried.

MODERN CRITICS

- social problems far too large for philanthropy to help
- philanthropists were self-serving
- philanthropy had effect of controlling labor class

AUTHOR

- Victorian philanthropists knew of the dangers of state charity
- they sacrificed

P1: Introduction of topic and criticisms. Victorian philanthropy was obsolete and ineffective.

P2: Second criticism. Victorian philanthropy was actually a means of controlling labor force.

P3: Criticism of the criticisms. Both criticisms treat Victorian philanthropy as an inferior prelude to state charity, symptomatic of a misguided view of history (the "Whig Fallacy").

P4: More criticism of the criticisms. The criticisms are condescending to Victorians, who were earnest and aware of potential criticisms of their charitable giving.

21. Which one of the following best summarizes the main idea of the passage? *(Synthesis)*

The author thinks the criticisms of Victorian philanthropists are condescending and off-base, and gives the Victorians credit for trying to help.

(A) While the motives of individual practitioners have been questioned by modern commentators, Victorian philanthropy successfully dealt with the social ills of nineteenth-century England.

This is extreme and contradicted. What would it mean to "successfully deal" with social ills? Those ills still existed, and the author acknowledges that philanthropists couldn't solve all the problems (lines 10–15).

(B) Philanthropy, inadequate to deal with the massive social and economic problems of the twentieth century, has slowly been replaced by state-sponsored charity.

We might infer this from the first paragraph, but it's much too narrow to be the main point.

(C) The practice of reading the past as a prelude to an enlightened present has fostered revisionist views of many institutions, among them Victorian philanthropy.

This seems close to the author's point about the "Whig fallacy" in the third paragraph, but now we're applying it to "many institutions." By focusing on this one aspect of the author's argument and then broadening it to include more than Victorian philanthropy, this answer choice manages to be both too narrow and too broad at the same time. Quite an accomplishment!

(D) Although modern commentators have perceived Victorian philanthropy as either inadequate or self-serving, the theoretical bias behind these criticisms leads to an incorrect interpretation of history.

This neatly sums up the ideas of the entire passage. We have the "two major criticisms" first mentioned in lines 4–5 (obsolete/inadequate, self-serving), theoretical bias (the "Whig fallacy"), and a clear statement that the critics are wrong, as the author asserts in the last paragraph.

(E) Victorian philanthropists, aware of public resentment of their self-congratulatory attitude, used devious methods to camouflage their self-serving motives.

Public resentment? Devious methods? This is an extreme version of the criticisms in the passage, and the author doesn't like those criticisms!

22. According to the passage, which one of the following is true of both modern criticisms made about Victorian philanthropy? *(Inference)*

The author thinks they're both misguided, but it's tough to prephrase a more specific answer here.

(A) Both criticisms attribute dishonorable motives to those privileged individuals who engaged in private philanthropy.

"Dishonorable" seems too strong, and at best this would apply to the second criticism.

(B) Both criticisms presuppose that the social rewards of charitable activity outweighed the economic benefits.

This is a comparison trap. While both the social and economic reasons for charity were mentioned, they were not compared. Furthermore, these rewards are mentioned only in relation to the second criticism.

(C) Both criticisms underemphasize the complacency and condescension demonstrated by the Victorians.

This is saying that the critics aren't critical enough of the Victorians! Contradicted.

(D) Both criticisms suggest that government involvement was necessary to cure social ills.

This doesn't seem obviously correct, so our first response here might be to defer. However, on second look, it does seem that the critics preferred government intervention to private philanthropy. This is central to the discussion of the first criticism in lines 8–12, but it comes up again in lines 37–39, where the author seems to be talking about all

6¾

"modern critics." Lines 42–45 go on to specifically connect resistance to state control with "commitment to a vested interest," which is a reference to the second criticism.

If we were unsure about this one, we might reassure ourselves by noting that this is the only answer choice with any connection to the first criticism.

(E) Both criticisms take for granted the futility of efforts by private individuals to enhance their social status by means of philanthropy.

While using philanthropy to enhance status was discussed in connection with the second criticism (lines 19–23), we never hear that it was a futile strategy.

25. It can be inferred from the passage that a social control theorist would be most likely to agree with which one of the following statements concerning the motives of Victorian philanthropists? *(Inference)*

Social control theorists saw philanthropy as a way of controlling the labor force and keeping the management class on top (lines 26–34).

(A) Victorian philanthropists were driven more by the desire for high social status than by the hope of economic gain.

We've already seen this comparison trap! Social status is mentioned (lines 20–23), but there's never a comparison between that and economic gain.

(B) Victorian philanthropists encouraged such values as thrift and temperance in order to instill in the working class the same acquisitiveness that characterized the management class.

This might look good initially—instilling those values is mentioned (lines 28–31)—but on second glance, we never learned that those are values that lead to acquisitiveness. Unsupported.

(C) Though basically well-intentioned, Victorian philanthropists faced problems that were far beyond the scope of private charitable organizations.

This is tempting, because we do learn in the first paragraph that the philanthropy was inadequate; however, this has nothing to do with what social control theorists think.

(D) By raising the living standards of the poor, Victorian philanthropists also sought to improve the intellectual status of the poor.

Intellectual status? Out of scope.

(E) Victorian philanthropists see philanthropy as a means to an end rather than as an end in itself.

This matches our prephrase: social control theorists think that Victorian philanthropists were using charity to maintain their own power.

26. Which of the following best describes the organization of the passage? *(Synthesis)*

Let's return to our passage map: introduce each criticism, and then criticize them!

(A) Two related positions are discussed, then both are subjected to the same criticism.

This is not very specific, but it does correctly represent disparate parts of the passage. The author presents two criticisms and then lumps them together at the end when he puts them down.

(B) Two opposing theories are outlined, then a synthesis between the two is proposed.

Opposing? Synthesis?

(C) A position is stated, and two differing evaluations of it are given.

One position and two evaluations? No.

(D) Three examples of the same logical inconsistency are given.

(E) A theory is outlined, and two supporting examples are given.

Not even close.

Chapter 7 of Reading Comprehension

Timing

Timing

If you're thinking, "Oh, great, we're finally going to talk about timing!" you've probably been nostalgic for the days of high school when you were one of the first in your class to finish tests. Or, alternatively, you've been wondering how to salvage your tried-and-true technique of slowly rereading until you figured it all out. Welcome to the LSAT, where time is of the essence!

For most test-takers, the LSAT is the first time they've been challenged to maintain a reading pace outside their comfort zone. Many find themselves rushing through the fourth passage, if they get to it at all! First off, please know that if that's happening to you, you're not alone. Also know that you can improve your timing. Let's talk about how.

Section Timing

Timing strategy, shmiming strategy... 35 Minutes ÷ 4 Passages = 8:45/passage, right?

Wouldn't it be lovely if we could simply divide our way to a timing strategy? Unfortunately, some passages and some questions take longer than others. In the Logic Games section, the difficulty tends to increase as we move through the four games. However, in Reading Comprehension, the difficulty order of the passages is less predictable, perhaps because what constitutes a difficult passage depends to a larger extent on the specific strengths of the test-taker. While RC may be somewhat less predictable than Logic Games in terms of section difficulty, for both section types, the LSAT tends to balance very tough passages with very easy ones. And for both sections, we recommend that you employ the **Time Bank**.

The idea of the Time Bank is that you start the section with 8 minutes per passage, leaving 3 minutes in the "bank." If the first passage takes only 7 minutes, you now have 4 minutes in the bank. If it requires 10, you have only 1 minute in your bank. (To track your bank, you might find it useful to note the time on your paper as you finish the question set for each passage.)

The benefit of the Time Bank strategy is that it allows you to handle fluctuations in passage difficulty while staying on top of your time both for individual passages and for the section as a whole. However, be warned that this timing strategy needs to be practiced many times before you will be able to use it under pressure. You will also need to develop and practice time-efficient strategies so that you are able to put time in the bank to spend on the tough passages, avoiding a time crunch at the end. That's what the rest of this chapter is about.

Speeding Up

The need for speed brings us to two important RC tensions: should we read faster or more carefully, and should we speed up on the passage or on the questions? You are going to have to wrestle with the first tension and find your reading pace sweet spot. It needs to be fast enough that you finish the section, but slow enough that you don't miss what's important. This tension is going to be harder to resolve if you haven't adopted strategies like reading for the scale and developing a passage map. As for whether to speed up on the passage or on the questions, you probably need to speed up on both, but you should spend more energy on moving through questions faster. An unproductive read can lead to confusion on most every question, while having to guess on a question or two leads to much more limited damage.

Speed Up by Speeding Up

Most of what we're about to say on speeding up is what you might expect—some smart tips about timing strategies—but here's the boot camp–style suggestion: READ FASTER. You have probably been reading academic texts at about the same pace for 10 years or more. Changing anything that you've been doing regularly for that long is tough, especially if it's something that has led you to academic success. However, "tough" is a far cry from "impossible."

The simple and powerful fact is that you can read and think faster.

Along with practicing all the other strategies in this chapter, you have to practice moving faster. Dust off that stopwatch, move your eyes faster, focus, and *go!* Your brain is designed to improve and adapt, so it will rise to the occasion as you steadily tighten the time you allow yourself for a passage. Be forewarned that your speed and accuracy will probably seesaw as you progress. Be patient each time you push the pace—your accuracy will creep back up after multiple sessions of practicing a certain pace of reading. Is there a limit to this? Yes. Will you hit that limit without pushing yourself to move faster? No.

Speed Up by Slowing Down

(Yes, this is the exact opposite of what we just told you above.)

The other simple and powerful fact is that if you read so fast that you are unable to understand what you read, you won't understand what you read.

You can't simply pass your eyes over the words at light speed and expect to identify the scale or the author's point of view, but you also can't sit back with a hot chocolate and savor every word (that's something to look forward to in between the LSAT and law school!). Clearly, this is a tension to be resolved, and like so many RC tensions, it's one in which the sweet spot keeps shifting. Some passages will require you to slow down, while others won't. But there's also a larger shift that will take place as you practice speeding up.

One reason people don't spend enough time reading the passage is that they mistakenly think that all the points are earned by focusing on the questions. In fact, at least half of the hard work in RC is done while reading the passage. That said—here's that tension again—the questions need some love, too. Take a moment to look over some indications that you're spending too much or too little time reading the passage:

Signs That You Are Spending too Little Time in the Reading Process	Signs That You Are Spending too Much Time in the Reading Process
You struggle to recognize the central argument.	You remember or notate every detail in the text.
You are unable to paraphrase what a paragraph is saying.	You relate what you're reading to the outside world or debate what the text says.
It is difficult for you to create a passage map.	You often spend time trying to understand aspects of the text that don't show up in the questions.
You don't notice the author when she speaks up.	You feel rushed while going through the questions.
You don't have a clear sense of which opinions contrast with one another.	You don't have time to work wrong-to-right.
You miss questions pertaining to the passage as a whole or you have to reread pieces of the text in order to answer questions about the entire passage.	You often answer questions by "gut" feeling.
You are unable to identify where to look back when asked about a specific detail.	

Speed Up by Reading for the Scale

Reading for the scale is not just a way to align your reading style with what the LSAT is asking of you. It's also a way to give your brain a mission, and your brain is much more effective when it's on a mission. Imagine that two people have been told to study a pile of photographs for a subsequent quiz. Laura is told to do her best, while Jerry is told that the quiz will ask about a political agenda that the photographer was advocating through that set of pictures. Jerry has a purpose as he flips through the stack, while Laura is probably going to spend an inordinate amount of time looking at some photograph and/or become overwhelmed and start flipping through the stack at lightning speed. Regardless of how Laura handles this amorphous assignment, she'll have a hard time feeling comfortable picking up the pace. Jerry, on the other hand, may not want to move faster, but he can do so by passing over information that is clearly not supporting a political agenda.

Similarly, if you are truly reading for the scale, you're sorting and prioritizing meaningfully. Complex details can be filed away quickly as support for this or that side rather than mined for every piece of information. Just as importantly, it becomes more apparent when to slow down: when you're reading something that helps to define the scale or when you can't figure out what role a section plays vis-à-vis the rest of the passage.

If you're struggling with timing and have been politely reading all of our advice about reading for the scale without earnestly attempting to put the strategy to work, it's time to look back at what you "read" and start putting the strategy into practice.

Speed Up by Not Spacing Out

We have all experienced moments when we're focused and on top of our game—when we're "on." It's great when we're one step ahead of the conversation, smoothly responding to questions because we've predicted what someone is about to ask, or avoiding pitfalls by anticipating them before they appear. The problem is that we may not feel we can turn on that "on" whenever we want. One issue is that we're "on" usually only when we're interested, and many LSAT passages may not fascinate us. The LSAT is a long and difficult test, and our brains are not designed to stay at peak attention level for very long. On top of that, test-day stress can make matters even worse! Given all these obstacles, it's worth spending some of our precious prep time improving our ability to focus under pressure.

We have already discussed some techniques for bringing our brains back online while reading: note-taking and visualizing the passage. While it can take a bit more time to read a sentence and then visualize it or write a note about it, if your struggles to grasp passage content are leading you to reread long paragraphs (or even entire passages!), then taking that little extra time every few sentences can save you time in the long run.

One technique that will not work on test day is to hire a Manhattan Prep teacher to sit next to you and ask you focusing questions the way we did in the last drill. However, you can get some of the same benefit by asking yourself the sort of questions we'd ask as you work through the passage and questions. In short, talk to yourself. When you get to the words "for example," ask yourself what you're seeing an example of. When you finish a paragraph, ask yourself what you think is coming next. When you face a question, ask yourself if you can prephrase the answer. As you work through the answer choices, quickly remark to yourself about how bad answer choices (B), (C), and (D) are, and then ask yourself whether you can find something fishy about (A). It's amazing what asking questions will unlock; go ahead and start asking them.

Meditation is a less test-specific technique that you may want to try as a brain-training exercise. There's been enough neurological research into the positive effect of meditation on attention and our ability to think clearly that you may want to give it a try. As you do full practice tests, see if working in short meditations before the test and during the break help you to stay calm and focused. Similarly, be sure to always get up, take a walk, snack, and stretch during the break.

Speed Up On the Easy Stuff

This is probably the most important recommendation in this entire chapter: **speed up on easy passages and questions, and slow down on tougher ones**.

It can be so wonderful when a passage is easy! The passage is on West African art history and, just your luck, you happen to have a PhD in that exact subject! It's tempting to slow down and think deeply about each detail concerning the different types of masks, since you are more than capable of following all of it. But this is exactly the opposite of what you want to do. This is your opportunity to shift into high gear and put some time in the bank to spend on other passages in the section. If you're a note-taker, perhaps the easy passage is your opportunity to let your pencil just watch for a change.

Similarly, let the easy questions be easy. Don't work too hard to support your elimination of obviously wrong answers—leave the deep analysis for review sessions.

Speed Up On the Impossible Stuff

Isn't there something fishy about the heading above—didn't we just say to slow down on the tough stuff? We did, but notice the term shift from tough to impossible. In general, your strategy should be to speed up on the easy stuff in order to save time for the tough stuff. However, you also need to know when a question has you beat. Each and every question is worth just one point—there's no reason to devote three minutes to one question and deprive two easier questions of the paltry 40 or so seconds they require of you. When a question is going to suck up too much time, make your best guess, put an asterisk next to the question in case you have time to come back to it, and move on.

In the many practice tests you're going to take, you can beat yourself up for being completely lost on a question, but if a self-administered beating is what you need, it's far better to do it for wasting time on a question that you still get wrong. Heck, if you run out of time on a section, you should be frustrated about the excess time you spent on questions that you got *right*. You want to see every question, spending just enough time on the easy ones to nail them, just enough time on the impossible ones to make an educated guess (or even an uneducated one—remember, they're *impossible*), and as much time as you can spare on the challenging-but-conquerable ones.

The recipe isn't too complicated: get the easy ones right, don't waste time on the killer questions, spend time on the ones you can answer with a bit more work. Are you going to put this plan into practice? If you're the type of person who's used to being right all the time, probably not—**unless you do multiple practice sessions with the specific goal of making smart choices about timing**.

Skipping Passages vs. Skipping Questions

It's relatively easy to give up on a single impossible question, but what about when you face what seems to be an impossible *passage*? In chapter 9 we'll look at strategies for handling the extreme passage, but to give you a short preview, you want to focus on identifying some sort of scale and placing the author on it, even if you're not clear on all the content. Be sure you don't shut down because of a complex first paragraph.

There are obvious score-limitation consequences to skipping an entire passage—if you haven't read the passage, you are going to get about 4/5 of the questions wrong! It's usually better to skip a few tough questions to allow yourself to get to every passage and give each question a shot. Most passages include a few easier questions, so it's best to sacrifice the few toughest questions to get to all the easier ones.

That said, some test-takers find that despite months of prep, they are never able to reach the last passage during a timed set, or that on the toughest passages, their accuracy isn't far enough above a random 20%

to warrant the time taken away from the other, more manageable passages. If that's the case, and you don't have another solid month or two to improve your performance, you will want to practice making strategic choices about which passages to skip. Some students insist that certain topics are "cursed" for them, and while this may seem the case, the truth is that the LSAT can deliver an easy passage in any topic. Instead of assuming that the science passage, for example, is too hard for you, spend about 30 seconds reading a passage before deciding it's best to skip it. (Since you're going to skip an entire passage, you have some time to spend choosing the right passage to skip.) Some students choose to skip whichever passage has the fewest questions, which makes sense numerically. However, that numerical advantage is outweighed by the benefit of working on easier passages and skipping the toughest one, as you'll be better prepared for the questions if you grasp what you've read. So if you must skip a passage, skip the one that you find most difficult to understand.

Last Resort Tips

Despite our best efforts, we may find ourselves rushing during the last five minutes of an RC section. Just as a pilot might use a flight simulator to practice landing an airplane with the landing gear stuck, we want to use our practice materials to make sure we're ready to handle this kind of timing emergency. Most of our focus should be on avoiding these kinds of "crash landings," but accidents happen! Below are some survival tools; try them out and see which ones help you speed up with the least impact on your accuracy.

To read as fast as you can:

1. Slow down on the first and last sentences of each paragraph and skim the rest (or, if you are in dire need of time, skip the middle entirely, trying to catch a few nouns on your way through the paragraph). It's likely that you can catch the drift of the paragraph from one of those two sentences.
2. As you skim, look for words that signal structure (but, however, for example, instead, etc.) and briefly slow down to absorb the point of those sentences. You may want to refer to our tip box on page 61.
3. Skip any list if you understand why it's there.

To do questions as fast as you can:

1. Prioritize questions. If the question is asking about something you don't remember, guess, and come back only if you have time. Skip Identification questions if you only skimmed the passage—they're time-consuming. Questions that you can prephrase deserve your attention.
2. Move the process of elimination into warp speed, eliminating answers with "fishy" phrases or extreme language.

In order to apply these tools successfully, it's important that you've actually practiced using them. Applying this kind of speed gets easier with practice, but also just knowing that you have a tried-and-true backup plan can help to alleviate the stress that might force you to use that backup plan! Thus, it's crucial that after you read this chapter you work some passages under a time crunch. For starters, try giving yourself only five or six minutes per passage (questions included, of course). Your accuracy will surely dip, but evaluate your performance based on your goals for the exercise. Were you able to speed up your reading? Did you make smart choices about the questions? If you were able to see each question, perhaps skipping some that were obviously tough, and got at least a few questions right, consider the exercise a success.

DRILL IT: Pick Up the Pace!

Use this passage either to practice simply moving fast (it's not a terribly difficult passage) or to apply some of the last-resort tips you just read. Give yourself 2:15 for the fast read, or 1:15 for the last-resort read.

PrepTest 36, Section 2, Passage 1

Traditionally, members of a community such as a town or neighborhood share a common location and a sense of necessary interdependence that includes, for example, mutual respect and emotional support. But as (5) modern societies grow more technological and sometimes more alienating, people tend to spend less time in the kinds of interactions that their communities require in order to thrive. Meanwhile, technology has made it possible for individuals to interact via personal (10) computer with others who are geographically distant. Advocates claim that these computer conferences, in which large numbers of participants communicate by typing comments that are immediately read by other participants and responding immediately to those (15) comments they read, function as communities that can substitute for traditional interactions with neighbors.

What are the characteristics that advocates claim allow computer conferences to function as communities? For one, participants often share (20) common interests or concerns; conferences are frequently organized around specific topics such as music or parenting. Second, because these conferences are conversations, participants have adopted certain conventions in recognition of the importance of (25) respecting each others' sensibilities. Abbreviations are used to convey commonly expressed sentiments of courtesy such as "pardon me for cutting in" ("pmfci") or "in my humble opinion" ("imho"). Because a humorous tone can be difficult to communicate in (30) writing, participants will often end an intentionally humorous comment with a set of characters that, when looked at sideways, resembles a smiling or winking face. Typing messages entirely in capital letters is avoided, because its tendency to demand the attention (35) of a reader's eye is considered the computer equivalent of shouting. These conventions, advocates claim, constitute a form of etiquette, and with this etiquette as a foundation, people often form genuine, trusting relationships, even offering advice and support during (40) personal crises such as illness or the loss of a loved one.

But while it is true that conferences can be both respectful and supportive, they nonetheless fall short of communities. For example, conferences discriminate (45) along educational and economic lines because participation requires a basic knowledge of computers and the ability to afford access to conferences. Further, while advocates claim that a shared interest makes computer conferences similar to traditional (50) communities—insofar as the shared interest is analogous to a traditional community's shared location—this analogy simply does not work. Conference participants are a self-selecting group; they are drawn together by their shared interest in the topic (55) of the conference. Actual communities, on the other hand, are "nonintentional": the people who inhabit towns or neighborhoods are thus more likely to exhibit genuine diversity—of age, career, or personal interests—than are conference participants. It might be (60) easier to find common ground in a computer conference than in today's communities, but in so doing it would be unfortunate if conference participants cut themselves off further from valuable interactions in their own towns or neighborhoods.

You're in a rush, so take just five seconds to do a passage map!

Now, on to the questions!

With these questions, let's simulate being short on time. Choose those questions that you can prephrase, guess and move on if you're stuck, make quick decisions, and be sure to get to all the questions so you're not missing any easy ones. **Six questions, four minutes.** Go!

1. Which one of the following most accurately expresses the central idea of the passage?

(A) Because computer conferences attract participants who share common interests and rely on a number of mutually acceptable conventions for communicating with one another, such conferences can substitute effectively for certain interactions that have become rarer within actual communities.
(B) Since increased participation in computer conferences threatens to replace actual communities, members of actual communities are returning to the traditional interactions that distinguish towns or neighborhoods.
(C) Because participants in computer conferences are geographically separated and communicate only by typing, their interactions cannot be as mutually respectful and supportive as are the kinds of interactions that have become rarer within actual communities.
(D) Although computer conferences offer some of the same benefits that actual communities do, the significant lack of diversity among conference participants makes such conferences unlike actual communities.
(E) Even if access to computer technology is broad enough to attract a more diverse group of people to participate in computer conferences, such conferences will not be acceptable substitutes for actual communities.

2. Based on the passage, the author would be LEAST likely to consider which one of the following a community?

(A) a group of soldiers who serve together in the same battalion and who come from a variety of geographic regions
(B) a group of university students who belong to the same campus political organization and who come from several different socioeconomic backgrounds
(C) a group of doctors who work at a number of different hospitals and who meet at a convention to discuss issues relevant to their profession
(D) a group of teachers who work interdependently in the same school with the same students and who live in a variety of cities and neighborhoods
(E) a group of worshipers who attend and support the same religious institution and who represent a high degree of economic and cultural diversity

3. The author's statement that "conferences can be both respectful and supportive" (lines 42–43) serves primarily to

(A) counter the claim that computer conferences may discriminate along educational or economic lines
(B) introduce the argument that the conventions of computer conferences constitute a form of social etiquette
(C) counter the claim that computer conferences cannot be thought of as communities
(D) suggest that not all participants in computer conferences may be equally respectful of one another
(E) acknowledge that computer conferences can involve interactions that are similar to those in an actual community

4. Given the information in the passage, the author can most reasonably be said to use which one of the following principles to refute the advocates' claim that computer conferences can function as communities (line 15)?

(A) A group is a community only if its members are mutually respectful and supportive of one another.
(B) A group is a community only if its members adopt conventions intended to help them respect each other's sensibilities.
(C) A group is a community only if its members inhabit the same geographic location.
(D) A group is a community only if its members come from the same educational or economic background.
(E) A group is a community only if its members feel a sense of interdependence despite different economic and educational backgrounds.

5. What is the primary function of the second paragraph of the passage?

(A) to add detail to the discussion in the first paragraph of why computer conferences originated
(B) to give evidence challenging the argument of the advocates discussed in the first paragraph
(C) to develop the claim of the advocates discussed in the first paragraph
(D) to introduce an objection that will be answered in the third paragraph
(E) to anticipate the characterization of computer conferences given in the third paragraph

6. Which one of the following, if true, would most weaken one of the author's arguments in the last paragraph?

(A) Participants in computer conferences are generally more accepting of diversity than is the population at large.
(B) Computer technology is rapidly becoming more affordable and accessible to people from a variety of backgrounds.
(C) Participants in computer conferences often apply the same degree of respect and support they receive from one another to interactions in their own actual communities.
(D) Participants in computer conferences often feel more comfortable interacting on the computer because they are free to interact without revealing their identities.
(E) The conventions used to facilitate communication in computer conferences are generally more successful than those used in actual communities.

SOLUTIONS: Pick Up the Pace!

The below real-time solution shows what a strong test-taker in a last-resort situation might have been thinking. Read these with a critical, eye, though—even a strong test-taker will get some questions wrong when rushing.

Read slowly to get a strong initial grasp of the passage

Traditionally, members of a community such as a town or neighborhood share a common location and a sense of necessary interdependence that includes, for example, mutual respect and emotional support. But as (5) modern societies grow more technological and sometimes more alienating, people tend to spend less

Move a bit faster

time in the kinds of interactions that their communities require in order to thrive. Meanwhile, technology has made it possible for individuals to interact via personal (10) computer with others who are geographically distant. Advocates claim that these computer conferences, in which large numbers of participants communicate by typing comments that are immediately read by other participants and responding immediately to those (15) comments they read, function as communities that can substitute for traditional interactions with neighbors.

I see what this is about: internet killing communities.

Advocates! Sounds like author will disagree with this. Point is whether online conferences are communities.

Slow down

What are the characteristics that advocates claim allow computer conferences to function as communities? For one, participants often share (20) common interests or concerns; conferences are

This is why conferences = community. Skip the list!

Skim/skip

frequently organized around specific topics such as music or parenting. Second, because these conferences are conversations, participants have adopted certain conventions in recognition of the importance of (25) respecting each others' sensibilities. Abbreviations are used to convey commonly expressed sentiments of courtesy such as "pardon me for cutting in" ("pmfci") or "in my humble opinion" ("imho"). Because a humorous tone can be difficult to communicate in (30) writing, participants will often end an intentionally humorous comment with a set of characters that, when looked at sideways, resembles a smiling or winking face. Typing messages entirely in capital letters is avoided, because its tendency to demand the attention (35) of a reader's eye is considered the computer equivalent of shouting. These conventions, advocates claim, constitute a form of etiquette, and with this etiquette as

Yup, the whole paragraph was pro conference as community. And something about relationships.

Slow down

a foundation, people often form genuine, trusting
relationships, even offering advice and support during
(40) personal crises such as illness or the loss of a loved
one.

Skim

But while it is true that conferences can be both
respectful and supportive, they nonetheless fall short of
communities. For example, conferences discriminate
(45) along educational and economic lines because
participation requires a basic knowledge of computers
and the ability to afford access to conferences. Further,
while advocates claim that a shared interest makes
computer conferences similar to traditional
(50) communities—insofar as the shared interest is
analogous to a traditional community's shared
location—this analogy simply does not work.
Conference participants are a self-selecting group; they
are drawn together by their shared interest in the topic
(55) of the conference. Actual communities, on the other

Author! Conferences ≠ community. Then an example of why not. Skim it.

Slow down

hand, are "nonintentional": the people who inhabit
towns or neighborhoods are thus more likely to exhibit
genuine diversity—of age, career, or personal
interests—than are conference participants. It might be
(60) easier to find common ground in a computer
conference than in today's communities, but in so
doing it would be unfortunate if conference participants
cut themselves off further from valuable interactions in
their own towns or neighborhoods.

Something about shared interests, self-selecting, intention, diversity.

Author voice strong here. Conferences = cutting off from real community.

Quick & Dirty Passage Map!

First, how the internet forms communities. Then author on how it doesn't (diversity issue).

1. Which one of the following most accurately expresses the central idea of the passage?

I know this one! Prephrase: Internet groups not community (diversity).

(A) Because computer conferences attract participants who share common interests and rely on a number of mutually acceptable conventions for communicating with one another, such conferences can substitute effectively for certain interactions that have become rarer within actual communities.

Can substitute? Eliminate.

(B) Since increased participation in computer conferences threatens to replace actual communities, members of actual communities are returning to the traditional interactions that distinguish towns or neighborhoods.

Threatens? Skip.

(C) Because participants in computer conferences are geographically separated and communicate only by typing, their interactions cannot be as mutually respectful and supportive as are the kinds of interactions that have become rarer within actual communities.

Nothing about diversity. Probably not.

(D) Although computer conferences offer some of the same benefits that actual communities do, the significant lack of diversity among conference participants makes such conferences unlike actual communities.

Love it. Quick scan of (E) to confirm.

(E) Even if access to computer technology is broad enough to attract a more diverse group of people to participate in computer conferences, such conferences will not be acceptable substitutes for actual communities.

Access? Wait, I see "diverse" here too! But this is making a prediction about the future. Stick with (D).

2. Based on the passage, the author would be LEAST likely to consider which one of the following a community?

I can do this. Author focused on diversity. So LEAST means not diverse. Eliminate diversity!

(A) a group of soldiers who serve together in the same battalion and who come from a <u>variety</u> of geographic regions

Variety of regions. Eliminate.

(B) a group of university students who belong to the same campus political organization and who come <u>from several different socioeconomic backgrounds</u>

Clearly out.

(C) a group of doctors who work at a number of <u>different hospitals</u> and who meet at a convention to discuss issues relevant to their profession

This might be about diversity, but it's just different workplaces. Leave it.

(D) a group of teachers who work interdependently in the same school with the same students and who live in a <u>variety of cities and neighborhoods</u>

Variety of cities. Same as (A). Out.

(E) a group of worshipers who attend and support the same religious institution and who represent a <u>high degree of economic and cultural diversity</u>

Definitely out. That leaves (C). No time to double-check.

3. The author's statement that "conferences can be both respectful and supportive" (lines 42–43) serves primarily to

That's from the last paragraph. Seems like the author conceding point before criticizing.

(A) <u>counter the claim</u> that computer conferences may discriminate along educational or economic lines

Counters a claim? Maybe.

(B) introduce the argument that the conventions of computer conferences constitute a form of <u>social etiquette</u>

Introduce? Maybe—but "social etiquette" is off.

(C) <u>counter the claim</u> that computer conferences cannot be thought of as communities

Another "counter." Seems fishy.

(D) suggest that not all participants in computer conferences may be <u>equally respectful</u> of one another

Equally respectful?

(E) acknowledge that computer conferences can involve interactions that are similar to those in an actual community

Acknowledge! Yes, this is it.

7

4. Given the information in the passage, the author can most reasonably be said to use which one of the following principles to refute the advocates' claim that computer conferences can function as communities (line 15)?

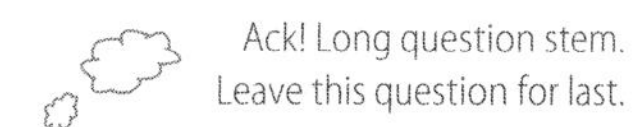

Ack! Long question stem. Leave this question for last.

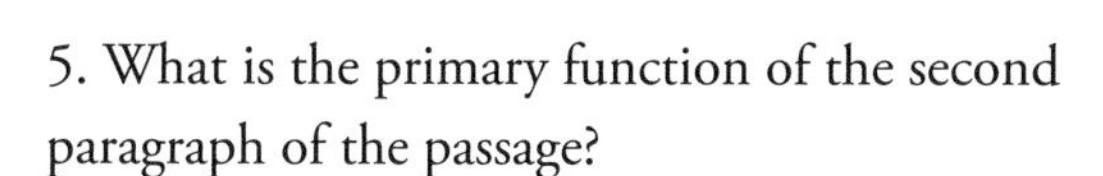

5. What is the primary function of the second paragraph of the passage?

Second paragraph is where we hear how internet = community.

(A) to add detail to the discussion in the first paragraph of why computer conferences originated

Add detail? Originated? Nope.

(B) to give evidence challenging the argument of the advocates discussed in the first paragraph

Challenging? Probably not.

(C) to develop the claim of the advocates discussed in the first paragraph

Looks good.

(D) to introduce an objection that will be answered in the third paragraph

Objection? No.

(E) to anticipate the characterization of computer conferences given in the third paragraph

Anticipate? No. Let's go with (C).

6. Which one of the following, if true, would most weaken one of the author's arguments in the last paragraph?

Weaken argument? Eek. What was the argument? That internet ≠community because of diversity issue. How to weaken that?

(A) Participants in computer conferences are generally more accepting of diversity than is the population at large.

Diversity! Keep it.

(B) Computer technology is rapidly becoming more affordable and accessible to people from a variety of backgrounds.

Affordable? Eliminate.

(C) Participants in computer conferences often apply the same degree of respect and support they receive from one another to interactions in their own actual communities.

Respect and support? Probably not.

(D) Participants in computer conferences often feel more comfortable interacting on the computer because they are free to interact without revealing their identities.

Comfortable interacting? No.

(E) The conventions used to facilitate communication in computer conferences are generally more successful than those used in actual communities.

Facilitate communication? No. Let's go with (A).

4. Given the information in the passage, the author can most reasonably be said to use which one of the following principles to refute the advocates' claim that computer conferences can function as communities (line 15)?

Back to this. What's it say? Author uses principle against the view that internet = community. Probably about diversity?

(A) A group is a community only if its members are mutually respectful and supportive of one another.

Respectful? Probably not.

(B) A group is a community only if its members adopt conventions intended to help them respect each other's sensibilities.

Sensibilities?

(C) A group is a community only if its members inhabit the same geographic location.

Same location? That's the opposite.

(D) A group is a community only if its members come from the same educational or economic background.

Same background? Again, that's the opposite.

(E) A group is a community only if its members feel a sense of interdependence despite different economic and educational backgrounds.

Interdependence despite differences. Yes, that sounds like diversity!

So, how did our student do in a rush? Missed one, but otherwise it was a pretty good performance. For question six, answer choice (A) is incorrect—*acceptance* of diversity is irrelevant to the author's argument—while (B) is correct since an increase in the diversity of who can access computers could address the author's concern that computer conferences are not diverse. Our student's choosing (A) demonstrates the danger of reacting quickly to specific words in an answer choice rather than taking the time to fully digest the answer's meaning. But regardless of the possibility of error, quick elimination on all the questions of a set is often the way to go in a timing emergency, as it affords the greatest chance of getting to all the easier questions.

You've now done one passage at an intentionally fast pace. Is that enough? Of course not! Be sure to mix some speed rounds into your practice sessions, practicing both speeding up on easy passages and applying your last-resort moves. Also, simply turning down your full section stopwatch from 35 minutes to 32 minutes is a great way to tighten the screws. Those lost 3 minutes might make you sweat, but you'll thank yourself on test day!

Chapter 8 of Reading Comprehension

Comparative Passages

Comparative Passages

So far, we've been focusing our attention on one passage at a time, but what about when the test gives us two passages to focus on at once? Ever since June 2007, every LSAT Reading Comprehension section has featured one of these "two-for-one deals" in which we see a set of questions based on two comparative passages written by two different authors. For the most part, the skills and habits you've built up so far will serve you well on comparative passages, too, but it's important to take a look at exactly what the test will be asking of you.

Read Like a Judge

Imagine that you are a judge preparing to hear a big case. You have two documents in front of you. You need to make sense of these documents, but you have limited time to review them. To get the most from your read, you should probably consider the following:

1. How does each document relate *to the central argument* of the case I'm about to hear?
Does it present one side of the argument?
Does it present objective information?
Does the author of the document make his or her opinion known?

2. How do the two documents relate *to each other*?
Do they work with each other or against each other?
What common evidence or information is presented across both documents?

This is essentially how you want to view your role as you read comparative passages on the LSAT. The questions will test your ability to understand how each passage relates *to the central argument* and how the two passages relate *to each other*.

The first type of question—how each passage relates to the central argument—is very similar to what we've been asking ourselves about each part of the passages we've worked on so far. For comparative passages, we're still reading for the scale; we just have two passages to work with. The second type of question might seem easy. Each passage will represent one side of the scale, right?

If you were reluctant to say yes to that question, you're getting a good feel for the complexity of the LSAT. Sure, you certainly may see comparative passages that present two sides of a scale, but there are plenty of more complex and subtle ways for the two passages to relate to each other. Here are a few of the possibilities:

1. Passage A describes a specific phenomenon, while Passage B relates that phenomenon to a larger movement or set of ideas.

2. Passage A provides one side of an argument, while Passage B provides objective historical information that supports the claim made in Passage A.

3. Passage A makes a straightforward point. Passage B makes a related point, but in a more nuanced way that leads us to suspect that the issue is more complicated than the author of Passage A acknowledges.

So, as always, we end up having to discern subtle differences in meaning and opinion. The only difference is that now we also have to navigate the relationship between the ideas presented in the two passages.

DRILL IT: Name That Relationship

This drill should give you a sense of the variety of relationships that can exist between two passages. Take a look at this miniature Passage A:

Passage A:

Jeffrey C. Goldfarb suggests public-spirited dialogue need not happen after a traditional theater show, as it is most successful when it happens through a show. He believes that the live component of the theater distinguishes it from other media objects, and allows meaning to arise from the interaction between performers and audience as the performance is happening. Whereas television or film, for instance, has no room for active dialogue, theater does because the performers and audience are present in the space together. The theatrical text becomes the medium, and the performers speak through the way in which they perform the text, while the audience does so through a number of culturally sanctioned actions: applause, laughter (both laughing with and laughing at), sighing, gasping, cheering, and booing.

Now compare this potential Passage B:

Passage B1:

Augusto Boal famously complained about how still everyone is expected to keep during any performance, constantly policed by other audience members. The high prices on professional theater tickets and an elitist value on cultural tradition (versus popular, technology-based mass media) combine to produce an aristocratic culture surrounding theater. In this manner, a "high class" code of etiquette is imposed upon the performance space, dictating that audience members are to remain quiet: the actors speak, the audience listens. As Boal criticizes in *Legislative Theatre*, traditional form sets up a relationship where "everything travels from stage to auditorium, everything is transported, transferred in that direction—emotions, ideas, morality!—and nothing goes the other way." He argues that this relationship encourages passivity and thus cancels theater's political potential.

How would you characterize the relationship between those two passages? Check your thoughts against the solution before continuing.

Now take a look at these alternative Passage B's. After reading each one, identify its relationship to Passage A. Note that the relationships modeled in this drill are not meant to represent all the possible relationships between the passages of a comparative passage set.

Passage B2:

In 1994, Ward Cunningham invented the first wiki, a website that can be edited by any viewer using an internet browser. Titled c2.com, this wiki allowed a new type of communication between software developers. Since that time wikis have grown exponentially in popularity not only because of their ability to foster efficient and ongoing improvement of information sources, but also because of their impact upon the nature of information sharing itself. While most wikis have few contributors and editors, the opportunity to become an active participant frames any form of participation as a conscious choice. Because any user could alter the text, the passive user is endorsing any information that he or she views without editing, thus becoming an active participant through what might otherwise be called inaction.

Passage B3:

Despite a widespread increase in the variety of low-cost and free recorded entertainment, attending live theater in some form continues to be a prominent component of many cultures. George Frentilo suggests that the enduring attraction can be traced to a basic need for approval and acceptance. He argues that sitting next to others and sharing in their reactions to the same event is interpreted subconsciously as joining in communal consideration and judgment of a potentially disruptive element in the community sphere. The fact that theater-goers remain anonymous allows them to avoid the risk and tension of having to individually proclaim their viewpoints and instead permits any attendee to passively join in the voicing of the majority opinion. Joining the act of shared judgment of the other, in this case the actors, gives each group member the sense that he or she is safe from the group's judgment and potential punishment.

Passage B4:

A production of *Dziady* (Forefather's Eve) in Poland in 1968 had been ordered to close and, on its last night, the theater was overcrowded with supporters. They were an enthusiastic, vocal audience who read into the play's anti-czarist language a critique of Soviet government. When the performance ended, the crowd went into the streets to protest. The play's content became political through the audience's interpretation of the content, and, in a way, the theater building held a public sphere where an anti-Soviet public gathered to affirm their political sentiment before taking it to the street in open, public protest.

SOLUTIONS: Name That Relationship

Passage B1: This passage directly counters Passage A, criticizing theater for not allowing for dialogue.

Passage B2: On the surface, this passage explores an entirely different topic, but both passages highlight a certain aspect of the phenomenon they describe. Both focus on the potential for dialogue through a specific medium or technology.

Passage B3: Like Passage A, this passage explores how the interactive nature of theater makes it different from other media, but here we see a new focus on the appeal and function of the experience for the individual theater-goer.

Passage B4: In some ways, this passage offers an example of the general phenomenon described in Passage A: the theater in Poland became a "public sphere" in which the anti-Soviet audience responded to the themes in the play. However, this example isn't a perfect match for Passage A—the audience *does* feel the need to engage in "public dialogue" after the play, and there is no real mention of the actual communication between the performers and the audience. So Passage B4 is looking at the same phenomenon in a way that only partially supports Goldfarb's position.

Making the Comparison

Scale and Passage Map

Because there are so many ways in which you may be asked to relate the two passages, it's important that you don't get too hung up on placing the passages on either end of a scale. Don't force it! Sometimes the passages are very close together, and sometimes the questions will focus more on differences or similarities in content than on differences in opinion. The scale is still a useful reading tool, and it's wise to take a PEAR moment between passages, anticipating how that second passage will relate to the one you just read. But since the passages can relate in so many different ways, it's usually hard to finalize the scale until at least the middle of the second passage. In many cases, you won't see a scale that includes both passages until you've finished them both and paused to reflect.

Because comparative passages can have so many paragraphs, and because the focus of the questions—as we're about to discuss—is often on the overlap or lack thereof between the passages, you will want to use most of your post-reading pause to address the questions we mentioned at the beginning:

1. How does each document relate to the central argument?
2. How do the two passages relate to each other?

With that in mind, it's smart to condense your mental passage map so that it doesn't eat up your attention. Essentially, treat each passage the way you would normally treat a paragraph. Identify briefly what role the passage is playing—explanation of a theory, argument for one side of a debate, review of several ideas and support for one in particular, etc.—and what the overall point seems to be. This brief passage map should serve, as usual, to help you respond to the questions more efficiently, in part by enabling you to answer the two questions above.

If you're having a hard time relating the passages to one another, you can take a look at the questions and see if they clarify what you're looking for. After all, the point of all this work is to answer the questions correctly! Maybe you already have all the understanding you need. In fact, because these questions tend to ask about elements that are mentioned in both passages (the overlap), you are often required to do twice as much work when it comes to verifying your answer choices using the text. Therefore, you want to allot a little extra time for answering the questions—ideally, you will read both passages in two to three minutes total and have five to seven minutes for the questions. The timing techniques you learned in the last chapter can help to keep you on track.

Questions

Many of the questions on comparative passages will look just like normal Reading Comprehension questions. You may well see a question about the main point of Passage A only, or a Local Inference question restricted to a few lines in Passage B. However, you are also going to see a number of questions that ask you to relate the two passages. Here are a few examples of what you might be asked to do:

1. Identify a point upon which the two passages agree or disagree.
2. Identify a purpose or concern that the two authors have in common.
3. Describe a difference (either general or specific) between the two passages.
4. Identify something that is mentioned in both passages, or mentioned in one but not the other.
5. Relate the opinion of one author to a view mentioned in the other passage.
6. Use information from one passage to support an opinion in the other.

HALF SCOPE ANSWERS

Because so many of the questions in comparative passages ask about commonalities between the two passages, we will be encountering a new wrong answer characteristic: the **half scope answer**. Watch out for answer choices that take an idea or attitude from one passage and try to apply it to both. Like narrow scope answers, half scope answers can be tempting because they present material that really is there—it just doesn't appear in both passages.

DRILL IT: Comparative Passages

Do your best to read both passages in a total of three minutes or less. Afterwards, try to answer all questions within six minutes total.

PrepTest 53, Section 4, Passage 3

The passages discuss relationships between business interests and university research.

Passage A

As university researchers working in a "gift economy" dedicated to collegial sharing of ideas, we have long been insulated from market pressures. The recent tendency to treat research findings as (5) commodities, tradable for cash, threatens this tradition and the role of research as a public good.

The nurseries for new ideas are traditionally universities, which provide an environment uniquely suited to the painstaking testing and revision of (10) theories. Unfortunately, the market process and values governing commodity exchange are ill suited to the cultivation and management of new ideas. With their shareholders impatient for quick returns, businesses are averse to wide-ranging experimentation. And, what (15) is even more important, few commercial enterprises contain the range of expertise needed to handle the replacement of shattered theoretical frameworks.

Further, since entrepreneurs usually have little affinity for adventure of the intellectual sort, they can (20) buy research and bury its products, hiding knowledge useful to society or to their competitors. The growth of industrial biotechnology, for example, has been accompanied by a reduction in the free sharing of research methods and results—a high price to pay for (25) the undoubted benefits of new drugs and therapies.

Important new experimental results once led university scientists to rush down the hall and share their excitement with colleagues. When instead the rush is to patent lawyers and venture capitalists, I (30) worry about the long-term future of scientific discovery.

Passage B

The fruits of pure science were once considered primarily a public good, available for society as a whole. The argument for this view was that most of (35) these benefits were produced through government support of universities, and thus no individual was entitled to restrict access to them.

Today, however, the critical role of science in the modern "information economy" means that what was (40) previously seen as a public good is being transformed into a market commodity. For example, by exploiting the information that basic research has accumulated about the detailed structures of cells and genes, the biotechnology industry can derive profitable (45) pharmaceuticals or medical screening technologies. In this context, assertion of legal claims to "intellectual property"—not just in commercial products but in the underlying scientific knowledge—becomes crucial.

Previously, the distinction between a scientific (50) "discovery" (which could not be patented) and a technical "invention" (which could) defined the limits of industry's ability to patent something. Today, however, the speed with which scientific discoveries can be turned into products and the large profits (55) resulting from this transformation have led to a blurring of both the legal distinction between discovery and invention and the moral distinction between what should and should not be patented.

Industry argues that if it has supported—either in (60) its own laboratories or in a university—the makers of a scientific discovery, then it is entitled to seek a return on its investment, either by charging others for using the discovery or by keeping it for its own exclusive use.

15. Which one of the following is discussed in Passage B but not in Passage A?

(A) the blurring of the legal distinction between discovery and invention
(B) the general effects of the market on the exchange of scientific knowledge
(C) the role of scientific research in supplying public goods
(D) new pharmaceuticals that result from industrial research
(E) industry's practice of restricting access to research findings

16. Both passages place in opposition the members of which one of the following pairs?

(A) commercially successful research and commercially unsuccessful research
(B) research methods and research results
(C) a marketable commodity and a public good
(D) a discovery and an invention
(E) scientific research and other types of inquiry

17. Both passages refer to which one of the following?

(A) theoretical frameworks
(B) venture capitalists
(C) physics and chemistry
(D) industrial biotechnology
(E) shareholders

18. It can be inferred from the passages that the authors believe that the increased constraint on access to scientific information and ideas arises from

(A) the enormous increase in the volume of scientific knowledge that is being generated
(B) the desire of individual researchers to receive credit for their discoveries
(C) the striving of commercial enterprises to gain a competitive advantage in the market
(D) moral reservations about the social impact of some scientific research
(E) a drastic reduction in government funding for university research

19. Which one of the following statements is most strongly supported by both passages?

(A) Many scientific researchers who previously worked in universities have begun to work in the biotechnology industry.
(B) Private biotechnology companies have invalidly patented the basic research findings of university researchers.
(C) Because of the nature of current scientific research, patent authorities no longer consider the distinction between discoveries and inventions to be clear cut.
(D) In the past, scientists working in industry had free access to the results of basic research conducted in universities.
(E) Government-funded research in universities has traditionally been motivated by the goals of private industry.

SOLUTIONS: Comparative Passages

Below is a real-time analysis of the passages, including annotations. As we read the passages, we'll take on the perspective of a judge looking for the central argument, the sides of this argument, and the evidence used to support either side of the argument. Because this is an example of comparative passages, we'll pay particular attention not only to how each passage relates to the central argument, but also to how the two passages relate to each other. Notice how the reader's understanding of the passages evolves throughout the process.

PrepTest 53, Section 4, Passage 3

The passages discuss relationships between business interests and university research.

Nice of them to provide this little intro for us. Too bad this feature hasn't shown up on subsequent comparative passages!

Passage A

As university researchers working in a "gift economy" dedicated to collegial sharing of ideas, we have long been insulated from market pressures. The recent tendency to treat research findings as commodities, tradable for cash, threatens this tradition and the role of research as a public good.

Strong statement right from the start. The author has spoken and it seems we already know one side of an argument. We'll guess the other side: that treating research findings as tradable commodities actually strengthens the role of research as a public good. We'll see, though...

The nurseries for new ideas are traditionally universities, which provide an environment uniquely suited to the painstaking testing and revision of theories. Unfortunately, the market process and values governing commodity exchange are ill suited to the cultivation and management of new ideas. With their shareholders impatient for quick returns, businesses are averse to wide-ranging experimentation. And, what is even more important, few commercial enterprises contain the range of expertise needed to handle the replacement of shattered theoretical frameworks.

More support for the idea that treating research findings as commodities is bad, and no opposing view yet. It's too soon to say if this scale is correct.

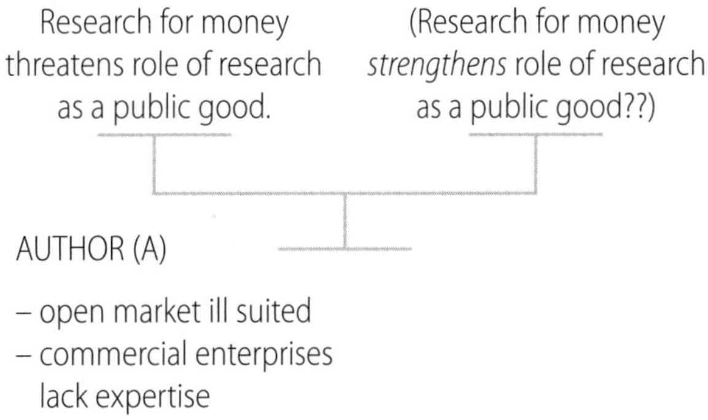

Research for money threatens role of research as a public good.

(Research for money *strengthens* role of research as a public good??)

AUTHOR (A)

- open market ill suited
- commercial enterprises lack expertise

Further, since entrepreneurs usually have little affinity for adventure of the intellectual sort, they can buy research and bury its products, hiding knowledge useful to society or to their competitors. The growth of industrial biotechnology, for example, has been accompanied by a reduction in the free sharing of research methods and results—a high price to pay for the undoubted benefits of new drugs and therapies.

More support for the author's position.

Research for money threatens role of research as a public good.

(Research for money *strengthens* role of research as a public good??)

AUTHOR (A)

- open market ill suited
- commercial enterprises lack expertise
- entrepreneurs hide knowledge (e.g., biotechnology)

Important new experimental results once led university scientists to rush down the hall and share their excitement with colleagues. When instead the rush is to patent lawyers and venture capitalists, I worry about the long-term future of scientific discovery.

A reiteration of the author's opinion. This doesn't change our understanding at all. So far we have one side of an argument and a guess at what the other side might be. Let's see what Passage B holds.

Passage B

The fruits of pure science were once considered primarily a public good, available for society as a whole. The argument for this view was that most of these benefits were produced through government support of universities, and thus no individual was entitled to restrict access to them.

The tone seems more objective here. So far the author is saying what people used to think. Is this author going to end up supporting the change that the first author finds so troubling?

Today, however, the critical role of science in the modern "information economy" means that what was previously seen as a public good is being transformed into a market commodity. For example, by exploiting the information that basic research has accumulated about the detailed structures of cells and genes, the biotechnology industry can derive profitable pharmaceuticals or medical screening technologies. In this context, assertion of legal claims to "intellectual property"—not just in commercial products but in the underlying scientific knowledge—becomes crucial.

This seems to document the same change mentioned in Passage A, except that the author doesn't seem to have much of an opinion on the matter at this point.

Previously, the distinction between a scientific "discovery" (which could not be patented) and a technical "invention" (which could) defined the limits of industry's ability to patent something. Today, however, the speed with which scientific discoveries can be turned into products and the large profits resulting from this transformation have led to a blurring of both the legal distinction between discovery and invention and the moral distinction between what should and should not be patented.

8

Industry argues that if it has supported—either in its own laboratories or in a university—the makers of a scientific discovery, then it is entitled to seek a return on its investment, either by charging others for using the discovery or by keeping it for its own exclusive use.

Hmm, the author seems to be staying neutral. We get a taste of the industry point of view, but it doesn't really refute the previous author's view that research for money is a threat. We simply see industry asserting its financial rights.

So we don't exactly end up with two points of view. We have a trend that the author of Passage A doesn't like, the author of Passage B describes, and industry asserts its right to pursue. This scale ought to work:

Research for money threatens role of research as a public good.

Research as marketable commodity.

AUTHOR (A)

- open market ill suited
- commercial enterprises lack expertise
- entrepreneurs hide knowledge (e.g., biotechnology)

INDUSTRY

- those who invest have a right to seek a financial return

P1: Opinion with explanation, examples, consequences. Treating research findings as commodities threatens research as a public good.

P2: Objective discussion. Explanation of change in treatment of research findings.

1. How does each passage relate to the central argument?
Passage A argues for the left side of the scale; Passage B explains the right side without actually taking sides in the argument.

2. How do the two passages relate to each other?
Passage A makes a strongly opinionated argument, and Passage B gives mostly objective information that seems to inform that argument. They present similar sorts of examples.

Note that *all five* of these questions test your ability to see the overlap, or the lack of overlap, across passages. In other words, they test your ability to *relate the two passages to each other.* You don't need to determine all the overlapping components up front, but see if annotating the various topics or examples used in each passage helps when it comes time to confirm your answers with the text.

15. Which one of the following is discussed in Passage B but not in Passage A? *(Identification)*

Hard to prephrase a question like this, but in this case we actually want a half scope answer!

(A) the blurring of the legal distinction between discovery and invention

This is a time-consuming sort of question, and there is no quick way to work wrong-to-right—to eliminate an answer, we have to confirm that whatever it describes is mentioned in both passages, or just in Passage A, or in neither! So if we had a feeling that (A) was correct, it might be worth taking a moment to confirm. The blurring of the legal distinction between "discovery and invention" is discussed in Passage B (lines 56–57) but not in Passage A.

(B) the general effects of the market on the exchange of scientific knowledge

Passage A discusses treating "research findings as commodities" (lines 4–6) and "the market process" (lines 10–12) as threats. In fact, most of Passage A is about the negative effects of this shift. Passage B documents the shift, too, and highlights the changes that have resulted (lines 52–58).

(C) the role of scientific research in supplying public goods

Both passages discuss scientific research as a public good (lines 6, 32–33), but not as a means of supplying public goods.

(D) new pharmaceuticals that result from industrial research

Passage A discusses "new drugs and therapies" (lines 21–25), while Passage B mentions "pharmaceuticals" (lines 44–45) resulting from industrial biotechnology.

(E) industry's practice of restricting access to research findings

Passage A mentions that entrepreneurs "can buy research and bury its products" (lines 18–21), while Passage B discusses industry's right to keep discoveries "for its own exclusive use" (lines 59–64).

16. Both passages place in opposition the members of which one of the following pairs? *(Synthesis)*

We can expect this to be about the tension between for-profit companies and not-for-profit institutions.

(A) commercially successful research and commercially unsuccessful research

Comparison trap! The issue here is commercial vs. noncommercial, not commercially successful vs. commercially unsuccessful.

(B) research methods and research results

Specific research methods are not discussed in either passage.

(C) a marketable commodity and a public good

Sure—this is what both passages are all about.

(D) a discovery and an invention

The legal distinction between discoveries and inventions is discussed in Passage B (lines 49-58) but not in Passage A. This is a half scope answer!

(E) scientific research and other types of inquiry

Another comparison trap. Scientific research is discussed in various places in both passages, but other types of inquiry are not discussed in either passage.

17. Both passages refer to which one of the following? *(Identification)*

Uh-oh, another comparison question—tough to prephrase, and, looking at the answer choices, the correct answer may be a small detail.

(A) theoretical frameworks

(B) venture capitalists

Half scope answers. Passage B never mentions theoretical frameworks or venture capitalists.

(C) physics and chemistry

While biotechnology is mentioned in both passages, there is no specific mention of physics or chemistry.

(D) industrial biotechnology

Both passages specifically refer to biotechnology undertaken by industry (lines 22 and 44).

(E) shareholders

Half scope. Passage B never mentions shareholders.

18. It can be inferred from the passages that the authors believe that the increased constraint on access to scientific information and ideas arises from *(Inference)*

This can be prephrased: something about business interests.

(A) the enormous increase in the volume of scientific knowledge that is being generated

(B) the desire of individual researchers to receive credit for their discoveries

These seem way off, especially since they each refer to something not discussed in either passage!

(C) the striving of commercial enterprises to gain a competitive advantage in the market

Similar to our prephrase and well supported by the text (lines 19–21 and 61–64).

(D) moral reservations about the social impact of some scientific research

Watch out! Passage B discusses a "moral distinction between what should and should not be patented" (lines 57–58), but neither passage gets into "moral reservations about the social impact of scientific research."

(E) a drastic reduction in government funding for university research

This is not discussed in either passage.

19. Which one of the following statements is most strongly supported by both passages? *(Inference)*

This is a very general question! Perhaps this answer is something about the main topic—industry vs. public research—but it seems like it might be a minor point of agreement.

(A) Many scientific researchers who previously worked in universities have begun to work in the biotechnology industry.

Though this would seem likely based on lines 28–29, there is no direct reference made to researchers switching jobs in either passage.

(B) Private biotechnology companies have invalidly patented the basic research findings of university researchers.

Neither passage discusses invalidly patenting research findings.

(C) Because of the nature of current scientific research, patent authorities no longer consider the distinction between discoveries and inventions to be clear cut.

Half scope. Passage A never mentions the distinction between discovery and invention.

(D) In the past, scientists working in industry had free access to the results of basic research conducted in universities.

This free access is mentioned throughout Passage A and in the first paragraph of Passage B.

(E) Government-funded research in universities has traditionally been motivated by the goals of private industry.

The motivations of government-funded research are not discussed in either passage.

TAKEAWAYS: Comparative Passages

Starting with this chapter, the focus has shifted from building your RC foundation to applying what you've learned to a variety of passage types. Are there major new techniques for you to learn? Not really. Will you continue to learn as you work through these chapters? Absolutely.

At the end of each of these chapters, rather than restate the main points, we're going to ask you to jot down some notes about what you've learned. Each chapter presents some new ideas (for example, in this chapter, you learned about a new approach to passage mapping and a new wrong-answer type), but at this point, it will also be really helpful for you to take a moment to consider your process during the drills. Is there anything you did particularly well this time? Is there something you wish you had done? What do you want to focus on during your next practice test?

Go ahead, write in your book. We won't tell.

Chapter 9 of Reading Comprehension

Extreme Passages

Extreme Passages

Beloved reader, on test day may all your RC passages be straightforward and may your pencil miraculously be guided to fill in only the correct answer bubbles!

Hopefully, by now, some passages really do feel like that. You breeze along, using your well-honed process to nail one answer after another, and you're even able to put a few extra minutes in the bank. But then... it happens. You turn the page and come up against a passage that makes your heart sink. What do you do? Slow down? Move into desperation mode and try to make educated guesses? In part, this depends on what's come before. If you really were able to breeze through the easier passages, you may have bought yourself enough time to dig deep and work up a strong understanding of this tougher material. If not, you will need to muster all your skills to make it through the questions alive. As we've said before, picking up the pace on the easier passages is one of the best ways to improve your performance on the harder ones. However, since we've already spotlighted timing, let's spend some time in this chapter preparing for the worst!

By now, you probably have a good idea of what makes a passage difficult for you, but here are a few strong signs:

1. The subject matter is unfamiliar, abstract, or otherwise confusing.

It can be very off-putting to feel from the beginning that we don't know exactly what the author is talking about. Sometimes the passage does a great job of making a new subject easy to understand, but at other times it feels as if we're being purposely shut out.

2. The vocabulary is difficult.

We've given you some practice working with tough terms, but it can still throw your comprehension if there are a lot of words you don't know. Also, the mere presence of technical language can make a passage more intimidating for some folks, especially if the terms look a lot like each other and/or are impossible to pronounce.

3. The scale is not clear.

Maybe the ideas expressed in the passage don't seem to sort themselves nicely into two sides, or maybe the author's opinion is hard to decipher.

4. The structure is confusing.

Can we identify the purpose of each paragraph? Do we know where the author is going from one paragraph to the next? If we struggle to map the passage as we go, it can be hard to walk away with a confident picture of the passage as a whole.

Naturally, a passage that is difficult in several, or perhaps *all,* of those ways is going to be quite a struggle to get through. But never fear! The skills you've been sharpening so far are designed to support you in cases like this. Here are a few more tips:

1. Stay curious!

Find something in the subject matter to latch onto and ask questions about. Okay, so maybe you have a hard time relating to a narrative about the competing classifications of fungi, but maybe you can get into the ways those geeky mycologists try to defeat their opponents' ideas. Staying curious is really what PEAR is all about. If you're imagining what might come next and taking a moment to react to each new revelation, you're more likely to overcome the intimidating terminology and abstract ideas and develop a strong grasp of the passage as a whole. You may not quite be able to convince yourself that you're reading a thriller, but you'll do a lot better than the person next to you who's just dutifully reading one word after another like a kid reading aloud in school.

2. Know what you know, and know what you don't.

Don't obsess over the elements of the passage that you don't understand. Focus on making sense of what you know and building it into a sensible whole. While you definitely want to recognize the limits of your knowledge, it may turn out that that intimidating word or concept is not as crucial as it seemed. However, if the questions bring up concepts that aren't coming together for you, defer judgment and use what you do know to narrow down the choices.

3. Read *for* the scale, not *through* the scale.

It's nice to be able to use the scale to heighten your understanding of each part of the passage, but that's not always possible—you can't necessarily expect to have a clear sense of the scale as you read. When your search for the scale gets challenging, use that energy to enliven and focus your reading process. At the end, you may need to look back over the passage to make sense of it all and decide what the scale might be. Even then, there might be more than one way to view the passage; you just need a strong enough sense of the whole to handle the questions. At the very least, make sure you are clear on the author's opinion. If you find you can't answer general Point/Purpose questions, you may need to spend a little more time with the passage.

4. Keep moving.

Don't let yourself get stuck on one difficult sentence, question, or answer choice. Remember that your goal is to maximize the total number of questions you get right, not to display your absolute mastery of the passage. Sometimes you'll have to go with your gut or make an educated guess in order to get through the passage in time. Having said that, remember that you can also buy yourself a little more time for the toughest passages by moving quickly through easier passages and questions. This applies to all sections of the LSAT—building up a reserve of time on easy, routine material leaves you with more time and energy to tackle the hard stuff. One of the major goals of your training should be to keep moving more material into the "easy, routine" category.

Difficult Content Areas

You may find that your difficulties in Reading Comprehension are mostly concentrated in one particular subject. Maybe you have never felt comfortable with science, or maybe you feel a little dizzy whenever you have to read about literary theory. It can be very helpful to get in some additional reading in this problem area to boost your comfort level. (If your weak area is law, this will be a good chance to either get more comfortable or save yourself a lot of money.) We have a list of suggested outside reading for each content area in your online Student Center. If you get in a little reading each day, you may begin to feel more at home with the style and content of passages in your chosen area. Even when you're reading material that doesn't come with built-in questions, make sure you're practicing all your core RC skills: PEAR, reading for the scale, and passage mapping. It won't do you any good just to *look* at the material—you need to really engage with it!

Of course, it's also very helpful to get practice on actual LSAT passages in your challenge area. You may want to skim through some of the PrepTests that you don't plan on using as full exams and pick out the passages in this area. Every type of content has its own ways of introducing difficulty; for instance, science passages can be very intimidating in terms of concepts and terminology, but once you get a handle on those elements, the questions can be a bit more straightforward. On the other hand, social science passages may get into nuanced layers of opinion that require you to interpret a very small amount of information accurately. If you get a feel for *how* and *why* particular passages are challenging, you will be one step closer to mastering them.

DRILL IT: Redacted Passage

We want to give you some practice working with material you don't fully grasp, but of course, at this point in your training, that kind of material may be hard to find! To keep the challenge up, we've looked to our friends in national security. Below is a passage from which material has been "redacted." See if you can use the tips above to develop a scale and passage map and work wrong-to-right through four questions. You're sure to feel that you're missing something here and there, so don't aim for perfection. Move on when you've gotten as far as you can with a question. You'll be surprised how many questions you can answer even with lots of material missing. This is good practice for trying to answer questions even when you don't understand vast swaths of the passage! And while this message won't self-destruct, give yourself six minutes to complete the exercise.

PrepTest 19, S3, P3

When the same habitat types (forests, oceans, grasslands, etc.) in regions of different latitudes are compared, it becomes apparent that the overall number of species increases from pole to equator. (5) the "time theory," holds that diverse species adapted to (10) today's climatic conditions have had more time to emerge in the tropical regions,

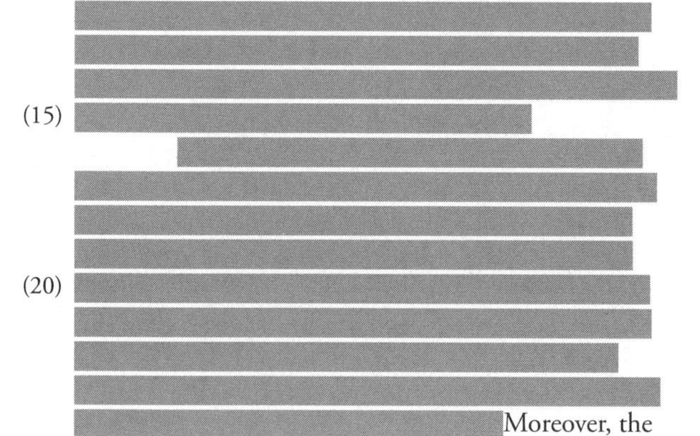

Moreover, the (25) mechanism proposed—greater energy influx leading to bigger populations, thereby lowering the probability of local extinction—remains untested.

(30) Species can thus survive even with few types of food, and competing species can tolerate greater overlap between their respective niches. Both capabilities enable more species to exist on the same resources. However, the ecology of local communities (35) cannot account for the origin of the latitudinal gradient.

A fourth and most plausible hypothesis focuses on regional speciation, and in particular on rates of speciation and extinction.

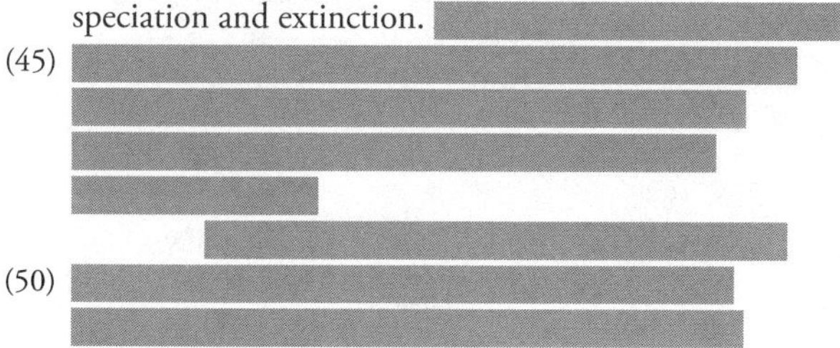

This subgroup evolves differently and eventually cannot interbreed with members of the original population. The uneven spread (55) of a species over a large geographic area promotes this mechanism: at the edges, small populations spread out and form isolated groups.

15. Which one of the following most accurately expresses the main idea of the passage?

(A) At present, no single hypothesis explaining the latitudinal gradient in numbers of species is more widely accepted than any other.
(B) The tropical climate is more conducive to promoting species diversity than are arctic or temperate climates.
(C) Several explanations have been suggested for global patterns in species distribution, but a hypothesis involving rates of speciation seems most promising.
(D) Despite their differences, the various hypotheses regarding a latitudinal gradient in species diversity concur in predicting that the gradient can be expected to increase.
(E) In distinguishing among the current hypotheses for distribution of species, the most important criterion is whether a hypothesis proposes a mechanism that can be tested and validated.

16. Which one of the following situations is most consistent with the species-energy hypothesis as described in the passage?

(A) The many plants in a large agricultural tract represent a limited range of species.
(B) An animal species experiences a death rate almost as rapid as its rate of growth and reproduction.
(C) Within the small number of living organisms in a desert habitat, many different species are represented.
(D) In a tropical rain forest, a species with a large population is found to exhibit instances of local extinction.
(E) In an arctic tundra, the plants and animals exhibit a slow rate of growth and reproduction.

17. As presented in the passage, the principles of the time theory most strongly support which one of the following predictions?

(A) In the absence of additional ice ages, the number of species at high latitudes could eventually increase significantly.
(B) No future ice ages are likely to change the climatic conditions that currently characterize temperate regions.
(C) If no further ice ages occur, climatic conditions at high latitudes might eventually resemble those at today's tropical latitudes.
(D) Researchers will continue to find many more new species in the tropics than in the arctic and temperate zones.
(E) Future ice ages are likely to interrupt the climatic conditions that now characterize high-latitude regions.

20. With which one of the following statements concerning possible explanations for the latitudinal gradient in number of species would the author be most likely to agree?

(A) The time theory is the least plausible of proposed hypotheses, since it does not correctly assess the impact of ice ages upon tropical conditions.
(B) The rate-of-speciation hypothesis addresses a principal objection to the climatic-stability hypothesis.
(C) The major objection to the time theory is that it does not accurately reflect the degree to which the latitudinal gradient exists, especially when undiscovered species are taken into account.
(D) Despite the claims of the species-energy hypothesis, a high rate of biological growth and reproduction is more likely to exist with low biomass than with high biomass.
(E) An important advantage of the rate-of-speciation theory is that it considers species competition in a regional rather than local context.

For more practice, log in to your Student Center!

SOLUTIONS: Redacted Passage

Scale and Passage Map

Were you able to come up with a scale for this one? The good news is that the scale is usually tied more closely to the overall structure of the passage than to small details, so even if we don't understand everything, we will usually have a good shot at the scale. Let's see how we do at passage mapping and go from there. Below is what our real-time process might look like.

P1: Presentation of a phenomenon. There are more species near the equator than near the poles. Odds are good we can expect the rest of the passage to give some kind of explanation for this phenomenon.

P2: Presentation of a theory to account for the phenomenon. Species in the tropics have had more time to adapt to today's conditions. It seems likely that the "time theory" is an explanation for what we saw in the last paragraph.

P3: Some kind of objection? We don't have enough here to know if this is an objection to the time theory mentioned in the previous paragraph, or if we've moved on to some other theory, but the author seems to be objecting to something. The word "moreover" indicates that the problem we see here is not the only problem.

P4: Elimination of a theory? The ecology of local communities cannot account for the origin of the latitudinal gradient. The author seems to be objecting to an explanation for the phenomenon presented in the first paragraph (now we're calling it the latitudinal gradient), but again, it's hard to tell if this is connected to the time theory or not.

P5: A fourth theory. Something about rates of speciation and extinction. Good news! The first sentence here tells us that we should already have seen three theories, so we now have a good idea of what was going on in the third and fourth paragraphs. We also know that the author prefers this fourth theory, because it's said to be the "most plausible." Maybe the author has been knocking off the other theories one by one.

P6: Explanation of fourth theory? Something about spreading out and forming groups that can't interbreed. Paragraph five is brief and mainly tells us that the author likes the fourth theory, so this paragraph is almost certainly an elaboration of that theory.

With this level of understanding, we can make a scale fairly comfortably, even if we don't understand either side fully:

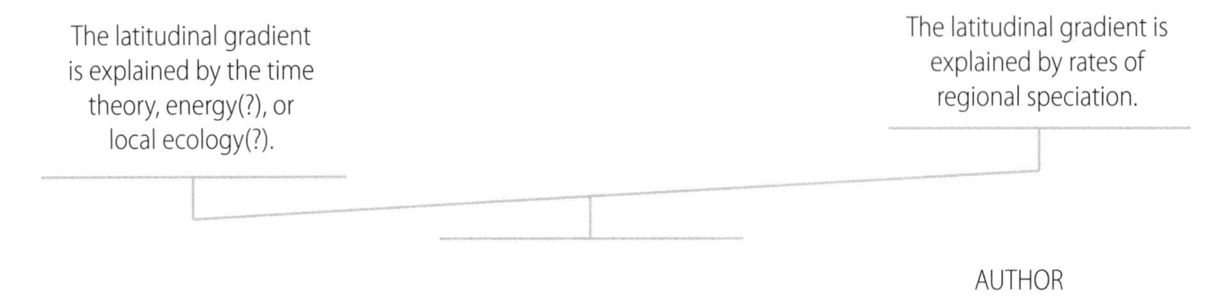

Questions

In a situation like this, it can be useful to take a moment to figure out where our time will best be spent. When we're not clear on all the details, the best technique is to focus on the most *general* possible questions, and leave the *specific* questions for later. Let's start by tackling the first and last questions, as these are much more general than the middle two.

15. Which one of the following most accurately expresses the main idea of the passage? *(Synthesis)*

This passage has given us four possible theories for the phenomenon in question, and the author prefers the fourth one, which has something to do with "regional speciation." We'll expect the correct answer to mention both the phenomenon and the preferred theory, though it may use synonyms or confusing language to do so.

9

(A) At present, no single hypothesis explaining the latitudinal gradient in numbers of species is more widely accepted than any other.

Well, we know that the author prefers one theory over the others, so this doesn't seem right, even if we don't know if the author's favorite is "widely accepted."

(B) The tropical climate is more conducive to promoting species diversity than are arctic or temperate climates.

This doesn't sound like the fourth theory.

(C) Several explanations have been suggested for global patterns in species distribution, but a hypothesis involving rates of speciation seems most promising.

This looks good. The fourth theory is about rates of speciation and it's being used to explain the distribution of species.

(D) Despite their differences, the various hypotheses regarding a latitudinal gradient in species diversity concur in predicting that the gradient can be expected to increase.

Nothing we can see says that the four theories make the same prediction. We can't be sure that isn't in the redacted portion, but even if it were, it wouldn't be the main point.

(E) In distinguishing among the current hypotheses for distribution of species, the most important criterion is whether a hypothesis proposes a mechanism that can be tested and validated.

This doesn't tell us which theory the author likes.

20. With which one of the following statements concerning possible explanations for the latitudinal gradient in number of species would the author be most likely to agree? *(Synthesis)*

This is a harder general question than the last one, but the right answer is likely to say something about the speciation theory being better than the others.

(A) The time theory is the least plausible of proposed hypotheses, since it does not correctly assess the impact of ice ages upon tropical conditions.

Comparison trap? The unredacted parts of the passage don't provide any comparison between the first three theories in terms of plausibility.

(B) The rate-of-speciation hypothesis addresses a principal objection to the climatic-stability hypothesis.

This has some details in it that we don't know much about, but it does say that the rate-of-speciation hypothesis does something good. Let's keep it.

(C) The major objection to the time theory is that it does not accurately reflect the degree to which the latitudinal gradient exists, especially when undiscovered species are taken into account.

We don't know what the major objection to the time theory is. Defer.

(D) Despite the claims of the species-energy hypothesis, a high rate of biological growth and reproduction is more likely to exist with low biomass than with high biomass.

This is very specific and we don't know anything about it. Maybe there's support for this in the missing text, but we have to defer.

(E) An important advantage of the rate-of-speciation theory is that it considers species competition in a regional rather than local context.

This also gives us a positive aspect of the speciation theory. Let's keep it.

At this point, we haven't eliminated many answers. This question wasn't as general as it looked! Our rough prephrase was that we wanted to see something positive about the speciation theory, and that would land us on a 50/50 split between (B) and (E). Not a perfect situation to be in, but not bad considering all that we don't know.

16. Which one of the following situations is most consistent with the species-energy hypothesis as described in the passage? *(Inference)*

It looks like we need to apply one of the theories to a specific situation. Let's see if we can locate the relevant paragraph. In this case, we can feel pretty confident that this is referring to the third paragraph, because that's the only one that mentions energy. What do we know? Someone seems to think that the greater energy available in the tropics would lead to bigger populations that would be less likely to go extinct. Hopefully, one of the answers will address this element, rather than the missing part that the author also objects to.

(A) The many plants in a large agricultural tract represent a limited range of species.

Where is this agricultural tract? There's nothing here to connect to what we have of the third paragraph. Also, wouldn't the plants in any area represent a limited range of species?

(B) An animal species experiences a death rate almost as rapid as its rate of growth and reproduction.

It's hard to see what to do with this. What does it have to do with energy? Maybe this connects to the author's preferred theory, which includes rates of extinction. And again, this seems like it could be true for any area, regardless of how much energy was available.

(C) Within the small number of living organisms in a desert habitat, many different species are represented.

Hmm, this seems plausible. Maybe the desert has more energy and so can produce more species. But wait—the passage is talking about large populations. This is talking about large numbers of different species within a small overall population. It's hard to say for sure, but this might be a closer match with the next paragraph.

(D) In a tropical rain forest, a species with a large population is found to exhibit instances of local extinction.

Contradicted! We've got this one–large populations are less likely to experience local extinction! It feels nice to be able to cross one off definitively.

(E) In an arctic tundra, the plants and animals exhibit a slow rate of growth and reproduction.

This seems to match what we have. If the tropics are getting more energy, leading to large populations, the opposite is probably happening in the arctic. Answer (E) is our best shot.

17. As presented in the passage, the principles of the time theory most strongly support which one of the following predictions? *(Inference)*

All we know about the time theory is that well-adapted species have had more time to evolve in the tropics, presumably because they have had the same type of climate for a longer time. Now we're supposed to use that to predict something. All we know is that if things stay the same in an area, we should see more species.

(A) In the absence of additional ice ages, the number of species at high latitudes could eventually increase significantly.

Maybe. If there are no more ice ages, perhaps creatures there will have time to adapt to new conditions.

(B) No future ice ages are likely to change the climatic conditions that currently characterize temperate regions.

This is actually saying that ice ages aren't likely to have an effect on the climate in some regions. We don't know anything about that, but it sounds kind of odd. Why wouldn't ice ages affect the climate?

(C) If no further ice ages occur, climatic conditions at high latitudes might eventually resemble those at today's tropical latitudes.

This could be true—serious global warming?—but this is like (B) in that it just seems to be about what will happen with the climate and doesn't say anything about the number of species.

(D) Researchers will continue to find many more new species in the tropics than in the arctic and temperate zones.

This is about scientists finding *new species. That's something else entirely.*

(E) Future ice ages are likely to interrupt the climatic conditions that now characterize high-latitude regions.

This is like answers (B) and (C)—it just makes a prediction about the climate without mentioning species. That leaves us with (A). Score another one for wrong-to-right!

Hopefully you were able to make your way correctly through some of the questions in that drill. While reading only bits of a passage is not the plan for test day, this experience should have reinforced that even during an extremely difficult (or rushed) passage, it's possible to cobble together sufficient understanding to eliminate some answer choices. Because the difficulty was part of the drill—it wasn't your fault the NSA redacted that passage!—you probably did not find it panic-inducing, and you may even have enjoyed the challenge. Indeed, your success in an extremely tough RC situation is determined in great part by how calmly you can approach the challenge, as well as by how much time you've built up in your time bank. As we said at the beginning of this chapter, great timing on the easier material is *essential* to success on the tougher stuff. Let's practice that right now.

DRILL IT: Extreme Passages

Here's a pair of full passages, the first of which is significantly easier than the second. Give yourself 18:00 to complete both, but allocate your time wisely. Push the pace on the first, and if the going gets tough on the second, either slow down for comprehension or use your hard-earned emergency skills to glean what you can from the passage and make smart choices on the questions! With this in mind, and before you even start the drill, make a quick mental note of how you think the timing ought to break down for this section. As you work through the drill, mark how much of your 18 minutes is left at each stage, so you'll be better positioned to review and learn from this exercise.

PrepTest 30, Section 3, Passage 1

The okapi, a forest mammal of central Africa, has presented zoologists with a number of difficult questions since they first learned of its existence in 1900. The first was how to classify it. Because it was (5) horselike in dimension, and bore patches of striped hide similar to a zebra's (a relative of the horse), zoologists first classified it as a member of the horse family. But further studies showed that, despite okapis' coloration and short necks, their closest relatives were (10) giraffes. The okapi's rightful place within the giraffe family is confirmed by its skin-covered horns (in males), two-lobed canine teeth, and long prehensile tongue.

The next question was the size of the okapi (15) population. Because okapis were infrequently captured by hunters, some zoologists believed that they were rare; however, others theorized that their habits simply kept them out of sight. It was not until 1985, when zoologists started tracking okapis by affixing collars (20) equipped with radio transmitters to briefly captured specimens, that reliable information about okapi numbers and habits began to be collected. It turns out that while okapis are not as rare as some zoologists suspected, their population is concentrated in an (25) extremely limited chain of forestland in northeastern central Africa, surrounded by savanna.

One reason for their seeming scarcity is that their coloration allows okapis to camouflage themselves even at close range. Another is that okapis do not travel (30) in groups or with other large forest mammals, and neither frequent open riverbanks nor forage at the borders of clearings, choosing instead to keep to the forest interior. This is because okapis, unlike any other animal in the central African forest, subsist entirely on (35) leaves: more than one hundred species of plants have been identified as part of their diet, and about twenty of these are preferred. Okapis never eat one plant to the exclusion of others; even where preferred foliage is abundant, okapis will leave much of it uneaten, (40) choosing to move on and sample other leaves. Because of this, and because of the distribution of their food, okapis engage in individual rather than congregated foraging.

But other questions about okapi behavior arise. (45) Why for example, do they prefer to remain within forested areas when many of their favorite plants are found in the open border between forest and savanna? One possibility is that this is a defense against predators; another is that the okapi was pushed into the (50) forest by competition with other large, hoofed animals, such as the bushbuck and bongo, that specialize on the forest edges and graze them more efficiently. Another question is why okapis are absent from other nearby forest regions that would seem hospitable to them. (55) Zoologists theorize that okapis are relicts of an era when forestland was scarce and that they continue to respect those borders even though available forestland has long since expanded.

Time Remaining: _______/ 18:00

1. Which one of the following most completely and accurately expresses the main idea of the passage?

(A) Information gathered by means of radio-tracking collars has finally provided answers to the questions about okapis that zoologists have been attempting to answer since they first learned of the mammal's existence.
(B) Because of their physical characteristics and their infrequent capture by hunters, okapis presented zoologists with many difficult questions at the start of the twentieth century.
(C) Research concerning okapis has answered some of the questions that have puzzled zoologists since their discovery, but has also raised other questions regarding their geographic concentration and feeding habits.
(D) A new way of tracking okapis using radio-tracking collars reveals that their apparent scarcity is actually a result of their coloration, their feeding habits, and their geographic concentration.
(E) Despite new research involving radio tracking, the questions that have puzzled zoologists about okapis since their discovery at the start of the twentieth century remain mostly unanswered.

2. The function of the third paragraph is to

(A) pose a question about okapi behavior
(B) rebut a theory about okapi behavior
(C) counter the assertion that okapis are rare
(D) explain why okapis appeared to be rare
(E) support the belief that okapis are rare

3. Based on the passage, in its eating behavior the okapi is most analogous to

(A) a child who eats one kind of food at a time, consuming all of it before going on to the next kind
(B) a professor who strictly follows the outline in the syllabus, never digressing to follow up on student questions
(C) a student who delays working on homework until the last minute, then rushes to complete it
(D) a newspaper reader who skips from story to story, just reading headlines and eye-catching paragraphs
(E) a deer that ventures out of the woods only at dusk and dawn, remaining hidden during the rest of the day

4. Suppose that numerous okapis are discovered living in a remote forest region in northeastern central Africa that zoologists had not previously explored. Based on their current views, which one of the following would the zoologists be most likely to conclude about this discovery?

(A) Okapis were pushed into this forest region by competition with mammals in neighboring forests.
(B) Okapis in this forest region forage in the border between forest and savanna.
(C) Okapis in this forest region are not threatened by the usual predators of okapis.
(D) Okapis moved into this forest region because their preferred foliage is more abundant there than in other forests.
(E) Okapis lived in this forest region when forestland in the area was scarce.

5. The passage provides information intended to help explain each of the following EXCEPT:

(A) why zoologists once believed that okapis were rare
(B) why zoologists classified the okapi as a member of the giraffe family
(C) why okapis choose to limit themselves to the interiors of forests
(D) why okapis engage in individual rather than congregated foraging
(E) why okapis leave much preferred foliage uneaten

6. Based on the passage, the author would be most likely to agree with which one of the following statements?

(A) The number of okapis is many times larger than zoologists had previously believed it to be.
(B) Radio-tracking collars have enabled scientists to finally answer all the questions about the okapi.
(C) Okapis are captured infrequently because their habits and coloration make it difficult for hunters to find them.
(D) Okapis are concentrated in a limited geographic area because they prefer to eat one plant species to the exclusion of others.
(E) The number of okapis would steadily increase if okapis began to forage in the open border between forest and savanna.

Time Remaining: _______/ 18:00

PrepTest 50, Section 1, Passage 4

One of the foundations of scientific research is that an experimental result is credible only if it can be replicated—only if performing the experiment a second time leads to the same result. But physicists (5) John Sommerer and Edward Ott have conceived of a physical system in which even the least change in the starting conditions—no matter how small, inadvertent, or undetectable—can alter results radically. The system is represented by a computer model of a (10) mathematical equation describing the motion of a particle placed in a particular type of force field.

Sommerer and Ott based their system on an analogy with the phenomena known as riddled basins of attraction. If two bodies of water bound a large (15) landmass and water is spilled somewhere on the land, the water will eventually make its way to one or the other body of water, its destination depending on such factors as where the water is spilled and the geographic features that shape the water's path and (20) velocity. The basin of attraction for a body of water is the area of land that, whenever water is spilled on it, always directs the spilled water to that body.

In some geographical formations it is sometimes impossible to predict, not only the exact destination (25) of the spilled water, but even which body of water it will end up in. This is because the boundary between one basin of attraction and another is riddled with fractal properties; in other words, the boundary is permeated by an extraordinarily high number of (30) physical irregularities such as notches or zigzags. Along such a boundary, the only way to determine where spilled water will flow at any given point is actually to spill it and observe its motion; spilling the water at any immediately adjacent point could give (35) the water an entirely different path, velocity, or destination.

In the system posited by the two physicists, this boundary expands to include the whole system: i.e., the entire force field is riddled with fractal properties, (40) and it is impossible to predict even the general destination of the particle given its starting point. Sommerer and Ott make a distinction between this type of uncertainty and that known as "chaos"; under chaos, a particle's general destination would be (45) predictable but its path and exact destination would not.

There are presumably other such systems because the equation the physicists used to construct the computer model was literally the first one they (50) attempted, and the likelihood that they chose the only equation that would lead to an unstable system is small. If other such systems do exist, metaphorical examples of riddled basins of attraction may abound in the failed attempts of scientists to replicate (55) previous experimental results—in which case, scientists would be forced to question one of the basic principles that guide their work.

Time Remaining: _______/ 18:00

22. Which one of the following most accurately expresses the main point of the passage?

(A) Sommerer and Ott's model suggests that many of the fundamental experimental results of science are unreliable because they are contaminated by riddled basins of attraction.
(B) Sommerer and Ott's model suggests that scientists who fail to replicate experimental results might be working within physical systems that make replication virtually impossible.
(C) Sommerer and Ott's model suggests that experimental results can never be truly replicated because the starting conditions of an experiment can never be re-created exactly.
(D) Sommerer and Ott's model suggests that most of the physical systems studied by scientists are in fact metaphorical examples of riddled basins of attraction.
(E) Sommerer and Ott's model suggests that an experimental result should not be treated as credible unless that result can be replicated.

23. The discussion of the chaos of physical systems is intended to perform which one of the following functions in the passage?

(A) emphasize the extraordinarily large number of physical irregularities in a riddled basin of attraction
(B) emphasize the unusual types of physical irregularities found in Sommerer and Ott's model
(C) emphasize the large percentage of a riddled basin of attraction that exhibits unpredictability
(D) emphasize the degree of unpredictability in Sommerer and Ott's model
(E) emphasize the number of fractal properties in a riddled basin of attraction

24. Given the information in the passage, Sommerer and Ott are most likely to agree with which one of the following?

(A) It is sometimes impossible to determine whether a particular region exhibits fractal properties.
(B) It is sometimes impossible to predict even the general destination of a particle placed in a chaotic system.
(C) It is sometimes impossible to re-create exactly the starting conditions of an experiment.
(D) It is usually possible to predict the exact path water will travel if it is spilled at a point not on the boundary between two basins of attraction.
(E) It is usually possible to determine the path by which a particle traveled given information about where it was placed and its eventual destination.

25. Which one of the following most accurately describes the author's attitude toward the work of Sommerer and Ott?

(A) skeptical of the possibility that numerous unstable systems exist but confident that the existence of numerous unstable systems would call into question one of the foundations of science
(B) convinced of the existence of numerous unstable systems and unsure if the existence of numerous unstable systems calls into question one of the foundations of science
(C) convinced of the existence of numerous unstable systems and confident that the existence of numerous unstable systems calls into question one of the foundations of science
(D) persuaded of the possibility that numerous unstable systems exist and unsure if the existence of numerous unstable systems would call into question one of the foundations of science
(E) persuaded of the possibility that numerous unstable systems exist and confident that the existence of numerous unstable systems would call into question one of the foundations of science

26. According to the passage, Sommerer and Ott's model differs from a riddled basin of attraction in which one of the following ways?

(A) In the model, the behavior of a particle placed at any point in the system is chaotic; in a riddled basin of attraction, only water spilled at some of the points behaves chaotically.
(B) In a riddled basin of attraction, the behavior of water spilled at any point is chaotic; in the model, only particles placed at some of the points in the system behave chaotically.
(C) In the model, it is impossible to predict the destination of a particle placed at any point in the system; in a riddled basin of attraction, only some points are such that it is impossible to predict the destination of water spilled at each of those points.
(D) In a riddled basin of attraction, water spilled at two adjacent points always makes its way to the same destination; in the model, it is possible for particles placed at two adjacent points to travel to different destinations.
(E) In the model, two particles placed successively at a given point always travel to the same destination; in a riddled basin of attraction, water spilled at the same point on different occasions may make its way to different destinations.

27. Which one of the following best defines the term "basin of attraction," as that term is used in the passage?

(A) the set of all points on an area of land for which it is possible to predict the destination, but not the path, of water spilled at that point
(B) the set of all points on an area of land for which it is possible to predict both the destination and the path of water spilled at that point
(C) the set of all points on an area of land that are free from physical irregularities such as notches and zigzags
(D) the set of all points on an area of land for which water spilled at each point will travel to a particular body of water
(E) the set of all points on an area of land for which water spilled at each point will travel to the same exact destination

28. Which one of the following is most clearly one of the "metaphorical examples of riddled basins of attraction" mentioned in lines 52–53?

(A) A scientist is unable to determine if mixing certain chemicals will result in a particular chemical reaction because the reaction cannot be consistently reproduced since sometimes the reaction occurs and other times it does not despite starting conditions that are in fact exactly the same in each experiment.
(B) A scientist is unable to determine if mixing certain chemicals will result in a particular chemical reaction because the reaction cannot be consistently reproduced since it is impossible to bring about starting conditions that are in fact exactly the same in each experiment.
(C) A scientist is unable to determine if mixing certain chemicals will result in a particular chemical reaction because the reaction cannot be consistently reproduced since it is impossible to produce starting conditions that are even approximately the same from one experiment to the next.
(D) A scientist is able to determine that mixing certain chemicals results in a particular chemical reaction because it is possible to consistently reproduce the reaction even though the starting conditions vary significantly from one experiment to the next.
(E) A scientist is able to determine that mixing certain chemicals results in a particular chemical reaction because it is possible to consistently reproduce the reaction despite the fact that the amount of time it takes for the reaction to occur varies significantly depending n the starting conditions of the experiment.

Time Remaining: _______/ 18:00

SOLUTIONS: Extreme Passages

How did it go? Do you feel you made the right choices? Take a look back at your time notations—did you give each part the amount of time that you planned to? Knowing in advance that the first passage was easier, were you able to push yourself to work faster? Did you use your time wisely on the second passage? Below, we've tried to model how a very well-prepared test-taker might have navigated the two extremes.

PrepTest 30, Section 3, Passage 1

Scale and Passage Map

Bravo if you kept wondering when the scale of this passage would reveal itself—that sort of active reading is what makes reading for the scale effective even when there is no scale! Indeed, this passage is simply informational and there is no argument (the initial question of how to classify okapi is just one of many questions that are discussed). Regardless of its lack of a scale, you probably found that the passage was not particularly difficult. Indeed, unusual passages—the subject of the next chapter—are not necessarily extreme.

P1: First of several questions about an animal. How to classify the okapi? It seemed horselike, but turned out to be closer to the giraffe.

P2: Second question. How many? This was up for debate, until radio tracking confirmed that okapis are not very rare, but concentrated in a small area.

P3: Explanation of a prior belief and further detail. Okapis seemed rare due to camouflage, small groups, and location in the forest interior. They stay in the forest because of their eating habits.

P4: More questions. Why do okapis stay in the forest when they like plants on the savanna border? Perhaps for defense, perhaps due to competition with other species, or perhaps because they stay within their historical borders.

Questions

1. Which one of the following most completely and accurately expresses the main idea of the passage? *(Synthesis)*

There's not much in the way of a scale here, so we need to work from our passage map. Basically, zoologists had a bunch of questions about okapis—some of them got answered, but others popped up in the process.

(A) Information gathered by means of radio-tracking collars has finally provided answers to the questions about okapis that zoologists have been attempting to answer since they first learned of the mammal's existence.

Hmm, this is awfully narrow and the collars answered one question—how rare are okapis? (lines 18–22)

(B) Because of their physical characteristics and their infrequent capture by hunters, okapis presented zoologists with many difficult questions at the start of the twentieth century.

Okay, but what about events after that? This only takes us up to line 18.

(C) Research concerning okapis has answered some of the questions that have puzzled zoologists since their discovery, but has also raised other questions regarding their geographic concentration and feeding habits.

Looking good—we've gotten some answers (lines 8–13, 18–26), but more questions have emerged (lines 44–54).

(D) A new way of tracking okapis using radio-tracking collars reveals that their apparent scarcity is actually a result of their coloration, their feeding habits, and their geographic concentration.

Two problems—first, this emphasis on the results of the collars is still too narrow; second, the passage doesn't say we learned all those details from the radio tracking.

(E) Despite new research involving radio tracking, the questions that have puzzled zoologists about okapis since their discovery at the start of the twentieth century remain mostly unanswered.

This is too extreme. We don't know what proportion of the questions remain unanswered. In fact, we don't know if any of the original questions remain at all. The questions in paragraph four are cited as examples of new questions that have arisen (line 44).

2. The function of the third paragraph is to *(Synthesis)*

Let's remind ourselves of what happened there: explanation of a prior belief and further detail. Okapis seemed rare due to camouflage, small groups, and location in the forest interior. They stay in the forest because of their eating habits.

(A) pose a question about okapi behavior

No question in paragraph three, just explanation.

(B) rebut a theory about okapi behavior

This could be seen as rebutting the idea that okapi were rare, but it's not about behavior.

(C) counter the assertion that okapis are rare

This looks good.

(D) explain why okapis appeared to be rare

Oh, this looks better. Glad we didn't just choose (C) and wander off like an okapi.

(E) support the belief that okapis are rare

Contradicted.

Looking at (C) and (D), (C) seems too extreme. The passage suggests that okapis are somewhat rare (lines 22–26). Answer (D) matches our prephrase perfectly—it's not so much an argument as an explanation.

3. Based on the passage, in its eating behavior the okapi is most analogous to *(Inference)*

From the second half of paragraph three we know that they eat a wide variety of leaves, moving on even when their favorite foods are around.

(A) a child who eats one kind of food at a time, consuming all of it before going on to the next kind

Contradicted!

(B) a professor who strictly follows the outline in the syllabus, never digressing to follow up on student questions

"Strictly follows" seems off, and the okapis do seem to digress.

(C) a student who delays working on homework until the last minute, then rushes to complete it

Procrastination and rushing have nothing to do with this.

(D) a newspaper reader who skips from story to story, just reading headlines and eye-catching paragraphs

This seems right. Moving around and sampling.

(E) a deer that ventures out of the woods only at dusk and dawn, remaining hidden during the rest of the day

Timing is never discussed.

4. Suppose that numerous okapis are discovered living in a remote forest region in northeastern central Africa that zoologists had not previously explored. Based on their current views, which one of the following would the zoologists be most likely to conclude about this discovery? *(Inference)*

This is hard to prephrase!

(A) Okapis were pushed into this forest region by competition with mammals in neighboring forests.

Maybe, but this doesn't seem supported.

(B) Okapis in this forest region forage in the border between forest and savanna.

We learn that okapis do NOT forage there (lines 31–33).

(C) Okapis in this forest region are not threatened by the usual predators of okapis.

Why?

(D) Okapis moved into this forest region because their preferred foliage is more abundant there than in other forests.

Contradicted. We know they don't put a premium on eating their preferred foliage (line 38–39).

(E) Okapis lived in this forest region when forestland in the area was scarce.

This ties in with the theory explained in the passage's last sentence.

9

5. The passage provides information intended to help explain each of the following EXCEPT: *(Identification)*

No way to prephrase this—just need to remember to eliminate what is explained.

(A) why zoologists once believed that okapis were rare

This was in the third paragraph.

(B) why zoologists classified the okapi as a member of the giraffe family

First paragraph.

(C) why okapis choose to limit themselves to the interiors of forests

Final paragraph.

(D) why okapis engage in individual rather than congregated foraging

Fourth.

(E) why okapis leave much preferred foliage uneaten

This was discussed but never explained!

6. Based on the passage, the author would be most likely to agree with which one of the following statements? *(Inference)*

Again, no way to prephrase.

(A) The number of okapis is many times larger than zoologists had previously believed it to be.

Many times? We know that there were more than previously thought (lines 23–26), but this answer is too extreme.

(B) Radio-tracking collars have enabled scientists to finally answer all the questions about the okapi.

All is too extreme. Man, they keep trotting out this idea!

(C) Okapis are captured infrequently because their habits and coloration make it difficult for hunters to find them.

This is supported by the explanation of their seeming scarcity (lines 28–33).

(D) Okapis are concentrated in a limited geographic area because they prefer to eat one plant species to the exclusion of others.

Contradicted!

(E) The number of okapis would steadily increase if okapis began to forage in the open border between forest and savanna.

This might be true, but it is unsupported.

PrepTest 50, Section 1, Passage 4

Scale and Passage Map

Well, if you didn't find this passage challenging, you probably use your Nobel Prize as a paperweight. For the rest of us, this passage was tough for a few reasons. Different readers may have different lists of grievances, but here are a few big ones:

1. The material is rather abstract. Sommerer and Ott have *conceived* of a system, but it's not clear whether we're dealing with something that actually exists.

2. There are multiple related concepts that are easy to mix together: basins of attraction, riddled basins of attraction, *metaphorical* riddled basins of attraction, chaos, Sommerer and Ott's model, force fields... How are we supposed to keep it all straight?

3. Some of the answer choices require us to make very fine distinctions.

4. It's tough to see the scale here. We get a taste at the beginning: "One of the foundations of scientific research is ... But ...." We are set up to expect Sommerer and Ott to upend one of the foundations of science. By the end, it's clear that they may have done that, but we have to get through all the technical descriptions in the middle to see it, and we still have a pretty tricky scale. Sommerer and Ott (and the author) aren't saying that this scientific principle is wrong, exactly. They're saying that because imperceptibly tiny differences in initial conditions can cause a completely different (and unpredictable) outcome, it may not always be possible to replicate a valid experimental result.

Part of the answer to keeping your head above water with this tough passage is to remember to categorize any overly-complex details in terms of what role they play in the passage. For example, lines 26–30—"This is because the boundary between one basin of attraction and another is riddled with fractal properties; in other words, the boundary is permeated by an extraordinarily high number of physical irregularities such as notches or zigzags."—are explaining the unpredictability of certain formations. It's a bonus if we "get" what that sentence said, but knowing its role is sufficient for survival.

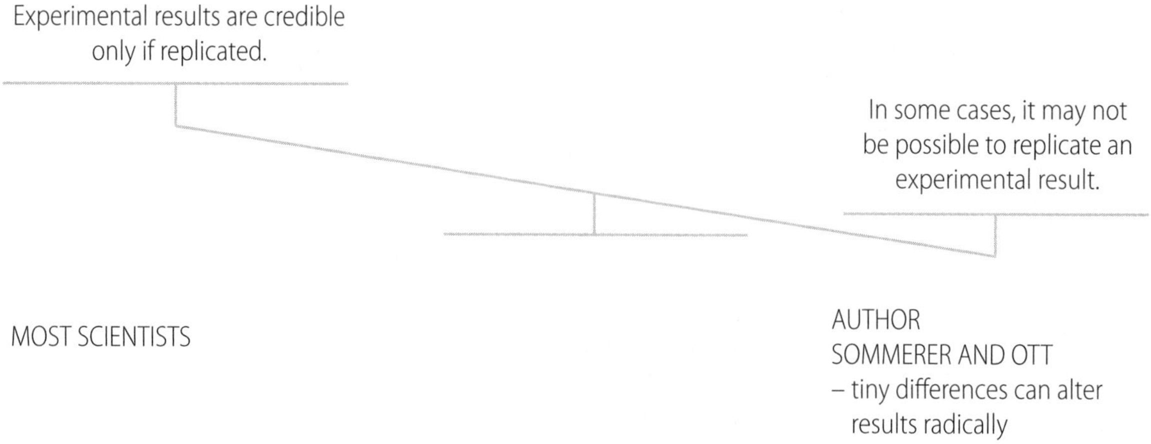

Experimental results are credible only if replicated.

In some cases, it may not be possible to replicate an experimental result.

MOST SCIENTISTS

AUTHOR
SOMMERER AND OTT
– tiny differences can alter results radically

P1: Introduction and challenges to a foundational idea. An experiment is considered credible only if its results can be replicated, but in the system described by Sommerer and Ott, very small changes can lead to a different result.

P2: Beginning of explanation through analogy. A basin of attraction is the area of land that drains into a particular body of water.

P3: Continuation of explanation. A riddled basin of attraction has irregular boundaries, and it's impossible to predict the direction of water spilled at these boundaries.

P4: Description of new system, comparison with chaos. The system described by Sommerer and Ott is unpredictable everywhere. This differs from chaos, under which we can still predict the general destination.

P5: Prediction of similar systems and their consequences. There are probably other unpredictable systems, and this kind of system may underlie scientists' difficulties in replicating experiments. If so, it would challenge the foundational idea in paragraph one.

Questions

22. Which one of the following most accurately expresses the main point of the passage? *(Synthesis)*

This is going to be a general point about unpredictability challenging a principle of science.

(A) Sommerer and Ott's model suggests that many of the fundamental experimental results of science are unreliable because they are contaminated by riddled basins of attraction.

Results contaminated by riddled basins? No—the basins are a metaphor! And the passage doesn't go so far as to say that many scientific results are unreliable.

(B) Sommerer and Ott's model suggests that scientists who fail to replicate experimental results might be working within physical systems that make replication virtually impossible.

This sounds a lot like what the author is saying at the end. If scientists are having trouble replicating results, maybe it's because they're working in unpredictable systems like the one described by Sommerer and Ott.

(C) Sommerer and Ott's model suggests that experimental results can never be truly replicated because the starting conditions of an experiment can never be re-created exactly.

This is too extreme. We aren't told that initial conditions can never be re-created—just that this may be hard to do in certain cases.

(D) Sommerer and Ott's model suggests that most of the physical systems studied by scientists are in fact metaphorical examples of riddled basins of attraction.

This is an answer we might defer judgment on, but on second glance, "most" is too extreme. True, the author does say that "metaphorical examples of riddled basins of attraction may abound in the failed attempts of scientists to replicate previous experimental results" (lines 52–55), but this is only about failed *attempts and is just a possibility that we may have to consider if there are many unpredictable systems like the one described by Sommerer and Ott. Also, this choice makes no mention of the implications for the foundational idea mentioned in paragraph one.*

(E) Sommerer and Ott's model suggests that an experimental result should not be treated as credible unless that result can be replicated.

This is contradicted. Sommerer and Ott's work challenges, rather than validates, the assumption that a result is only credible if it can be replicated.

23. The discussion of the chaos of physical systems is intended to perform which one of the following functions in the passage? *(Synthesis)*

Here's a great example of when we may have to look back and squeeze a more detailed understanding out of something we skimmed earlier. Chaos shows up in the fourth paragraph as a point of comparison: according to lines 42–46, the system described by Sommerer and Ott is less predictable than chaos, because we can't even predict a particle's general destination.

(A) emphasize the extraordinarily large number of physical irregularities in a riddled basin of attraction

This answer seems to have nothing to do with unpredictability. Under time pressure, we'd be likely to note that and defer, looking for a better answer elsewhere. Looking more closely, we might see that physical irregularities are discussed in the previous paragraph—they occur at the boundaries between basins. The current paragraph states that the system described by S&O also displays these "fractal properties," but the discussion of chaos does not do anything to support this. Also, this portion is about S&O's system, not actual riddled basins. This is a good example of an answer choice that can trip us up if we're not focused on answering the specific question at hand. Our prephrase saved us a lot of work!

(B) emphasize the unusual types of physical irregularities found in S&O's model

Again, this seems far from our prephrase. There is also no indication that the irregularities in S&O's system are particularly unusual.

(C) emphasize the large percentage of a riddled basin of attraction that exhibits unpredictability

Good answer to defer on during a first pass, as it mentions unpredictability. However, as we mentioned above, this portion of the passage is about S&O's system, not a riddled basin. It's true that this system is unpredictable everywhere, but this is not true of riddled basins—their unpredictability occurs at the boundaries.

(D) emphasize the degree of unpredictability in Sommerer and Ott's model

Exactly! The discussion of chaos serves to emphasize the unpredictability of the model. By deferring on a few of the trickier choices, we can get to the correct answer much more efficiently.

(E) emphasize the number of fractal properties in a riddled basin of attraction

How does the part about chaos emphasize this? Also, this answer has the same error as (A) and (C)—the lines we're looking at are about S&O's system, not riddled basins!

24. Given the information in the passage, Sommerer and Ott are most likely to agree with which one of the following? *(Inference)*

Hard to prephrase this sort of question—the answer could be anything from a small inference to a broader synthesis of the passage. Let's dial up the wrong-to-right.

(A) It is sometimes impossible to determine whether a particular region exhibits fractal properties.

This is unsupported—the author never says that these properties themselves are hard to detect.

(B) It is sometimes impossible to predict even the general destination of a particle placed in a chaotic system.

Lines 43–46 state that under chaos, we can tell the general direction a particle will take. Contradicted!

(C) It is sometimes impossible to re-create exactly the starting conditions of an experiment.

The passage tells us that in S&O's system, even "small, inadvertent, or undetectable" changes in initial conditions "can alter results radically" (lines 6–8). This is the explanation behind our answer to #22: we can't always replicate results because it may be impossible to replicate the starting conditions precisely, and even the tiniest difference can produce a different result.

(D) It is usually possible to predict the exact path water will travel if it is spilled at a point not on the boundary between two basins of attraction.

Paragraph three makes it clear that the boundaries are where the most unpredictability lies, but that doesn't mean we know the path that water spilled elsewhere will take. For water spilled elsewhere than a boundary of a riddled basin, we are likely to know which basin the water will end up in, but not necessarily its exact destination (lines 23–25) or, by extension, the specific path it will take.

(E) It is usually possible to determine the path by which a particle traveled given information about where it was placed and its eventual destination.

The reasoning for (D) knocks out (E), too. We don't always know much about specific paths,

25. Which one of the following most accurately describes the author's attitude toward the work of Sommerer and Ott? *(Synthesis)*

The answer choices here are very close together, so our best response is to do some fine-tuning! Let's start by finding the author. In line 47, we are told that "there are presumably other such systems." The author then goes on to say what may happen if such systems exist (lines 52–57). So we can conclude that the author is persuaded that multiple systems may exist, but is not 100% certain. Just glancing down at the opening of each answer choice, we can see a three-way split: (A) is negative, (B) and (C) are 100% positive, and (D) and (E) are mildly positive ("persuaded of the possibility").

(A) skeptical of the possibility that numerous unstable systems exist but confident that the existence of numerous unstable systems would call into question one of the foundations of science

(B) convinced of the existence of numerous unstable systems and unsure if the existence of numerous unstable systems calls into question one of the foundations of science

(C) convinced of the existence of numerous unstable systems and confident that the existence of numerous unstable systems calls into question one of the foundations of science

Our preliminary work eliminates (A)–(C).

9

(D) persuaded of the possibility that numerous unstable systems exist and unsure if the existence of numerous unstable systems would call into question one of the foundations of science

(E) persuaded of the possibility that numerous unstable systems exist and confident that the existence of numerous unstable systems would call into question one of the foundations of science.

We don't usually focus on directly comparing answer choices—it's generally best to go back to the question or passage—but in this case, the answers are identical except for "unsure" vs. "confident." So what does the author think will happen if these systems exist? We are told that if such systems "abound" (line 53)—in other words, if many of them exist—"scientists would be forced to question one of the basic principles that guide their work" (lines 56–57). The author may not be sure of the existence of these systems, but seems sure of what will happen if they exist. "Unsure" rules (D) out; (E) is the answer.

26. According to the passage, Sommerer and Ott's model differs from a riddled basin of attraction in which one of the following ways? *(Inference)*

We should look back to paragraph four, where we learn that S&O's system is unpredictable everywhere.

(A) In the model, the behavior of a particle placed at any point in the system is chaotic; in a riddled basin of attraction, only water spilled at some of the points behaves chaotically.

S&O's system is not chaotic—it's more unpredictable than that.

(B) In a riddled basin of attraction, the behavior of water spilled at any point is chaotic; in the model, only particles placed at some of the points in the system behave chaotically.

This answer is again talking about chaos. It also reverses the model and riddled basins—it's riddled basins that are unpredictable only at the boundaries.

(C) In the model, it is impossible to predict the destination of a particle placed at any point in the system; in a riddled basin of attraction, only some points are such that it is impossible to predict the destination of water spilled at each of those points.

A riddled basin is unpredictable at the boundaries, while S&O's model is unpredictable everywhere. Bingo!

(D) In a riddled basin of attraction, water spilled at two adjacent points always makes its way to the same destination; in the model, it is possible for particles placed at two adjacent points to travel to different destinations.

This is contradicted. Two adjacent spills in a riddled basin might end up in different places.

(E) In the model, two particles placed successively at a given point always travel to the same destination; in a riddled basin of attraction, water spilled at the same point on different occasions may make its way to different destinations.

The passage suggests that it's difficult to place two particles at exactly the same point, but there is no indication that if this is successfully done, either in the model or in a riddled basin, the particles will end up in different places.

27. Which one of the following best defines the term "basin of attraction," as that term is used in the passage? *(Identification)*

Notice that we are being asked for a general definition of "basin of attraction"—it doesn't have to be a "riddled" one. This is defined in lines 20–22.

(A) the set of all points on an area of land for which it is possible to predict the destination, but not the path, of water spilled at that point

(B) the set of all points on an area of land for which it is possible to predict both the destination and the path of water spilled at that point

Answers (A) and (B) talk about the destination of the water. All we know is what body it will end up in. We don't necessarily know its exact destination, and we don't know anything about its path.

(C) the set of all points on an area of land that are free from physical irregularities such as notches and zigzags

Contradicted! We know that a basin of attraction can have these irregularities—that's the "riddled" part.

(D) the set of all points on an area of land for which water spilled at each point will travel to a particular body of water

This is a solid rephrase of the definition in lines 20–22.

(E) the set of all points on an area of land for which water spilled at each point will travel to the same exact destination

This is wrong for the same reason as (A) and (B).

28. Which one of the following is most clearly one of the "metaphorical examples of riddled basins of attraction" mentioned in lines 52–53? *(Synthesis)*

If the passage was very difficult for you, this would have been a smart question to skip if you needed time for others.

We've had basins of attraction, riddled basins of attraction, chaos, and Sommerer & Ott's model. Now we're asked for a metaphorical example of a riddled basin of attraction! To find this, we need to take what we know about riddled basins and make it a bit more abstract and generalizable. What do we know? Water dropped at seemingly similar points may end up in different places due to little irregularities. (Jeff Goldblum actually demonstrates this in Jurassic Park.*) The more general idea is that two actions that look the same may have different results, again due to tiny differences at the outset. Note that the author mentions this metaphorical idea as an explanation of scientists' inability to replicate experimental results, and a quick glance shows us that all of the answer choices are built on this theme. We want one in which tiny initial differences make it hard to get the same result twice.*

(A) A scientist is unable to determine if mixing certain chemicals will result in a particular chemical reaction because the reaction cannot be consistently reproduced since sometimes the reaction occurs and other times it does not despite starting conditions that are in fact exactly the same in each experiment.

This is saying that even with the exact same starting conditions, a different result might occur. That is taking things too far. (It's the same trap as 26(E).)

(B) A scientist is unable to determine if mixing certain chemicals will result in a particular chemical reaction because the reaction cannot be consistently reproduced since it is impossible to bring about starting conditions that are in fact exactly the same in each experiment.

This seems a bit extreme. It's impossible *to have the same starting conditions?*

(C) A scientist is unable to determine if mixing certain chemicals will result in a particular chemical reaction because the reaction cannot be consistently reproduced since it is impossible to produce starting conditions that are even approximately the same from one experiment to the next.

This is even worse. Now we can't have even approximately the same starting conditions!

(D) A scientist is able to determine that mixing certain chemicals results in a particular chemical reaction because it is possible to consistently reproduce the reaction even though the starting conditions vary significantly from one experiment to the next.

This is an odd one. It's saying that despite differences in the starting conditions, we'll end up with the same result. Well, perhaps that occurs sometimes, even in a riddled basin—after all, there are only so many places for the water to end up—but it doesn't really get at what the example of riddled basins is about. It certainly wouldn't explain scientists' difficulties in replicating results.

(E) A scientist is able to determine that mixing certain chemicals results in a particular chemical reaction because it is possible to consistently reproduce the reaction despite the fact that the amount of time it takes for the reaction to occur varies significantly depending n the starting conditions of the experiment.

This one continues the theme of successfully *replicating results and adds in something about how long the process takes. Fortunately, since we know that successful replication is going in the wrong direction, we don't even have to start thinking about time!*

So what does that leave us with? Answers (D) and (E) are the opposite of what we want. Answer (A) is finding error in the wrong place. That leaves (B) and (C). Answer (C) is more extreme than (B), so we should probably consider (B) again. We didn't like that it said it was impossible to re-create the starting conditions. But we did say in question 24 that this was sometimes impossible. If we're looking for an explanation of why scientists have trouble replicating some results, an inability to re-create the starting conditions would make sense. Answer (B) is the one.

NOTES

Chapter 10
of
Reading Comprehension

Unusual Passages

Unusual Scales

So far, we've concentrated on passages for which we can identify two clear sides of a scale. We've already seen some exceptions, such as the three-sided Greek tragedies passage in Chapter 3 and the purely informative okapis passage in Chapter 9. We want to build on those experiences in this chapter, because it's important to recognize that some passages put up quite a bit of resistance to our efforts to identify a scale. This doesn't automatically make a passage difficult—maybe the ideas the author is presenting are still easy for us to understand—but if we have a hard time seeing the overall structure or determining the author's opinion, we may stumble on a few of the questions.

With that in mind, here are a few tips for handling oddball scales:

1. Don't force it.

It's possible that a seemingly offbeat passage will resolve itself into two clear positions by the end, but some passages resist such categorization. In that case, make sure you understand the structure of the passage on a paragraph-by-paragraph basis, and then take a moment to relate the ideas in the passage to one another, even if you don't land on a typical two-headed scale. Maybe it's simply an informational passage, maybe there are more than two sides to the issue, or maybe there is more than one major issue under discussion. Maybe the scale is traditional until the end, when the author changes direction. Take note of these complexities and don't panic. The scale is simply a tool for understanding the passage, so if there are more (or fewer) ideas than you'd normally see in a scale, just make sure you know how they relate to one another.

2. Find the author (or at least the big points).

As always, when a passage gets complicated, make sure to identify the author's opinion, if any. If the author is holding back, map out any major opinions expressed in the passage. If you know what ideas are being advocated, you will be better able to stitch together the content presented in the passage. Some passages have no opinions at all, and for those you need to keep your eye on the major topics.

3. Use the questions.

If you're worried about your understanding of the scale, test it out by tackling any general questions first. Use your sense of the scope of the passage and the author's opinion to work wrong-to-right and identify the best answer choices. These might help you refine your thinking about what's going on in the passage.

DRILL IT: Unusual Passages

Here are two challenging passages that may give you some trouble at the scale-building stage. Try to complete both and answer all the questions in 19 minutes. (We're suggesting a bit more than half of 35 minutes as these are challenging examples).

PrepTest 32, Section 2, Passage 2

Many educators in Canada and the United States advocate multicultural education as a means of achieving multicultural understanding. There are, however, a variety of proposals as to what multicultural (5) education should consist of. The most modest of these proposals holds that schools and colleges should promote multicultural understanding by teaching about other cultures, teaching which proceeds from within the context of the majority culture. Students should (10) learn about other cultures, proponents claim, but examination of these cultures should operate with the methods, perspectives, and values of the majority culture. These values are typically those of liberalism: democracy, tolerance, and equality of persons.

(15) Critics of this first proposal have argued that genuine understanding of other cultures is impossible if the study of other cultures is refracted through the distorting lens of the majority culture's perspective. Not all cultures share liberal values. Their value (20) systems have arisen in often radically different social and historical circumstances, and thus, these critics argue, cannot be understood and adequately appreciated if one insists on approaching them solely from within the majority culture's perspective.

(25) In response to this objection, a second version of multicultural education has developed that differs from the first in holding that multicultural education ought to adopt a neutral stance with respect to the value differences among cultures. The values of one culture (30) should not be standards by which others are judged; each culture should be taken on its own terms. However, the methods of examination, study, and explanation of cultures in this second version of multicultural education are still identifiably Western. (35) They are the methods of anthropology, social psychology, political science, and sociology. They are, that is, methods which derive from the Western scientific perspective and heritage.

Critics of this second form of multicultural (40) education argue as follows: The Western scientific heritage is founded upon an epistemological system that prizes the objective over the subjective, the logical over the intuitive, and the empirically verifiable over the mystical. The methods of social-scientific (45) examination of cultures are thus already value laden; the choice to examine and understand other cultures by these methods involves a commitment to certain values such as objectivity. Thus, the second version of multicultural education is not essentially different from (50) the first. Scientific discourse has a privileged place in Western cultures, but the discourses of myth, tradition, religion, and mystical insight are often the dominant forms of thought and language of non-Western cultures. To insist on trying to understand nonscientific (55) cultures by the methods of Western science is not only distorting, but is also an expression of an attempt to maintain a Eurocentric cultural chauvinism: the chauvinism of science. According to this objection, it is only by adopting the (often nonscientific) perspectives (60) and methods of the cultures studied that real understanding can be achieved.

8. Which one of the following most accurately states the main point of the passage?

(A) Proponents of two proposals for promoting multicultural understanding disagree about both the goal of multicultural education and the means for achieving this goal.
(A) Proponents of two proposals for promoting multicultural understanding claim that education should be founded upon an epistemological system that recognizes the importance of the subjective, the intuitive, and the mystical.
(A) Proponents of two proposals for promoting multicultural understanding claim that it is not enough to refrain from judging non-Western cultures if the methods used to study these cultures are themselves Western.
(A) Critics of two proposals for promoting multicultural understanding disagree about the extent to which a culture's values are a product of its social and historical circumstances.
(B) Critics of two proposals for promoting multicultural understanding claim these proposals are not value neutral and are therefore unable to yield a genuine understanding of cultures with a different value system.

9. Critics who raise the objection discussed in the second paragraph would be most likely to agree with which one of the following?

(A) The social and historical circumstances that give rise to a culture's values cannot be understood by members of a culture with different values.
(B) The historical and social circumstances of a culture can play an important role in the development of that culture's values.
(C) It is impossible for one culture to successfully study another culture unless it does so from more than one cultural perspective.
(D) Genuine understanding of another culture is impossible unless that culture shares the same cultural values.
(E) The values of liberalism cannot be adequately understood if we approach them solely through the methods of Western science.

10. Which one of the following most accurately describes the organization of the passage as a whole?

(A) Difficulties in achieving a goal are contrasted with the benefits of obtaining that goal.
(B) A goal is argued to be unrealizable by raising objections to the means proposed to achieve it.
(C) Two means for achieving a goal are presented along with an objection to each.
(D) Difficulties in achieving a goal are used to defend several radical revisions to that goal.
(E) The desirability of a goal is used to defend against a number of objections to its feasibility.

11. The version of multicultural education discussed in the first paragraph is described as "modest" (line 5) most likely because it

(A) relies on the least amount of speculation about non-Western cultures
(B) calls for the least amount of change in the educational system
(C) involves the least amount of Eurocentric cultural chauvinism
(D) is the least distorting since it employs several cultural perspectives
(E) deviates least from a neutral stance with respect to differences in values

12. Given the information in the passage, which one of the following would most likely be considered objectionable by proponents of the version of multicultural education discussed in the third paragraph?

(A) a study of the differences between the moral codes of several Western and non-Western societies
(B) a study of a given culture's literature to determine the kinds of personal characteristics the culture admires
(C) a study that employs the methods of Western science to investigate a nonscientific culture
(D) a study that uses the literary theories of one society to criticize the literature of a society that has different values
(E) a study that uses the methods of anthropology and sociology to criticize the values of Western culture

13. Which one of the following, if true, would provide the strongest objection to the criticism in the passage of the second version of multicultural education?

(A) It is impossible to adopt the perspectives and methods of a culture unless one is a member of that culture.

(B) Many non-Western societies have value systems that are very similar to one another.

(C) Some non-Western societies use their own value system when studying cultures that have different values.

(D) Students in Western societies cannot understand their culture's achievements unless such achievements are treated as the subject of Western scientific investigations.

(E) Genuine understanding of another culture is necessary for adequately appreciating that culture.

PrepTest 31, Section 4, Passage 4

Some philosophers find the traditional, subjective approach to studying the mind outdated and ineffectual. For them, the attempt to describe the sensation of pain or anger, for example, or the (5) awareness that one is aware, has been surpassed by advances in fields such as psychology, neuroscience, and cognitive science. Scientists, they claim, do not concern themselves with how a phenomenon feels from the inside; instead of investigating private evidence (10) perceivable only to a particular individual, scientists pursue hard data—such as the study of how nerves transmit impulses to the brain—which is externally observable and can be described without reference to any particular point of view. With respect to features of (15) the universe such as those investigated by chemistry, biology, and physics, this objective approach has been remarkably successful in yielding knowledge. Why, these philosophers ask, should we suppose the mind to be any different?

(20) But philosophers loyal to subjectivity are not persuaded by appeals to science when such appeals conflict with the data gathered by introspection. Knowledge, they argue, relies on the data of experience, which includes subjective experience. Why (25) should philosophy ally itself with scientists who would reduce the sources of knowledge to only those data that can be discerned objectively?

On the face of it, it seems unlikely that these two approaches to studying the mind could be reconciled. (30) Because philosophy, unlike science, does not progress inexorably toward a single truth, disputes concerning the nature of the mind are bound to continue. But what is particularly distressing about the present debate is that genuine communication between the two sides is (35) virtually impossible. For reasoned discourse to occur, there must be shared assumptions or beliefs. Starting from radically divergent perspectives, subjectivists and objectivists lack a common context in which to consider evidence presented from each other's (40) perspectives.

The situation may be likened to a debate between adherents of different religions about the creation of the universe. While each religion may be confident that its cosmology is firmly grounded in its respective (45) sacred text, there is little hope that conflicts between their competing cosmologies could be resolved by recourse to the texts alone. Only further investigation into the authority of the texts themselves would be sufficient.

(50) What would be required to resolve the debate between the philosophers of mind, then, is an investigation into the authority of their differing perspectives. How rational is it to take scientific description as the ideal way to understand the nature of (55) consciousness? Conversely, how useful is it to rely solely on introspection for one's knowledge about the workings of the mind? Are there alternative ways of gaining such knowledge? In this debate, epistemology—the study of knowledge—may itself (60) lead to the discovery of new forms of knowledge about how the mind works.

21. Which one of the following most accurately summarizes the main point of the passage?

(A) In order to gain new knowledge of the workings of the mind, subjectivists must take into consideration not only the private evidence of introspection but also the more objective evidence obtainable from disciplines such as psychology, neuroscience, and cognitive science.

(B) In rejecting the traditional, subjective approach to studying the mind, objectivists have made further progress virtually impossible because their approach rests on a conception of evidence that is fundamentally incompatible with that employed by subjectivists.

(C) Because the subjectivist and objectivist approaches rest on diametrically opposed assumptions about the kinds of evidence to be used when studying the mind, the only way to resolve the dispute is to compare the two approaches' success in obtaining knowledge.

(D) Although subjectivists and objectivists appear to employ fundamentally irreconcilable approaches to the study of the mind, a common ground for debate may be found if both sides are willing to examine the authority of the evidence on which their competing theories depend.

(E) While the success of disciplines such as chemistry, biology, and physics appears to support the objectivist approach to studying the mind, the objectivist approach has failed to show that the data of introspection should not qualify as evidence.

22. Which one of the following most likely reflects the author's belief about the current impasse between subjectivists and objectivists?

(A) It cannot be overcome because of the radically different conceptions of evidence favored by each of the two sides.
(B) It is resolvable only if the two sides can find common ground from which to assess their competing conceptions of evidence.
(C) It is unavoidable unless both sides recognize that an accurate understanding of the mind requires both types of evidence.
(D) It is based on an easily correctable misunderstanding between the two sides about the nature of evidence.
(E) It will prevent further progress until alternate ways of gaining knowledge about the mind are discovered

23. The author's primary purpose in writing the passage is to

(A) suggest that there might be valid aspects to both the subjective and the objective approaches to studying the mind
(B) advocate a possible solution to the impasse undermining debate between subjectivists and objectivists
(C) criticize subjectivist philosophers for failing to adopt a more scientific methodology
(D) defend the subjective approach to studying the mind against the charges leveled against it by objectivists
(E) evaluate the legitimacy of differing conceptions of evidence advocated by subjectivists and objectivists

24. According to the passage, subjectivists advance which one of the following claims to support their charge that objectivism is faulty?

(A) Objectivism rests on evidence that conflicts with the data of introspection.
(B) Objectivism restricts the kinds of experience from which philosophers may draw knowledge.
(C) Objectivism relies on data that can be described and interpreted only by scientific specialists.
(D) Objectivism provides no context in which to view scientific data as relevant to philosophical questions.
(E) Objectivism concerns itself with questions that have not traditionally been part of philosophical inquiry.

25. The author discusses the work of scientists in lines 7–14 primarily to

(A) contrast the traditional approach to studying the mind with the approach advocated by objectivists
(B) argue that the attempt to describe the sensation of pain should be done without reference to any particular point of view
(C) explain why scientists should not concern themselves with describing how a phenomenon feels from the inside
(D) criticize subjectivists for thinking there is little to be gained from studying the mind scientifically
(E) clarify why the objectivists' approach has been successful in disciplines such as chemistry, biology, and physics

26. The author characterizes certain philosophers as "loyal to subjectivity" (line 20) for each of the following reasons EXCEPT:

(A) These philosophers believe scientists should adopt the subjective approach when studying phenomena such as how nerves transmit impulses to the brain.
(B) These philosophers favor subjective evidence about the mind over objective evidence about the mind when the two conflict.
(C) These philosophers maintain that subjective experience is essential to the study of the mind.
(D) These philosophers hold that objective evidence is only a part of the full range of experience.
(E) These philosophers employ evidence that is available only to a particular individual.

27. Based on the passage, which one of the following is most clearly an instance of the objectivist approach to studying the mind?

(A) collecting accounts of dreams given by subjects upon waking in order to better understand the nature of the subconscious
(B) interviewing subjects during extremes of hot and cold weather in order to investigate a connection between weather and mood
(C) recording subjects' evaluation of the stress they experienced while lecturing in order to determine how stress affects facility at public speaking
(D) analyzing the amount of a certain chemical in subjects' bloodstreams in order to investigate a proposed link between the chemical and aggressive behavior
(E) asking subjects to speak their thoughts aloud as they attempt to learn a new skill in order to test the relationship between mental understanding and physical performance

28. Which one of the following is most closely analogous to the debate described in the hypothetical example given by the author in the fourth paragraph?

(A) a debate among investigators attempting to determine a criminal's identity when conflicting physical evidence is found at the crime scene
(B) a debate among jurors attempting to determine which of two conflicting eyewitness accounts of an event is to be believed
(C) a debate between two archaeologists about the meaning of certain written symbols when no evidence exists to verify either's claim
(D) a debate between two museum curators about the value of a painting that shows clear signs of both genuineness and forgery
(E) a debate between two historians who draw conflicting conclusions about the same event based on different types of historical data

SOLUTIONS: Unusual Passages

Let's look at how a successful reader might have worked through this passage in real time. After each passage discussion, we've included full solutions to the questions. Check your answers and, more importantly, your reasoning about why answers are right and wrong.

PrepTest 32, Section 2, Passage 2

Many educators in Canada and the United States advocate multicultural education as a means of achieving multicultural understanding. There are, however, a variety of proposals as to what multicultural (5) education should consist of. The most modest of these proposals holds that schools and colleges should promote multicultural understanding by teaching about other cultures, teaching which proceeds from within the context of the majority culture. Students should (10) learn about other cultures, proponents claim, but examination of these cultures should operate with the methods, perspectives, and values of the majority culture. These values are typically those of liberalism: democracy, tolerance, and equality of persons.

Okay, so there are several possible approaches, and the author finds this one the most modest. We'll probably see support for something more ambitious.

It looks like this approach is very limited. The author is probably just setting this one up to knock it down.

(15) Critics of this first proposal have argued that genuine understanding of other cultures is impossible if the study of other cultures is refracted through the distorting lens of the majority culture's perspective. Not all cultures share liberal values. Their value (20) systems have arisen in often radically different social and historical circumstances, and thus, these critics argue, cannot be understood and adequately appreciated if one insists on approaching them solely from within the majority culture's perspective.

Critics! Here comes side two?

Got it: not all cultures have the same values, so if the majority culture sticks to its perspective, it won't really understand other cultures. Is a solution next?

(25) In response to this objection, a second version of multicultural education has developed that differs from the first in holding that multicultural education ought to adopt a neutral stance with respect to the value differences among cultures. The values of one culture (30) should not be standards by which others are judged; each culture should be taken on its own terms. However, the methods of examination, study, and explanation of cultures in this second version of multicultural education are still identifiably Western. (35) They are the methods of anthropology, social

The revised version: study cultures in terms of their own values. Is this one going to get the stamp of approval?

Looks like no!

psychology, political science, and sociology. They are, that is, methods which derive from the Western scientific perspective and heritage.

I'm not sure what this is about. It's bad that the methods are identifiably Western?

Critics of this second form of multicultural (40) education argue as follows: The Western scientific heritage is founded upon an epistemological system that prizes the objective over the subjective, the logical over the intuitive, and the empirically verifiable over the mystical. The methods of social-scientific (45) examination of cultures are thus already value laden; the choice to examine and understand other cultures by these methods involves a commitment to certain values such as objectivity. Thus, the second version of multicultural education is not essentially different from (50) the first. Scientific discourse has a privileged place in Western cultures, but the discourses of myth, tradition, religion, and mystical insight are often the dominant forms of thought and language of non-Western cultures. To insist on trying to understand nonscientific (55) cultures by the methods of Western science is not only distorting, but is also an expression of an attempt to maintain a Eurocentric cultural chauvinism: the chauvinism of science. According to this objection, it is only by adopting the (often nonscientific) perspectives (60) and methods of the cultures studied that real understanding can be achieved.

Ah! Western methods are still pushing one set of values.

This seems important, but it's still the critics. Where's the author?

More about how Westerners are stuck in their perspective.

A third method? Use the perspectives *and* the methods of other cultures.

Scale and Passage Map

The scale of this passage is difficult to pin down! We could envision a multitiered scale, with each of the two forms of multicultural education taking a side across from its critics. However, the last paragraph makes it clear that to some critics, both forms are pretty much the same. If we wanted to add something about the commonality, we'd end up with a pretty complicated scale! Perhaps what's more important is to pit those who think multicultural education is effective against those who point out its flaws. The scale below captures that divide without getting too complex. But as always, keep in mind that the scale is just a tool for improving our engagement and understanding, and multiple versions could be considered "correct." The real test of our scale and passage map is in the questions—does our work allow us to keep all the many perspectives in this passage straight? The answer choices here are full of misquotes!

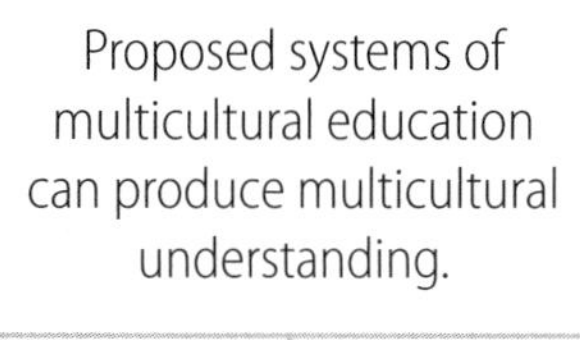

Multicultural education that uses Western methods/perspectives (science) is inherently flawed.

ADVOCATES FOR EACH FORM

CRITICS OF EACH FORM

P1: Introduction of first of two approaches to a problem. One of several multicultural education approaches is to simply teach about other cultures.

P2: Criticism of first approach. Genuine understanding of another culture is impossible within one's own cultural perspective.

P3: Introduction and criticism of second approach. Adopting a neutral stance towards culture is essentially a Western approach.

P4: Further criticism of second approach and potential solution. Studying a non-Western culture through an inherently Western scientific lens is inevitably distorting; the solution is to adopt the perspective of the studied culture.

Questions

8. Which one of the following most accurately states the main point of the passage? *(Synthesis)*

We see two versions of multicultural education get set up and knocked down, perhaps to make way for a third version that is capable of providing true understanding. However, the author never comes out with an opinion, so the main point must just be to let us know about these differing proposals and critiques.

(A) Proponents of two proposals for promoting multicultural understanding disagree about both the goal of multicultural education and the means for achieving this goal.

Contradicted. We're told up front that the goal of multicultural education is to achieve understanding (lines 1–3), and that original message never changes. The scope here is also too narrow—what about the critics of the second approach?

(B) Proponents of two proposals for promoting multicultural understanding claim that education should be founded upon an epistemological system that recognizes the importance of the subjective, the intuitive, and the mystical.

This is a misquote. The critics in the last paragraph like these ideas (39–44), but it's unlikely that the proponents of the two proposals advanced in the first and third paragraphs feel this way. If they did, the critics at the end would have nothing to object to.

(C) Proponents of two proposals for promoting multicultural understanding claim that it is not enough to refrain from judging non-Western cultures if the methods used to study these cultures are themselves Western.

Another misquote from the critics in the last paragraph (54–58). This can't be the perspective of the proponents of the two proposals, since they advocate the use of Western methods (lines 9–13, 32–38).

(D) Critics of two proposals for promoting multicultural understanding disagree about the extent to which a culture's values are a product of its social and historical circumstances.

This is too narrow. Only the critics of the first proposal bring up the origin of values (lines 19–24), and there is no indication that the other critics disagree with this assertion.

(E) Critics of two proposals for promoting multicultural understanding claim these proposals are not value neutral and are therefore unable to yield a genuine understanding of cultures with a different value system.

The critics of both proposals stress the bias in values built into each approach (lines 19–24, 44–50) and claim that this bias prevents genuine understanding (lines 15–18, 58–61).

9. Critics who raise the objection discussed in the second paragraph would be most likely to agree with which one of the following? *(Inference)*

The critics in paragraph two stress that different cultures have different values due to their differing social and historical circumstances, so we can't truly understand another culture through our own perspective.

(A) The social and historical circumstances that give rise to a culture's values cannot be understood by members of a culture with different values.

Too extreme. We may be able to understand other cultures, just not if we stick to our own perspective (lines 21–24).

(B) The historical and social circumstances of a culture can play an important role in the development of that culture's values.

This looks like a rephrase of lines 19–24. The situation described by the author comes about because value systems have arisen in different circumstances, so these circumstances must have played an important role.

(C) It is impossible for one culture to successfully study another culture unless it does so from more than one cultural perspective.

Unsupported. We don't know if we need more than one perspective—maybe we can just use the perspective of the culture in question.

(D) Genuine understanding of another culture is impossible unless that culture shares the same cultural values.

Too extreme and a lot like (A). This seems to assume that we can't take on other perspectives.

(E) The values of liberalism cannot be adequately understood if we approach them solely through the methods of Western science.

This is a misquote. Liberalism and Western science are both concepts associated with the majority culture (lines 9–13, 32–38), and there is no indication that they interfere with one another.

10. Which one of the following most accurately describes the organization of the passage as a whole? *(Synthesis)*

We are presented with two proposals for multicultural education, each of which is followed by criticism.

(A) Difficulties in achieving a goal are contrasted with the benefits of obtaining that goal.

Out of scope. The passage presents and knocks down methods for achieving understanding through multicultural education, but it doesn't address the benefits or difficulties of actually obtaining that goal.

(B) A goal is argued to be unrealizable by raising objections to the means proposed to achieve it.

Too extreme. At the end, it looks like there is a way to achieve understanding (lines 58–61). Besides, the author is presenting the views of critics, not making an argument.

(C) Two means for achieving a goal are presented along with an objection to each.

Great match for our prephrase.

(D) Difficulties in achieving a goal are used to defend several radical revisions to that goal.

Unsupported. There is no revision of the goal—everyone wants to achieve multicultural understanding.

(E) The desirability of a goal is used to defend against a number of objections to its feasibility.

Out of scope. The objections made by the critics are never countered.

11. The version of multicultural education discussed in the first paragraph is described as "modest" (line 5) most likely because it *(Inference)*

By using the words "most modest" to describe the first proposal (lines 5–9), the author implies that other approaches will ask us to go beyond this approach.

(A) relies on the least amount of speculation about non-Western cultures

Out of scope. There is nothing here about the degree of speculation.

(B) calls for the least amount of change in the educational system

This looks good. All of the subsequent critics want us to do more in teaching multicultural education.

(C) involves the least amount of Eurocentric cultural chauvinism

Contradicted. The second approach is supposed to be less centered on the majority culture than the first (lines 25–31), and even the second approach is criticized as chauvinistic (lines 54–58).

(D) is the least distorting since it employs several cultural perspectives

(E) deviates least from a neutral stance with respect to differences in values

These are both contradicted. This first approach sticks with the majority culture's values and perspective (lines 15–20).

12. Given the information in the passage, which one of the following would most likely be considered objectionable by proponents of the version of multicultural education discussed in the third paragraph? *(Inference)*

The proponents of the second version think that it's wrong to judge one culture through the values of another (lines 29–31).

(A) a study of the differences between the moral codes of several Western and non-Western societies

(B) a study of a given culture's literature to determine the kinds of personal characteristics the culture admires

These both look like attempts to understand other cultures' values—nothing to object to.

(C) a study that employs the methods of Western science to investigate a nonscientific culture

Misquote. This sounds like something the critics in the last paragraph would object to (lines 54–58).

(D) a study that uses the literary theories of one society to criticize the literature of a society that has different values

This sounds like exactly what they don't want to see—using one society's values to judge another.

(E) a study that uses the methods of anthropology and sociology to criticize the values of Western culture

Contradicted. The folks in paragraph three still like anthropology and sociology (lines 32–36), and since these are Western disciplines (lines 36–38), none of the critics in the passage would be likely to worry about using them to criticize Western culture.

13. Which one of the following, if true, would provide the strongest objection to the criticism in the passage of the second version of multicultural education? *(Inference)*

Critics of the second version think that it doesn't really succeed in being value-neutral because its methods are based in Western values (lines 40–48), so they want us to study other cultures using the "perspectives and methods" of those cultures (lines 58–61).

(A) It is impossible to adopt the perspectives and methods of a culture unless one is a member of that culture.

Uh-oh. That would make the critics' idea impossible to implement.

(B) Many non-Western societies have value systems that are very similar to one another.

Comparison trap. We're not concerned with how similar one non-Western society is to another.

(C) Some non-Western societies use their own value system when studying cultures that have different values.

Unsupported. The fact that non-Western societies proceed differently from what the critics suggest doesn't weaken the critics' point about understanding.

(D) Students in Western societies cannot understand their culture's achievements unless such achievements are treated as the subject of Western scientific investigations.

Out of scope. We aren't concerned with how Westerners study Western culture.

(E) Genuine understanding of another culture is necessary for adequately appreciating that culture.

Out of scope. These critics (and everyone else in the passage) are talking about understanding (lines 58–61), not appreciation.

PrepTest 31, Section 4, Passage 4

Some philosophers find the traditional, subjective approach to studying the mind outdated and ineffectual. For them, the attempt to describe the sensation of pain or anger, for example, or the (5) awareness that one is aware, has been surpassed by advances in fields such as psychology, neuroscience, and cognitive science. Scientists, they claim, do not concern themselves with how a phenomenon feels from the inside; instead of investigating private evidence (10) perceivable only to a particular individual, scientists pursue hard data—such as the study of how nerves transmit impulses to the brain—which is externally observable and can be described without reference to any particular point of view. With respect to features of (15) the universe such as those investigated by chemistry, biology, and physics, this objective approach has been remarkably successful in yielding knowledge. Why, these philosophers ask, should we suppose the mind to be any different?

Some philosophers are criticizing the subjective approach to studying the mind.

This was anti-subjective stuff; hard data/science is better. We'll probably see something about the other side now.

(20) But philosophers loyal to subjectivity are not persuaded by appeals to science when such appeals conflict with the data gathered by introspection. Knowledge, they argue, relies on the data of experience, which includes subjective experience. Why (25) should philosophy ally itself with scientists who would reduce the sources of knowledge to only those data that can be discerned objectively?

Yep, here comes the other side. The scale seems to be subjective vs. objective approaches to studying mind.

Subjectivists: objectivists too limited and subjective important. No author yet—maybe she'll show up now.

On the face of it, it seems unlikely that these two approaches to studying the mind could be reconciled. (30) Because philosophy, unlike science, does not progress inexorably toward a single truth, disputes concerning the nature of the mind are bound to continue. But what is particularly distressing about the present debate is that genuine communication between the two sides is (35) virtually impossible. For reasoned discourse to occur, there must be shared assumptions or beliefs. Starting from radically divergent perspectives, subjectivists and objectivists lack a common context in which to consider evidence presented from each other's (40) perspectives.

It looks like the author is setting this idea up just to knock it down. In that case, the scale is changing.

The author is loud and clear here!

The two sides need to find common ground. What's the scale? Can be reconciled vs. can't? No idea what's next...

The situation may be likened to a debate between adherents of different religions about the creation of the universe. While each religion may be confident that its cosmology is firmly grounded in its respective (45) sacred text, there is little hope that conflicts between their competing cosmologies could be resolved by recourse to the texts alone. Only further investigation into the authority of the texts themselves would be sufficient.

An analogy! Basic idea: to resolve debate, look at the authority of your data. Seems like this is the author's message. Scale?

(50) What would be required to resolve the debate between the philosophers of mind, then, is an investigation into the authority of their differing perspectives. How rational is it to take scientific description as the ideal way to understand the nature of (55) consciousness? Conversely, how useful is it to rely solely on introspection for one's knowledge about the workings of the mind? Are there alternative ways of gaining such knowledge? In this debate, epistemology—the study of knowledge—may itself (60) lead to the discovery of new forms of knowledge about how the mind works.

The author is driving the point home—both sides need to be investigated.

Epistemology, huh? So we need to know more about knowledge.

Scale and Passage Map

Well, we started off with what looked like a clear scale—the objective vs. the subjective approach to studying the mind. Then the author came in and muddled things up. Can these views be reconciled? Yes, but only if the subjectivists and objectivists look into the authority of each approach. Apparently, epistemology is going to save the day. This is kind of like the Greek tragedies passage in chapter 3: two sides, with a middle position that gets the last word. In this case, the author is there in the middle. So maybe our scale should look like this:

Use only observable data to study mind.

OBJECTIVISTS

Debate impasse reconcilable only by evaluating authority of respective perspectives.

AUTHOR

Objectivists too limited. Introspection valuable.

SUBJECTIVISTS

P1: Introduction of a debate & the views of one side. Objectivists believe that the subjectivist approach to mind is outdated and ineffectual.

P2: Response by other side. Subjectivists think that objectivist data is insufficient.

P3: Author's reframing of the debate. The debate is at an impasse because the two sides lack common ground.

P4: Analogy to support author's position. The debate can't be resolved without looking at the authority of information.

P5: Possible solutions/implications. To resolve, we must evaluate each perspective's authority and perhaps discover new forms of knowledge.

Questions

21. Which one of the following most accurately summarizes the main point of the passage? *(Synthesis)*

The author thinks that subjectivists and objectivists are at an impasse and that in order to move on they need to examine the authority of their information.

(A) In order to gain new knowledge of the workings of the mind, subjectivists must take into consideration not only the private evidence of introspection but also the more objective evidence obtainable from disciplines such as psychology, neuroscience, and cognitive science.

(B) In rejecting the traditional, subjective approach to studying the mind, objectivists have made further progress virtually impossible because their approach rests on a conception of evidence that is fundamentally incompatible with that employed by subjectivists.

These are both too narrow. Answer (A) addresses only the subjectivists, and (B) addresses only the objectivists. The assertions here aren't supported, either, but we don't have to get into that to eliminate these two and move on.

(C) Because the subjectivist and objectivist approaches rest on diametrically opposed assumptions about the kinds of evidence to be used when studying the mind, the only way to resolve the dispute is to compare the two approaches' success in obtaining knowledge.

This looks good, and we'd probably keep it on a first pass, but the author wants to investigate the two approaches' authority, not compare their success in obtaining knowledge. After all, a big part of the debate is what counts as useful knowledge (lines 23–27).

(D) Although subjectivists and objectivists appear to employ fundamentally irreconcilable approaches to the study of the mind, a common ground for debate may be found if both sides are willing to examine the authority of the evidence on which their competing theories depend.

This basically matches our prephrase and is supported by the passage (lines 47–49, 50–57).

(E) While the success of disciplines such as chemistry, biology, and physics appears to support the objectivist approach to studying the mind, the objectivist approach has failed to show that the data of introspection should not qualify as evidence.

Another one-sided attack, like (A) and (B).

22. Which one of the following most likely reflects the author's belief about the current impasse between subjectivists and objectivists? *(Synthesis)*

This question is not too different from the last. The author thinks that the impasse is distressing, and that to find common ground, it's important to look at the authority of each perspective.

(A) It cannot be overcome because of the radically different conceptions of evidence favored by each of the two sides.

Extreme/contradicted. This ignores the author's suggested solution.

(B) It is resolvable only if the two sides can find common ground from which to assess their competing conceptions of evidence.

This focuses just on the common ground part, and that's fine. This isn't a main point question—we've just been asked what the author believes, and this matches very well.

(C) It is unavoidable unless both sides recognize that an accurate understanding of the mind requires both types of evidence.

Unsupported. The author wants us to investigate the authority of both approaches—maybe one will turn out to be no good!

(D) It is based on an easily correctable misunderstanding between the two sides about the nature of evidence.

Extreme modifier. The author suggests that we may be able to resolve the impasse (lines 50–53), but that's a long way from saying that the situation is easily correctable. Also, the author never says that the two sides misunderstand each other.

(E) It will prevent further progress until alternate ways of gaining knowledge about the mind are discovered.

Out of scope. The author finds the impasse distressing, but never suggests that it prevents any further progress in the study of the mind. Maybe each side can make progress on its own.

23. The author's primary purpose in writing the passage is to *(Synthesis)*

We're just doing variations on the same idea here. The author wants to explain an impasse between two sides and suggest a solution.

(A) suggest that there might be valid aspects to both the subjective and the objective approaches to studying the mind

Unsupported. This is like (C) in the last question—the author is not weighing in on the validity of the two approaches or saying that we need to combine them.

(B) advocate a possible solution to the impasse undermining debate between subjectivists and objectivists

Perfect.

(C) criticize subjectivist philosophers for failing to adopt a more scientific methodology

(D) defend the subjective approach to studying the mind against the charges leveled against it by objectivists

As before, we see answer choices trying to push the author to one side. The author is not attacking or defending one side.

(E) evaluate the legitimacy of differing conceptions of evidence advocated by subjectivists and objectivists

This seems to be doing just what the author suggests. But the author doesn't actually perform that evaluation! Out of scope.

24. According to the passage, subjectivists advance which one of the following claims to support their charge that objectivism is faulty? *(Identification)*

The subjectivists think that the objectivists ignore the valuable data gathered through introspection.

(A) Objectivism rests on evidence that conflicts with the data of introspection.

This looks like a close match with the beginning of the second paragraph, but this isn't why *objectivism is faulty. That comes in the next sentence.*

(B) Objectivism restricts the kinds of experience from which philosophers may draw knowledge.

Yes (lines 24–27).

(C) Objectivism relies on data that can be described and interpreted only by scientific specialists.

Out of scope. There is no discussion of who can handle the data that objectivists prefer.

(D) Objectivism provides no context in which to view scientific data as relevant to philosophical questions.

(E) Objectivism concerns itself with questions that have not traditionally been part of philosophical inquiry.

These are both extreme and out of scope! While the passage describes a philosophical debate (note that the objectivists are philosophers, too), that debate is about how to study the mind, not about philosophical questions or inquiries in general.

25. The author discusses the work of scientists in lines 7–14 primarily to *(Inference)*

The first paragraph presents the objectivist side. In the cited lines, the objectivists are supporting their approach by saying that scientists focus on external data rather than the private perceptions favored by subjectivists.

(A) contrast the traditional approach to studying the mind with the approach advocated by objectivists

Looks good. "Contrast" is an easy way to convey the author's neutral tone; "traditional approach" is a reference to the subjective approach (line 1).

(B) argue that the attempt to describe the sensation of pain should be done without reference to any particular point of view

(C) explain why scientists should not concern themselves with describing how a phenomenon feels from the inside

(D) criticize subjectivists for thinking there is little to be gained from studying the mind scientifically

These all look like criticisms of the subjectivist approach, but the author is simply presenting *the objectivist position, not arguing for it. Wrong degree of opinion!*

(E) clarify why the objectivists' approach has been successful in disciplines such as chemistry, biology, and physics

Like the three answers above, this suggests that the author supports the objectivist position. While the objectivists *might say that lines 7–14 clarify the success of fields that rely on their approach, the* author *is not trying to do that.*

26. The author characterizes certain philosophers as "loyal to subjectivity" (line 20) for each of the following reasons EXCEPT: *(Identification)*

Any preparation for this EXCEPT Identification question may seem useless at first glance (and now comes the "however" that an active reader expects after reading "at first glance"). However, a closer look at the question stem reveals that the four wrong answers will all be characterizations of subjectivists. The majority of that description can be found in the second paragraph.

(A) These philosophers believe scientists should adopt the subjective approach when studying phenomena such as how nerves transmit impulses to the brain.

True, subjectivists like the subjective approach, but they aren't trying to tell scientists how to study neural impulses. They just don't want to leave out subjective experience (lines 23–24). This answer is unsupported, which here means it's correct.

(B) These philosophers favor subjective evidence about the mind over objective evidence about the mind when the two conflict.

(C) These philosophers maintain that subjective experience is essential to the study of the mind.

(D) These philosophers hold that objective evidence is only a part of the full range of experience.

These are all directly supported by the second paragraph.

(E) These philosophers employ evidence that is available only to a particular individual.

This shows up when the objectivists contrast scientists with subjectivists (line 7–10).

27. Based on the passage, which one of the following is most clearly an instance of the objectivist approach to studying the mind? *(Inference)*

Here, we're asked to apply the objectivist approach by matching it to an example. If we weren't sure what the question wanted, we could take a quick look at the answers and notice that they are all descriptions of studies. To match the objectivist approach, we want a study that relies on objective data rather than subjective personal experience.

(A) collecting accounts of dreams given by subjects upon waking in order to better understand the nature of the subconscious

(B) interviewing subjects during extremes of hot and cold weather in order to investigate a connection between weather and mood

(C) recording subjects' evaluation of the stress they experienced while lecturing in order to determine how stress affects facility at public speaking

These all seem pretty subjective.

(D) analyzing the amount of a certain chemical in subjects' bloodstreams in order to investigate a proposed link between the chemical and aggressive behavior

The amount of a chemical? We can measure that objectively.

(E) asking subjects to speak their thoughts aloud as they attempt to learn a new skill in order to test the relationship between mental understanding and physical performance

More subjective experience—assessing understanding through individual thoughts spoken aloud.

28. Which one of the following is most closely analogous to the debate described in the hypothetical example given by the author in the fourth paragraph? *(Inference)*

Wow, this question is asking us to identify something analogous to an analogous example! In the fourth paragraph, two religions are citing their conflicting texts, and we can't resolve the debate unless we look into the authority of the texts themselves. So we want something where two sides are fighting because they are looking at different data.

(A) a debate among investigators attempting to determine a criminal's identity when conflicting physical evidence is found at the crime scene

Hmm, this has conflicting evidence, but we don't see two sides each using just one part of that evidence, the way that people in the example are citing different texts.

(B) a debate among jurors attempting to determine which of two conflicting eyewitness accounts of an event is to be believed

This seems closer. Defer.

(C) a debate between two archaeologists about the meaning of certain written symbols when no evidence exists to verify either's claim

No evidence at all? Out.

(D) a debate between two museum curators about the value of a painting that shows clear signs of both genuineness and forgery

Here, they're debating the value, but there's no sign that they are drawing on different data or that they need to evaluate their data sources to come to an agreement. It's possible that the two curators agree on the painting's authenticity but disagree over something else, like aesthetic issues.

(E) a debate between two historians who draw conflicting conclusions about the same event based on different types of historical data

This looks good. They're drawing on different data. Looking back, this is better than (B). In (B), both sides are evaluating both sets of data. That sort of investigation into the authority of each side's information is what the author would like to see happen, but that's not what's actually happening in the example in paragraph four—both sides are just looking at their own information.

NOTES

Chapter 11 of Reading Comprehension

Putting It All Together

Grade Yourself Again!

Let's take another look at the self-assessment from chapter 6¾. See where you'd place yourself now, but don't peek at your old answers! Once you've filled out the whole thing, you can compare to your previous assessment on page 138.

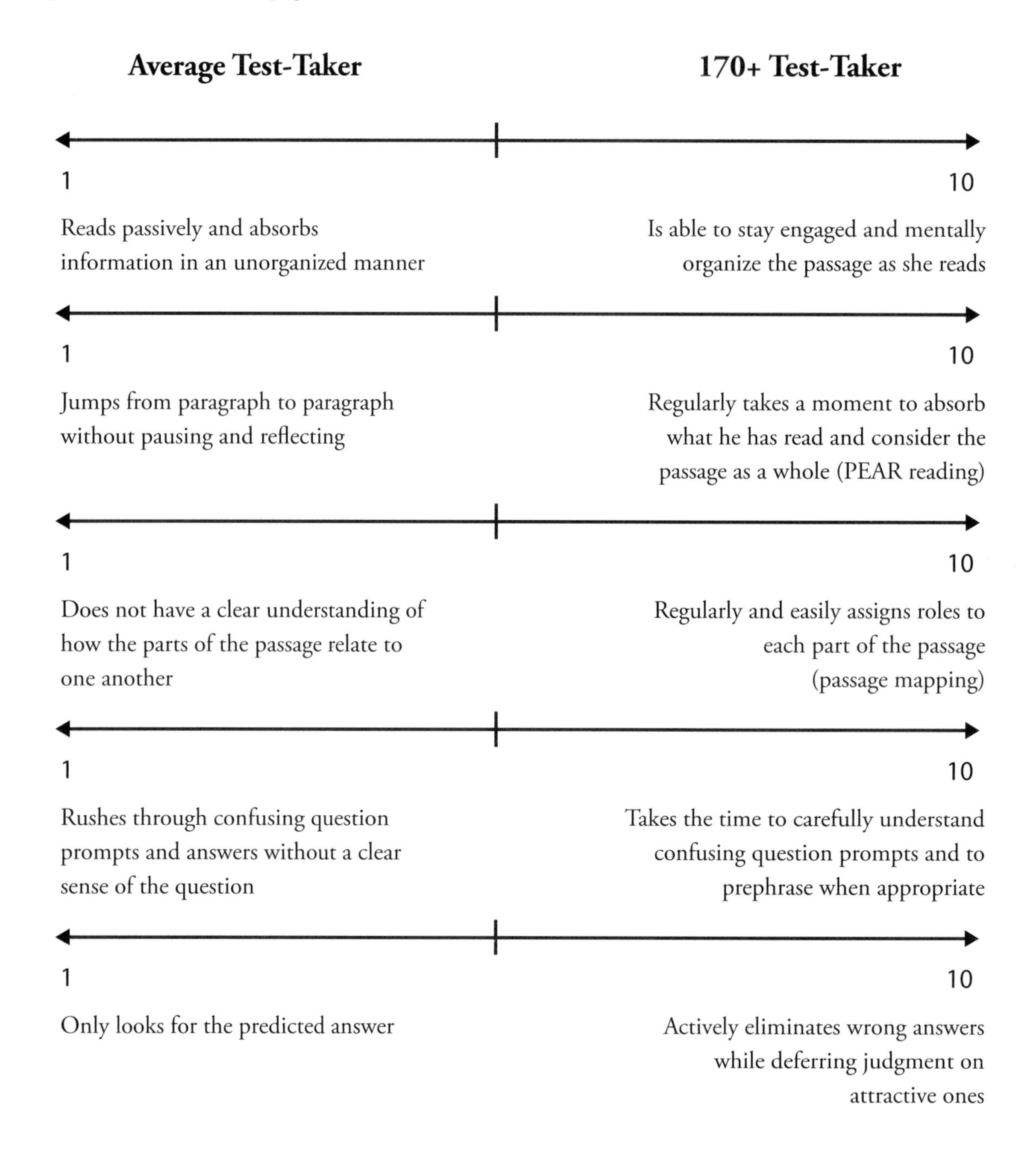

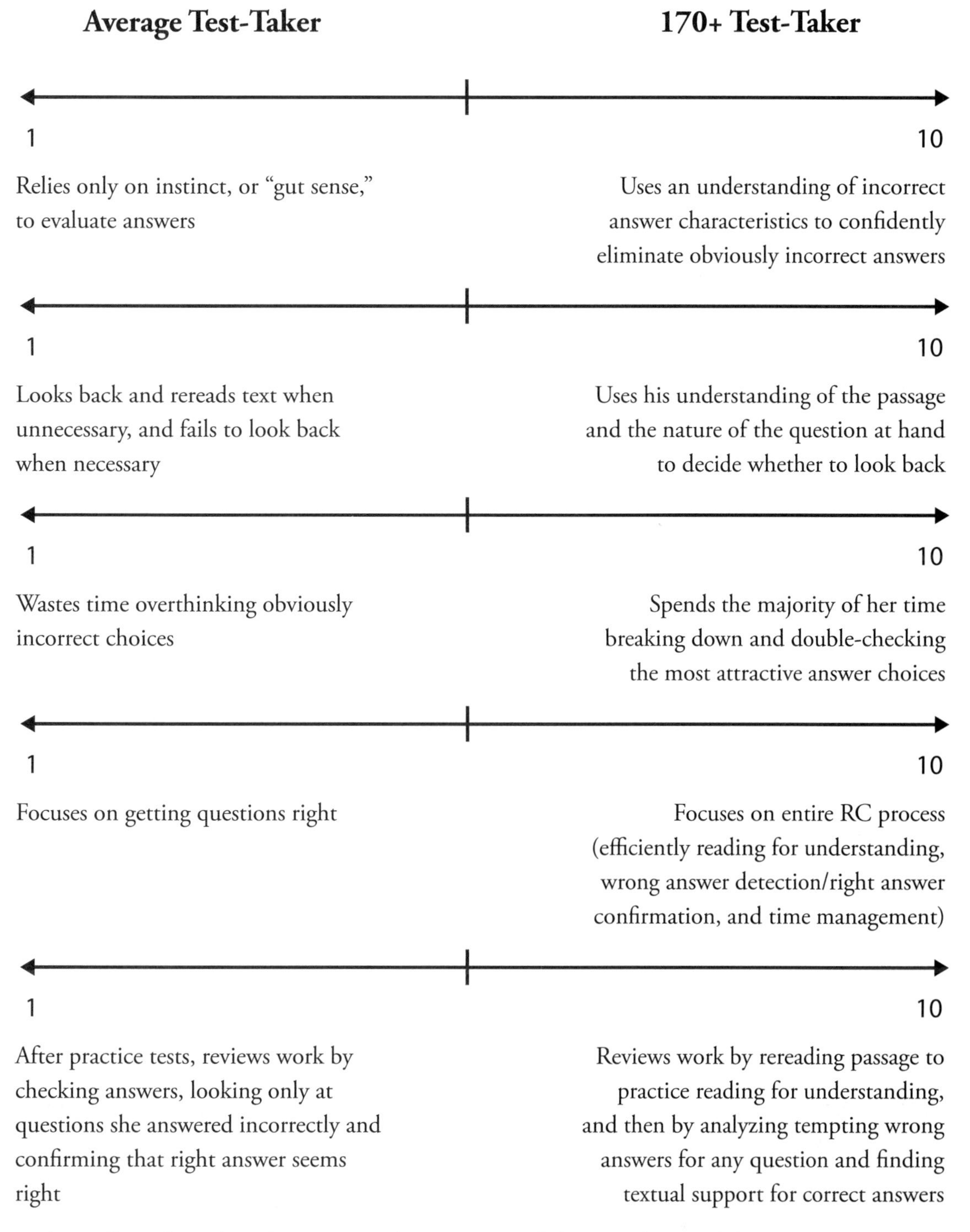

So what still needs work at this point? Pick one or two of the areas that need the most improvement and make them the point of focus for your next practice set, which it just so happens is going to occur... right now!

This page has been left intentionally blank.

Go right ahead and doodle on it.

DRILL IT: The Final Set

On the following pages is a complete Reading Comprehension section from a past LSAT exam (PrepTest 40). This should be a good representation of what you will experience on test day (the only difference is that this drill does not contain comparative passages, whereas your test will include one set of comparative passages).

Complete the drill as if you were in the actual exam. Give yourself 35 minutes, and don't take any breaks! Remember to focus on one or two improvement areas: maybe you need to pay more attention to prephrasing or maybe you need to try to move on faster when you're pretty confident an answer is wrong.

Following the drill, we have provided a solution set that we call The 180 Experience. Instead of presenting the kind of full solutions you've seen in the last few chapters—scale and passage map followed by full explanations for each answer choice—we are going to take you into the head of a 180 test-taker. These more minimal notes are designed to indicate a real-time thought process. When and how do we make quick eliminations, and when do we need to take a second look at a portion of the passage or at a few similar answer choices? Of course, even 180 test-takers can differ over how to approach a given problem. These solutions don't represent the "correct" way to handle this section; they're just one way to get all the answers right in 35 minutes! If you're interested in a more thorough solution for any portion of this drill, check out our forums.

PrepTest 40, Section 4

27 Questions, 35 minutes

Social scientists have traditionally defined multipolar international systems as consisting of three or more nations, each of roughly equal military and economic strength. Theoretically, the members of such (5) systems create shifting, temporary alliances in response to changing circumstances in the international environment. Such systems are, thus, fluid and flexible. Frequent, small confrontations are one attribute of multipolar systems and are usually the result of less (10) powerful members grouping together to counter threats from larger, more aggressive members seeking hegemony. Yet the constant and inevitable counterbalancing typical of such systems usually results in stability. The best-known example of a (15) multipolar system is the Concert of Europe, which coincided with general peace on that continent lasting roughly 100 years beginning around 1815.

Bipolar systems, on the other hand, involve two major members of roughly equal military and (20) economic strength vying for power and advantage. Other members of lesser strength tend to coalesce around one or the other pole. Such systems tend to be rigid and fixed, in part due to the existence of only one axis of power. Zero-sum political and military (25) maneuverings, in which a gain for one side results in an equivalent loss for the other, are a salient feature of bipolar systems. Overall superiority is sought by both major members which can lead to frequent confrontations, debilitating armed conflict, and, (30) eventually, to the capitulation of one or the other side. Athens and Sparta of ancient Greece had a bipolar relationship, as did the United States and the USSR during the Cold War.

However, the shift in the geopolitical landscape (35) following the end of the Cold War calls for a reassessment of the assumptions underlying these two theoretical concepts. The emerging but still vague multipolar system in Europe today brings with it the unsettling prospect of new conflicts and shifting (40) alliances that may lead to a diminution, rather than an enhancement, of security. The frequent, small confrontations that are thought to have kept the Concert of Europe in a state of equilibrium would today, as nations arm themselves with modern (45) weapons, create instability that could destroy the system. And the larger number of members and shifting alliance patterns peculiar to multipolar systems would create a bewildering tangle of conflicts.

This reassessment may also lead us to look at the (50) Cold War in a new light. In 1914 smaller members of the multipolar system in Europe brought the larger members into a war that engulfed the continent. The aftermath—a crippled system in which certain members were dismantled, punished, or voluntarily (55) withdrew—created the conditions that led to World War II. In contrast, the principal attributes of bipolar systems—two major members with only one possible axis of conflict locked in a rigid yet usually stable struggle for power—may have created the necessary (60) parameters for general peace in the second half of the twentieth century.

1. Which one of the following most accurately expresses the main point of the passage?

(A) Peace can be maintained in Europe only if a new bipolar system emerges to replace Cold War alliances.

(B) All kinds of international systems discussed by social scientists carry within themselves the seeds of their own collapse and ultimately endanger international order.

(C) The current European geopolitical landscape is a multipolar system that strongly resembles the Concert of Europe which existed through most of the nineteenth century.

(D) Multipolarity fostered the conditions that led to World War II and is incompatible with a stable, modern Europe.

(E) The characterization of multipolar systems as stable and bipolar systems as open to debilitating conflict needs to be reconsidered in light of the realities of post-Cold War Europe.

2. Which one of the following statements most accurately describes the function of the final paragraph?

(A) The weaknesses of both types of systems are discussed in the context of twentieth-century European history.

(B) A prediction is made regarding European security based on the attributes of both types of systems.

(C) A new argument is introduced in favor of European countries embracing a new bipolar system.

(D) Twentieth-century European history is used to expand on the argument in the previous paragraph.

(E) The typical characteristics of the major members of a bipolar system are reviewed.

3. The author's reference to the possibility that confrontations may lead to capitulation (lines 27–30) serves primarily to

(A) indicate that bipolar systems can have certain unstable characteristics
(B) illustrate how multipolar systems can transform themselves into bipolar systems
(C) contrast the aggressive nature of bipolar members with the more rational behavior of their multipolar counterparts
(D) indicate the anarchic nature of international relations
(E) suggest that military and economic strength shifts in bipolar as frequently as in multipolar systems

4. With respect to the Cold War, the author's attitude can most accurately be described as

(A) fearful that European geopolitics may bring about a similar bipolar system
(B) surprised that it did not end with a major war
(C) convinced that it provides an important example of bipolarity maintaining peace
(D) regretful that the major European countries were so ambivalent about it
(E) confident it will mark only a brief hiatus between long periods of European multipolarity

5. Which one of the following statements concerning the Concert of Europe (lines 14–17) can most reasonably be inferred from the passage?

(A) Each of the many small confrontations that occurred under the Concert of Europe threatened the integrity of the system.
(B) It provided the highest level of security possible for Europe in the late nineteenth century.
(C) All the factors contributing to stability during the late nineteenth century continue to contribute to European security.
(D) Equilibrium in the system was maintained as members grouped together to counterbalance mutual threats.
(E) It was more stable than most multipolar systems because its smaller members reacted promptly to aggression by its larger members.

In spite of a shared language, Latin American poetry written in Spanish differs from Spanish poetry in many respects. The Spanish of Latin American poets is more open than that of Spanish poets, more exposed (5) to outside influences—indigenous, English, French, and other languages. While some literary critics maintain that there is as much linguistic unity in Latin American poetry as there is in Spanish poetry, they base this claim on the fact that Castilian Spanish, the (10) official and literary version of the Spanish language based largely on the dialect originally spoken in the Castile region of Spain, was transplanted to the Americas when it was already a relatively standardized idiom. Although such unity may have characterized the (15) earliest Latin American poetry, after centuries in the Americas the language of Latin American poetry cannot help but reveal the influences of its unique cultural history.

Latin American poetry is critical or irreverent in its (20) attitude toward language, where that of Spanish poets is more accepting. For example, the Spanish-language incarnations of modernism and the avant-garde, two literary movements that used language in innovative and challenging ways, originated with Latin American (25) poets. By contrast, when these movements later reached Spain, Spanish poets greeted them with reluctance. Spanish poets, even those of the modern era, seem to take their language for granted, rarely using it in radical or experimental ways.

(30) The most distinctive note in Latin American poetry is its enthusiastic response to the modern world, while Spanish poetry displays a kind of cultural conservatism—the desire to return to an ideal culture of the distant past. Because no Spanish-language (35) culture lies in the equally distant (i.e., pre-Columbian) past of the Americas, but has instead been invented by Latin Americans day by day, Latin American poetry has no such long-standing past to romanticize. Instead, Latin American poetry often displays a curiosity about (40) the literature of other cultures, an interest in exploring poetic structures beyond those typical of Spanish poetry. For example, the first Spanish-language haiku—a Japanese poetic form—were written by José Juan Tablada, a Mexican. Another of the Latin (45) American poets' responses to this absence is the search for a world before recorded history—not only that of Spain or the Americas, but in some cases of the planet; the Chilean poet Pablo Neruda's work, for example, is noteworthy for its development of an ahistorical (50) mythology for the creation of the earth. For Latin American poets there is no such thing as the pristine cultural past affirmed in the poetry of Spain: there is only the fluid interaction of all world cultures, or else the extensive time before cultures began.

6. The discussion in the second paragraph is intended primarily to

(A) argue that Latin American poets originated modernism and the avant-garde
(B) explain how Spanish poetry and Latin American poetry differ in their attitudes toward the Spanish language
(C) demonstrate why Latin American poetry is not well received in Spain
(D) show that the Castilian Spanish employed in Spanish poetry has remained relatively unchanged by the advent of modernism and the avant-garde
(E) illustrate the extent to which Spanish poetry romanticizes Spanish-language culture

7. Given the information in the passage, which one of the following is most analogous to the evolution of Latin American poetry?

(A) A family moves its restaurant to a new town and incorporates local ingredients into its traditional recipes.
(B) A family moves its business to a new town after the business fails in its original location.
(C) A family with a two-hundred-year-old house labors industriously in order to restore the house to its original appearance.
(D) A family does research into its ancestry in order to construct its family tree.
(E) A family eagerly anticipates its annual vacation but never takes photographs or purchases souvenirs to preserve its memories.

8. The passage's claims about Spanish poetry would be most weakened if new evidence indicating which one of the following were discovered?

(A) Spanish linguistic constructs had greater influence on Latin American poets than had previously been thought.
(B) Castilian Spanish was still evolving linguistically at the time of the inception of Latin American poetry.
(C) Spanish poets originated an influential literary movement that used language in radical ways.
(D) Castilian Spanish was influenced during its evolution by other Spanish dialects.
(E) Spanish poets rejected the English and French incarnations of modernism.

9. The passage affirms each of the following EXCEPT:

(A) The first haiku in the Spanish language were written by a Latin American poet.
(B) Spanish poetry is rarely innovative or experimental in its use of language.
(C) Spanish poetry rarely incorporates poetic traditions from other cultures.
(D) Latin American poetry tends to take the Spanish language for granted.
(E) Latin American poetry incorporates aspects of various other languages.

10. Which one of the following can most reasonably be inferred from the passage about Latin American poetry's use of poetic structures from other world cultures?

(A) The use of poetic structures from other world cultures is an attempt by Latin American poets to create a cultural past.
(B) The use of poetic structures from other world cultures by Latin American poets is a response to their lack of a long-standing Spanish-language cultural past in the Americas.
(C) The use of poetic structures from other world cultures has led Latin American poets to reconsider their lack of a long-standing Spanish-language cultural past in the Americas.
(D) Latin American poets who write about a world before recorded history do not use poetic structures from other world cultures.
(E) Latin American poetry does not borrow poetic structures from other world cultures whose literature exhibits cultural conservatism.

11. Based on the passage, the author most likely holds which one of the following views toward Spanish poetry's relationship to the Spanish cultural past?

(A) This relationship has inspired Spanish poets to examine their cultural past with a critical eye.
(B) This relationship forces Spanish poets to write about subjects with which they feel little natural affinity.
(C) This relationship is itself the central theme of much Spanish poetry.
(D) This relationship infuses Spanish poetry with a romanticism that is reluctant to embrace the modern era.
(E) This relationship results in poems that are of little interest to contemporary Spanish readers.

12. Which one of the following inferences is most supported by the passage?

(A) A tradition of cultural conservatism has allowed the Spanish language to evolve into a stable, reliable form of expression.
(B) It was only recently that Latin American poetry began to incorporate elements of other languages.
(C) The cultural conservatism of Spanish poetry is exemplified by the uncritical attitude of Spanish poets toward the Spanish language.
(D) Lain American poets' interest in other world cultures is illustrated by their use of Japanese words and phrases.
(E) Spanish poetry is receptive to the influence of some Spanish-language poets outside of Spain.

According to the theory of gravitation, every particle of matter in the universe attracts every other particle with a force that increases as either the mass of the particles increases, or their proximity to one (5) another increases, or both. Gravitation is believed to shape the structures of stars, galaxies, and the entire universe. But for decades cosmologists (scientists who study the universe) have attempted to account for the finding that at least 90 percent of the universe seems to (10) be missing: that the total amount of observable matter—stars, dust, and miscellaneous debris—does not contain enough mass to explain why the universe is organized in the shape of galaxies and clusters of galaxies. To account for this discrepancy, cosmologists (15) hypothesize that something else, which they call "dark matter," provides the gravitational force necessary to make the huge structures cohere.

What is dark matter? Numerous exotic entities have been postulated, but among the more attractive (20) candidates—because they are known actually to exist—are neutrinos, elementary particles created as a by-product of nuclear fusion, radioactive decay, or catastrophic collisions between other particles. Neutrinos, which come in three types, are by far the (25) most numerous kind of particle in the universe; however, they have long been assumed to have no mass. If so, that would disqualify them as dark matter. Without mass, matter cannot exert gravitational force; without such force, it cannot induce other matter to (30) cohere.

But new evidence suggests that a neutrino does have mass. This evidence came by way of research findings supporting the existence of a long-theorized but never observed phenomenon called oscillation, (35) whereby each of the three neutrino types can change into one of the others as it travels through space. Researchers held that the transformation is possible only if neutrinos also have mass. They obtained experimental confirmation of the theory by generating (40) one neutrino type and then finding evidence that it had oscillated into the predicted neutrino type. In the process, they were able to estimate the mass of a neutrino at from 0.5 to 5 electron volts.

While slight, even the lowest estimate would yield (45) a lot of mass given that neutrinos are so numerous, especially considering that neutrinos were previously assumed to have no mass. Still, even at the highest estimate, neutrinos could only account for about 20 percent of the universe's "missing" mass. (50) Nevertheless, that is enough to alter our picture of the universe even if it does not account for all of dark matter. In fact, some cosmologists claim that this new evidence offers the best theoretical solution yet to the dark matter problem. If the evidence holds up, these (55) cosmologists believe, it may add to our understanding of the role elementary particles play in holding the universe together.

13. Which one of the following most accurately expresses the main idea of the passage?

(A) Although cosmologists believe that the universe is shaped by gravitation, the total amount of observable matter in the universe is greatly insufficient to account for the gravitation that would be required to cause the universe to be organized into galaxies.

(B) Given their inability to account for more than 20 percent of the universe's "missing" mass, scientists are beginning to speculate that our current understanding of gravity is significantly mistaken.

(C) Indirect evidence suggesting that neutrinos have mass may allow neutrinos to account for up to 20 percent of dark matter, a finding that could someday be extended to a complete solution of the dark matter problem.

(D) After much speculation, researchers have discovered that neutrinos oscillate from one type into another as they travel through space, a phenomenon that proves that neutrinos have mass.

(E) Although it has been established that neutrinos have mass, such mass does not support the speculation of cosmologists that neutrinos constitute a portion of the universe's "missing" mass.

14. Which one of the following titles most completely and accurately expresses the contents of the passage?

(A) "The Existence of Dark Matter: Arguments For and Against"

(B) "Neutrinos and the Dark Matter Problem: A Partial Solution?"

(C) "Too Little, Too Late: Why Neutrinos Do Not Constitute Dark Matter"

(D) "The Role of Gravity: How Dark Matter Shapes Stars"

(E) "The Implications of Oscillation: Do Neutrinos Really Have Mass?"

15. Based on the passage, the author most likely holds which one of the following views?

(A) Observable matter constitutes at least 90 percent of the mass of the universe.
(B) Current theories are incapable of identifying the force that causes all particles in the universe to attract one another.
(C) The key to the problem of dark matter is determining the exact mass of a neutrino.
(D) It is unlikely that any force other than gravitation will be required to account for the organization of the universe into galaxies.
(E) Neutrinos probably account for most of the universe's "missing" mass.

16. As described in the last paragraph of the passage, the cosmologists' approach to solving the dark matter problem is most analogous to which one of the following?

(A) A child seeking information about how to play chess consults a family member and so learns of a book that will instruct her in the game.
(B) A child seeking to earn money by delivering papers is unable to earn enough money for a bicycle and so decides to buy a skateboard instead.
(C) A child hoping to get a dog for his birthday is initially disappointed when his parents bring home a cat but eventually learns to love the animal.
(D) A child seeking money to attend a movie is given some of the money by one of his siblings and so decides to go to each of his other siblings to ask for additional money.
(E) A child enjoys playing sports with the neighborhood children but her parents insist that she cannot participate until she has completed her household chores.

17. The author's attitude towards oscillation can most accurately be characterized as being

(A) satisfied that it occurs and that it suggests that neutrinos have mass
(B) hopeful that it will be useful in discovering other forms of dark matter
(C) concerned that it is often misinterpreted to mean that neutrinos account for all of dark matter
(D) skeptical that it occurs until further research can be done
(E) convinced that it cannot occur outside an experimental setting

18. Which one of the following phrases could replace the world "cohere" at line 30 without substantively altering the author's meaning?

(A) exert gravitational force
(B) form galactic structures
(C) oscillate into another type of matter
(D) become significantly more massive
(E) fuse to produce new particles

19. The passage states each of the following EXCEPT:

(A) There are more neutrinos in the universe than there are non-neutrinos.
(B) Observable matter cannot exert enough gravitational force to account for the present structure of the universe.
(C) Scientific experiments support the theory of neutrino oscillation.
(D) Neutrinos likely cannot account for all of the universe's "missing" mass.
(E) Dark matter may account for a large portion of the universe's gravitational force.

Leading questions—questions worded in such a way as to suggest a particular answer—can yield unreliable testimony either by design, as when a lawyer tries to trick a witness into affirming a particular (5) version of the evidence of a case, or by accident, when a questioner unintentionally prejudices the witness's response. For this reason, a judge can disallow such questions in the courtroom interrogation of witnesses. But their exclusion from the courtroom by no means (10) eliminates the remote effects of earlier leading questions on eyewitness testimony. Alarmingly, the beliefs about an event that a witness brings to the courtroom may often be adulterated by the effects of leading questions that were introduced intentionally or (15) unintentionally by lawyers, police investigators, reporters, or others with whom the witness has already interacted.

Recent studies have confirmed the ability of leading questions to alter the details of our memories (20) and have led to a better understanding of how this process occurs and, perhaps, of the conditions that make for greater risks that an eyewitness's memories have been tainted by leading questions. These studies suggest that not all details of our experiences become (25) clearly or stably stored in memory—only those to which we give adequate attention. Moreover, experimental evidence indicates that if subtly introduced new data involving remembered events do not actively conflict with our stored memory data, we (30) tend to process such new data similarly whether they correspond to details as we remember them, or to gaps in those details. In the former case, we often retain the new data as a reinforcement of the corresponding aspect of the memory, and in the latter case, we often (35) retain them as a construction to fill the corresponding gap. An eyewitness who is asked, prior to courtroom testimony, "How fast was the car going when it passed the stop sign?" may respond to the query about speed without addressing the question of the stop sign. But (40) the "stop sign" datum has now been introduced, and when later recalled, perhaps during courtroom testimony, it may be processed as belonging to the original memory even if the witness actually saw no stop sign.

(45) The farther removed from the event, the greater the chance of a vague or incomplete recollection and the greater the likelihood of newly suggested information blending with original memories. Since we can be more easily misled with respect to fainter and more (50) uncertain memories, tangential details are more apt to become constructed out of subsequently introduced information than are more central details. But what is tangential to a witness's original experience of an event may nevertheless be crucial to the courtroom issues (55) that the witness's memories are supposed to resolve. For example, a perpetrator's shirt color or hairstyle might be tangential to one's shocked observance of an armed robbery, but later those factors might be crucial to establishing the identity of the perpetrator.

20. Which one of the following most accurately expresses the main point of the passage?

(A) The unreliability of memories about incidental aspects of observed events makes eyewitness testimony especially questionable in cases in which the witness was not directly involved.
(B) Because of the nature of human memory storage and retrieval, the courtroom testimony of eyewitnesses may contain crucial inaccuracies due to leading questions asked prior to the courtroom appearance.
(C) Researchers are surprised to find that courtroom testimony is often dependent on suggestion to fill gaps left by insufficient attention to detail at the time that the incident in question occurred.
(D) Although judges can disallow leading questions from the courtroom, it is virtually impossible to prevent them from being used elsewhere, to the detriment of many cases.
(E) Stricter regulation should be placed on lawyers whose leading questions can corrupt witnesses' testimony by introducing inaccurate data prior to the witnesses' appearance in the courtroom.

21. It can be reasonably inferred from the passage that which of the following, if it were effectively implemented, would most increase the justice system's ability to prevent leading questions from causing mistaken court decisions?

(A) a policy ensuring that witnesses have extra time to answer questions concerning details that are tangential to their original experiences of events
(B) thorough revision of the criteria for determining which kinds of interrogation may be disallowed in courtroom testimony under the category of "leading questions"
(C) increased attention to the nuances of all witnesses' responses to courtroom questions, even those that are not leading questions
(D) extensive interviewing of witnesses by all lawyers for both sides of a case prior to those witnesses' courtroom appearance
(E) availability of accurate transcripts of all interrogations of witnesses that occurred prior to those witnesses' appearance in court

22. Which one of the following is mentioned in the passage as a way in which new data suggested to a witness by a leading question are sometimes processed?

(A) They are integrated with current memories as support for those memories.
(B) They are stored tentatively as conjectural data that fade with time.
(C) They stay more vivid in memory than do previously stored memory data.
(D) They are reinterpreted so as to be compatible with the details already stored in memory.
(E) They are retained in memory even when they conflict with previously stored memory data.

23. In discussing the tangential details of events, the passage contrasts their original significance to witnesses with their possible significance in the courtroom (lines 52–59). That contrast is most closely analogous to which one of the following?

(A) For purposes of flavor and preservation, salt and vinegar are important additions to cucumbers during the process of pickling, but these purposes could be attained by adding other ingredients instead.
(B) For the purpose of adding a mild stimulant effect, caffeine is included in some types of carbonated drinks, but for the purposes of appealing to health-conscious consumers, some types of carbonated drinks are advertised as being caffeine-free.
(C) For purposes of flavor and tenderness, the skins of apples and some other fruits are removed during preparation for drying, but grape skins are an essential part of raisins, and thus grape skins are not removed.
(D) For purposes of flavor and appearance, wheat germ is not needed in flour and is usually removed during milling, but for purposes of nutrition, the germ is an important part of the grain.
(E) For purposes of texture and appearance, some fat may be removed from meat when it is ground into sausage, but the removal of fat is also important for purposes of health.

24. Which one of the following questions is most directly answered by information in the passage?

(A) In witnessing what types of crimes are people especially likely to pay close attention to circumstantial details?
(B) Which aspects of courtroom interrogation cause witnesses to be especially reluctant to testify in extensive detail?
(C) Can the stress of having to testify in a courtroom situation affect the accuracy of memory storage and retrieval?
(D) Do different people tend to possess different capacities for remembering details correctly?
(E) When is it more likely that a detail of an observed event will be accurately remembered?

25. The second paragraph consists primarily of material that

(A) corroborates and adds detail to a claim made in the first paragraph
(B) provides examples illustrating the applications of a theory discussed in the first paragraph
(C) forms an argument in support of a proposal that is made in the final paragraph
(D) anticipates and provides grounds for the rejection of a theory alluded to by the author in the final paragraph
(E) explains how newly obtained data favor one of two traditional theories mentioned elsewhere in the second paragraph

26. It can be most reasonably inferred from the passage that the author holds that the recent studies discussed in the passage

(A) have produced some unexpected findings regarding the extent of human reliance on external verification of memory details
(B) shed new light on a longstanding procedural controversy in the law
(C) may be of theoretical interest despite their tentative nature and inconclusive findings
(D) provide insights into the origins of several disparate types of logically fallacious reasoning
(E) should be of more than abstract academic interest to the legal profession

Continued on the following page...

27. Which one of the following can be most reasonably inferred from the information in the passage?

(A) The tendency of leading questions to cause unreliable courtroom testimony has no correlation with the extent to which witnesses are emotionally affected by the events that they have observed.
(B) Leading questions asked in the process of a courtroom examination of a witness are more likely to cause inaccurate testimony than are leading questions asked outside the courtroom.
(C) The memory processes by which newly introduced data tend to reinforce accurately remembered details of events are not relevant to explaining the effects of leading questions.
(D) The risk of testimony being inaccurate due to certain other factors tends to increase as an eyewitness's susceptibility to giving inaccurate testimony due to the effects of leading questions increases.
(E) The traditional grounds on which leading questions can be excluded from courtroom interrogation of witnesses have been called into question by the findings of recent studies.

SOLUTIONS: The 180 Experience

WARNING! As you read these real-time solutions, notice how the lessons presented earlier in this book come together to carry our 180 scorer successfully through an entire timed section. Through hours of practice, review, and analysis, this test-taker has internalized the approaches outlined in the preceding chapters and is able to work wrong-to-right in a quick and intuitive way while maintaining high (often perfect) accuracy. In some cases, a strong prephrase enables our hero to spot the correct answer without reading the full text of each answer choice—we've indicated these quick scans by lightening the skipped text in the answer choices. However, at other times, the reader is only able to navigate the answers through a combination of detailed recall and fine-grained rereading of the passage.

That all sounds great, right? So why have we attached a warning to these solutions? Because while this is the level of comprehension we may all aspire to, this performance is not going to be realistic in 35 minutes for every reader. A solid 170+ scorer might well have taken a strategic guess or two in this section and still ended up at a top-notch law school. Remember that we're always navigating that tension between detailed comprehension and time-efficient performance.

Social scientists have traditionally defined multipolar international systems as consisting of three or more nations, each of roughly equal military and economic strength. Theoretically, the members of such (5) systems create shifting, temporary alliances in response to changing circumstances in the international environment. Such systems are, thus, fluid and flexible. Frequent, small confrontations are one attribute of multipolar systems and are usually the result of less (10) powerful members grouping together to counter threats from larger, more aggressive members seeking hegemony. Yet the constant and inevitable counterbalancing typical of such systems usually results in stability. The best-known example of a (15) multipolar system is the Concert of Europe, which coincided with general peace on that continent lasting roughly 100 years beginning around 1815.

"Traditionally…" So this is probably going to change or be questioned.

Yep. "Theoretically."

Oh! It looks like this really does happen—it's not just a theory. So what's the scale? Will there be some exceptions?

Bipolar systems, on the other hand, involve two major members of roughly equal military and (20) economic strength vying for power and advantage. Other members of lesser strength tend to coalesce around one or the other pole. Such systems tend to be rigid and fixed, in part due to the existence of only one axis of power. Zero-sum political and military (25) maneuverings, in which a gain for one side results in an equivalent loss for the other, are a salient feature of bipolar systems. Overall superiority is sought by both major members which can lead to frequent confrontations, debilitating armed conflict, and, (30) eventually, to the capitulation of one or the other side. Athens and Sparta of ancient Greece had a bipolar relationship, as did the United States and the USSR during the Cold War.

Now we're on bipolar systems, but I don't see a scale yet. Mutipolar vs. bipolar isn't an argument unless people are making differing claims about them.

Okay, so the theory says that multipolar is stable and bipolar is not, because one side can collapse. So the author is probably going to come in and question the theory.

However, the shift in the geopolitical landscape (35) following the end of the Cold War calls for a reassessment of the assumptions underlying these two theoretical concepts. The emerging but still vague multipolar system in Europe today brings with it the unsettling prospect of new conflicts and shifting (40) alliances that may lead to a diminution, rather than an enhancement, of security. The frequent, small confrontations that are thought to have kept the Concert of Europe in a state of equilibrium would

Yep. "However," and now we're reassessing.

Multipolar systems are not such a good thing in modern times.

today, as nations arm themselves with modern
(45) weapons, create instability that could destroy the system. And the larger number of members and shifting alliance patterns peculiar to multipolar systems would create a bewildering tangle of conflicts.

This reassessment may also lead us to look at the
(50) Cold War in a new light. In 1914 smaller members of the multipolar system in Europe brought the larger members into a war that engulfed the continent. The aftermath—a crippled system in which certain members were dismantled, punished, or voluntarily
(55) withdrew—created the conditions that led to World War II. In contrast, the principal attributes of bipolar systems—two major members with only one possible axis of conflict locked in a rigid yet usually stable struggle for power—may have created the necessary
(60) parameters for general peace in the second half of the twentieth century.

So multipolar systems are responsible for the World Wars and bipolar systems cause peace? It's definitely the author vs. the theory.

To sum up, paragraph one is about how multipolar systems work, paragraph two is about how bipolar is less stable, and paragraphs three and four are about how multipolar is less stable in the modern world, with paragraph four adding that bipolar is more stable than we thought. The scale is the author challenging the idea that multipolar is more stable than bipolar in modern times.

1. Which one of the following most accurately expresses the main point of the passage?

The author is questioning traditional thinking—multipolar systems are less stable than people thought, and bipolar systems might actually be sustainable.

~~(A)~~ Peace can be maintained in Europe only if a new bipolar system emerges to replace Cold War alliances.

The author isn't making a prediction.

~~(B)~~ All kinds of international systems discussed by social scientists carry within themselves the seeds of their own collapse and ultimately endanger international order.

All kinds? No.

~~(C)~~ The current European geopolitical landscape is a multipolar system that strongly resembles the Concert of Europe which existed through most of the nineteenth century.

I think this is contradicted, but it's too fine a detail to be the point anyway.

~~(D)~~ Multipolarity fostered the conditions that led to World War II and is incompatible with a stable, modern Europe.

Same as (C). Even if it's true, it's too narrow to be the main point.

(E) The characterization of multipolar systems as stable and bipolar systems as open to debilitating conflict needs to be reconsidered in light of the realities of post-Cold War Europe.

Couldn't have said it better myself.

2. Which one of the following statements most accurately describes the function of the final paragraph?

It's where they make the point I just picked in (E) in the last problem: multipolar systems made a mess and a bipolar system may have kept the peace.

~~(A)~~ The weaknesses of both types of systems are discussed in the context of twentieth-century European history.

Weaknesses of both? No.

~~(B)~~ A prediction is made regarding European security based on the attributes of both types of systems.

Prediction?

~~(C)~~ A new argument is introduced in favor of European countries embracing a new bipolar system.

The author isn't trying to get us to do anything.

(D) Twentieth-century European history is used to expand on the argument in the previous paragraph.

The author is reassessing in the third paragraph and supporting that with examples in the final paragraph. Looks good, but let's look at (E).

~~(E)~~ The typical characteristics of the major members of a bipolar system are reviewed.

Characteristics of the members? Never happens.

3. The author's reference to the possibility that confrontations may lead to capitulation (lines 27–30) serves primarily to

If one side gives in, there's the end of the bipolar system.

(A) indicate that bipolar systems can have certain unstable characteristics.

Unstable sounds right.

~~(B)~~ illustrate how multipolar systems can transform themselves into bipolar systems.

I don't want anything about multipolar.

~~(C)~~ contrast the aggressive nature of bipolar members with the more rational behavior of their multipolar counterparts.

Multipolar again.

~~(D)~~ indicate the anarchic nature of international relations.

This is really out there.

~~(E)~~ suggest that military and economic strength shifts in bipolar as frequently as in multipolar systems.

More multipolar.

4. With respect to the Cold War, the author's attitude can most accurately be described as

More peaceful than it gets credit for?

~~(A)~~ fearful that European geopolitics may bring about a similar bipolar system.

The author is only looking backward.

~~(B)~~ surprised that it did not end with a major war.

Wrong direction.

(C) convinced that it provides an important example of bipolarity maintaining peace.

Right direction, but seems a little strong. Defer.

~~(D)~~ regretful that the major European countries were so ambivalent about it.

Regretful? Ambivalent? I don't see any of this.

(E) confident it will mark only a brief hiatus between long periods of European multipolarity.

Another prediction.

(C) is the only one that makes the right point, so I'll go with it even though I wanted a milder answer.

5. Which one of the following statements concerning the Concert of Europe (lines 14–17) can most reasonably be inferred from the passage?

Let me look back. There's not much there—it was a long period of multipolar peace, mostly in the nineteenth century.

(A) Each of the many small confrontations that occurred under the Concert of Europe threatened the integrity of the system.

Contradicted. Small confrontations are supposed to help the system maintain stability.

(B) It provided the highest level of security possible for Europe in the late nineteenth century.

Highest level possible? Way too extreme.

(C) All the factors contributing to stability during the late nineteenth century continue to contribute to European security.

No, the author says this wouldn't work now.

(D) Equilibrium in the system was maintained as members grouped together to counterbalance mutual threats.

Hmm, did that happen? Oh yeah, right above this it says that's what multipolar systems are like and then cites the Concert of Europe as an example.

(E) It was more stable than most multipolar systems because its smaller members reacted promptly to aggression by its larger members.

Comparison trap. We know it lasted a long time, but we don't really know how it compares to other multipolar systems.

In spite of a shared language, Latin American poetry written in Spanish differs from Spanish poetry in many respects. The Spanish of Latin American poets is more open than that of Spanish poets, more exposed (5) to outside influences—indigenous, English, French, and other languages. While some literary critics maintain that there is as much linguistic unity in Latin American poetry as there is in Spanish poetry, they base this claim on the fact that Castilian Spanish, the (10) official and literary version of the Spanish language based largely on the dialect originally spoken in the Castile region of Spain, was transplanted to the Americas when it was already a relatively standardized idiom. Although such unity may have characterized the (15) earliest Latin American poetry, after centuries in the Americas the language of Latin American poetry cannot help but reveal the influences of its unique cultural history.

Latin American poetry is critical or irreverent in its (20) attitude toward language, where that of Spanish poets is more accepting. For example, the Spanish-language incarnations of modernism and the avant-garde, two literary movements that used language in innovative and challenging ways, originated with Latin American (25) poets. By contrast, when these movements later reached Spain, Spanish poets greeted them with reluctance. Spanish poets, even those of the modern era, seem to take their language for granted, rarely using it in radical or experimental ways.

(30) The most distinctive note in Latin American poetry is its enthusiastic response to the modern world, while Spanish poetry displays a kind of cultural conservatism—the desire to return to an ideal culture of the distant past. Because no Spanish-language (35) culture lies in the equally distant (i.e., pre-Columbian) past of the Americas, but has instead been invented by Latin Americans day by day, Latin American poetry has no such long-standing past to romanticize. Instead, Latin American poetry often displays a curiosity about (40) the literature of other cultures, an interest in exploring poetic structures beyond those typical of Spanish poetry. For example, the first Spanish-language haiku—a Japanese poetic form—were written by José

Wow—instant scale! I hope the passage sticks with this.

Wait, is the scale going to pit Spanish poetry vs. Latin American, or is it going to be the author and critics arguing about the differences? That would be more complicated.

So some critics think Latin American poetry is no more diverse than Spanish poetry, but the author dismisses this.

Wait, this bit was not about diversity. It was about how Latin American poets played with language more than Spanish poets.

The author sees Spanish poetry as more cautious and conservative—maybe the original scale is going to hold.

Now we're on to why Latin American poetry is different. I think the critics above were a side note—the author basically wants to tell us that Latin American poetry is cooler than Spanish poetry because it doesn't have an extensive past on which to focus obsessively.

Juan Tablada, a Mexican. Another of the Latin
(45) American poets' responses to this absence is the search for a world before recorded history—not only that of Spain or the Americas, but in some cases of the planet; the Chilean poet Pablo Neruda's work, for example, is noteworthy for its development of an ahistorical
(50) mythology for the creation of the earth. For Latin American poets there is no such thing as the pristine cultural past affirmed in the poetry of Spain: there is only the fluid interaction of all world cultures, or else the extensive time before cultures began.

Paragraph one says that Latin American poetry is different from Spanish poetry in that it's more open to outside influences. Paragraph two adds that Latin American poets experiment with language, while Spanish poetry is more conservative. Paragraph three continues that comparison and adds an explanation for the difference: Spanish poetry looks toward the past, but since Latin America doesn't have a very long history, poets there look elsewhere for inspiration. So the scale is that Latin American poetry is bold and experimental and inclusive, while Spanish poetry is narrow and tradition-bound.

6. The discussion in the second paragraph is intended primarily to

Let's see, basically it says that Latin American poets play with language a lot more than Spanish poets do.

(A) argue that Latin American poets originated modernism and the avant-garde.

Didn't they say this in paragraph two? Oh no, just the Spanish-language versions, not the movements themselves. Anyway, it's not the point of the whole paragraph.

(B) explain how Spanish poetry and Latin American poetry differ in their attitudes toward the Spanish language.

This seems exactly right.

(C) demonstrate why Latin American poetry is not well received in Spain.

Another misquote. Just the movements were not well received—we don't know what people in Spain think of Latin American poetry.

(D) show that the Castilian Spanish employed in Spanish poetry has remained relatively unchanged by the advent of modernism and the avant-garde.

Nothing about that in paragraph two.

(E) illustrate the extent to which Spanish poetry romanticizes Spanish-language culture.

Again, nothing about that here, and this paragraph is only about language, not culture.

7. Given the information in the passage, which one of the following is most analogous to the evolution of Latin American poetry?

Okay, an analogy. Well, Latin American poetry evolved from Spanish poetry , but it's more playful and more open to outside influences.

(A) A family moves its restaurant to a new town and incorporates local ingredients into its traditional recipes.

I guess so. They brought in indigenous culture.

~~(B)~~ A family moves its business to a new town after the business fails in its original location.

Harsh. Spain didn't fail!

~~(C)~~ A family with a two-hundred-year-old house labors industriously in order to restore the house to its original appearance.

They're not trying to re-create anything—I think that's Spain.

~~(D)~~ A family does research into its ancestry in order to construct its family tree.

This also sounds like they're focused on the past.

~~(E)~~ A family eagerly anticipates its annual vacation but never takes photographs or purchases souvenirs to preserve its memories.

I'm not sure how this analogy even relates. What does the vacation stand for? These poets live *in Latin America—they're not just visiting. And how could anything evolve this way?*

8. The passage's claims about Spanish poetry would be most weakened if new evidence indicating which one of the following were discovered?

The author thinks Spanish poetry is backward-looking and conservative compared to Latin American poetry. So we need evidence to the contrary.

~~(A)~~ Spanish linguistic constructs had greater influence on Latin American poets than had previously been thought.

We're not disputing this influence.

~~(B)~~ Castilian Spanish was still evolving linguistically at the time of the inception of Latin American poetry.

Evolution of the language?

(C) Spanish poets originated an influential literary movement that used language in radical ways.

Looks good—it's exactly what the author says Spanish poets don't do.

~~(D)~~ Castilian Spanish was influenced during its evolution by other Spanish dialects.

More evolution stuff.

~~(E)~~ Spanish poets rejected the English and French incarnations of modernism.

Wrong direction.

9. The passage affirms each of the following EXCEPT:

This could be anything. I need to confirm the other four.

~~(A)~~ The first haiku in the Spanish language were written by a Latin American poet.

42–44.

~~(B)~~ Spanish poetry is rarely innovative or experimental in its use of language.

Paragraph 2.

~~(C)~~ Spanish poetry rarely incorporates poetic traditions from other cultures.

39–42.

(D) Latin American poetry tends to take the Spanish language for granted.

Misquote! This is Spanish poetry (27–28).

~~(E)~~ Latin American poetry incorporates aspects of various other languages.

3–6.

10. Which one of the following can most reasonably be inferred from the passage about Latin American poetry's use of poetic structures from other world cultures?

I don't know where they're going with this—I just know that Latin America borrows from other cultures and Spain doesn't. Let me see what the answer choices are talking about.

(A) The use of poetic structures from other world cultures is an attempt by Latin American poets to create a cultural past.

Create a past? That doesn't seem familiar. Let me keep looking.

(B) The use of poetic structures from other world cultures by Latin American poets is a response to their lack of a long-standing Spanish-language cultural past in the Americas.

Okay, so we're pulling from the last paragraph. Let me see—yes, this is there. Lines 34–40 and 50–53 say that Latin American poets look to other cultures because they don't have a long cultural history of their own. I see where (A) is coming from now, but they're not actually creating a past—they're replacing it with something else.

~~(C)~~ The use of poetic structures from other world cultures has led Latin American poets to reconsider their lack of a long-standing Spanish-language cultural past in the Americas.

Reconsider their lack? What would that even mean?

~~(D)~~ Latin American poets who write about a world before recorded history do not use poetic structures from other world cultures.

It looks like Latin American poets do both of these things. Maybe no one poet does both, but I don't know about that.

~~(E)~~ Latin American poetry does not borrow poetic structures from other world cultures whose literature exhibits cultural conservatism.

This is nowhere to be seen.

11. Based on the passage, the author most likely holds which one of the following views toward Spanish poetry's relationship to the Spanish cultural past?

Well, they're really into it. The author seems a bit judgmental about it, describing them as backward-looking and conservative.

~~(A)~~ This relationship has inspired Spanish poets to examine their cultural past with a critical eye.

Opposite.

~~(B)~~ This relationship forces Spanish poets to write about subjects with which they feel little natural affinity.

No—maybe Spanish poets like those traditional subjects.

(C) This relationship is itself the central theme of much Spanish poetry.

This seems reasonable, but I'm not sure the passage ever quite says this. Defer.

(D) This relationship infuses Spanish poetry with a romanticism that is reluctant to embrace the modern era.

Again, sounds reasonable, but I don't see this exactly.

~~(E)~~ This relationship results in poems that are of little interest to contemporary Spanish readers.

Kinda like (B). Maybe Spanish readers love this stuff.

Okay, so I don't have an answer choice I love. It has to be (C) or (D). Let me look back…

Lines 30–34 say Spanish poetry isn't really into the modern world, so that helps with (D). But is Spanish poetry romantic? Lines 37–38 say that unlike Spain, Latin America doesn't have a long-standing past to romanticize. I don't see any support for (C)—"central theme" is pretty extreme. I'd have to see something that says Spanish poets write mostly about their relationship to the past. I guess (D) is it.

12. Which one of the following inferences is most supported by the passage?

~~(A)~~ A tradition of cultural conservatism has allowed the Spanish language to evolve into a stable, reliable form of expression.

Spanish evolved through conservatism? Doesn't make much sense to me, plus this is about the whole Spanish language, which includes the Latin Americans.

~~(B)~~ It was only recently that Latin American poetry began to incorporate elements of other languages.

That doesn't sound familiar at all.

(C) The cultural conservatism of Spanish poetry is exemplified by the uncritical attitude of Spanish poets toward the Spanish language.

I don't know if this exemplifies their conservatism, but I know they don't mess with the language much.

~~(D)~~ Latin American poets' interest in other world cultures is illustrated by their use of Japanese words and phrases.

Someone wrote a haiku in Spanish, but there's nothing about Japanese words and phrases.

~~(E)~~ Spanish poetry is receptive to the influence of some Spanish-language poets outside of Spain.

Well, I would imagine they're not totally closed off, especially to Spanish-language poetry, but I don't see anything about this. The author's emphasis is on their not *bringing in outside influences, and no time is spent on exceptions.*

Answer (C) is the only one that comes close.

According to the theory of gravitation, every particle of matter in the universe attracts every other particle with a force that increases as either the mass of the particles increases, or their proximity to one (5) another increases, or both. Gravitation is believed to shape the structures of stars, galaxies, and the entire universe. But for decades cosmologists (scientists who study the universe) have attempted to account for the finding that at least 90 percent of the universe seems to (10) be missing: that the total amount of observable matter—stars, dust, and miscellaneous debris—does not contain enough mass to explain why the universe is organized in the shape of galaxies and clusters of galaxies. To account for this discrepancy, cosmologists (15) hypothesize that something else, which they call "dark matter," provides the gravitational force necessary to make the huge structures cohere.

We're starting with a theory again. Are we going to attack the theory?

This is heavy stuff. Maybe I should take notes.

Space is missing 90% of mass predicted by theory.

Dark matter!

What is dark matter? Numerous exotic entities have been postulated, but among the more attractive (20) candidates—because they are known actually to exist—are neutrinos, elementary particles created as a by-product of nuclear fusion, radioactive decay, or catastrophic collisions between other particles. Neutrinos, which come in three types, are by far the (25) most numerous kind of particle in the universe; however, they have long been assumed to have no mass. If so, that would disqualify them as dark matter. Without mass, matter cannot exert gravitational force; without such force, it cannot induce other matter to (30) cohere.

Neutrinos = dark matter?

but no mass!

But new evidence suggests that a neutrino does have mass. This evidence came by way of research findings supporting the existence of a long-theorized but never observed phenomenon called oscillation, (35) whereby each of the three neutrino types can change into one of the others as it travels through space. Researchers held that the transformation is possible only if neutrinos also have mass. They obtained experimental confirmation of the theory by generating (40) one neutrino type and then finding evidence that it had oscillated into the predicted neutrino type. In the process, they were able to estimate the mass of a neutrino at from 0.5 to 5 electron volts.

maybe they do have mass...

oscillation → mass

Neut. theory good start, but mass still low

While slight, even the lowest estimate would yield
(45) a lot of mass given that neutrinos are so numerous, especially considering that neutrinos were previously assumed to have no mass. Still, even at the highest estimate, neutrinos could only account for about 20 percent of the universe's "missing" mass.
(50) Nevertheless, that is enough to alter our picture of the universe even if it does not account for all of dark matter. In fact, some cosmologists claim that this new evidence offers the best theoretical solution yet to the dark matter problem. If the evidence holds up, these
(55) cosmologists believe, it may add to our understanding of the role elementary particles play in holding the universe together.

Paragraph one says that we can only find 10 percent of the matter predicted by the theory of gravitation; the rest must be dark matter. Paragraph two asks what dark matter is and suggests neutrinos, but they would need mass. Paragraph three says that because neutrinos oscillate, they must have mass. The last paragraph says that even still, they'd only make up about 20 percent of the missing mass—it's not a complete solution, but it seems to be a promising start. There are opinions here, but this has remained pretty one-sided. The author seems to agree with the cosmologists that neutrinos might be part of dark matter, and that we can eventually explain the rest.

13. Which one of the following most accurately expresses the main idea of the passage?

There's a bunch of missing mass in the universe, and neutrinos may account for some of it.

(A) Although cosmologists believe that the universe is shaped by gravitation, the total amount of observable matter in the universe is greatly insufficient to account for the gravitation that would be required to cause the universe to be organized into galaxies.

This doesn't get past paragraph one.

(B) Given their inability to account for more than 20 percent of the universe's "missing" mass, scientists are beginning to speculate that our current understanding of gravity is significantly mistaken.

Understanding of gravity is mistaken? No.

(C) Indirect evidence suggesting that neutrinos have mass may allow neutrinos to account for up to 20 percent of dark matter, a finding that could someday be extended to a complete solution of the dark matter problem.

This is a good summary.

(D) After much speculation, researchers have discovered that neutrinos oscillate from one type into another as they travel through space, a phenomenon that proves that neutrinos have mass.

This is one point from the third paragraph.

(E) Although it has been established that neutrinos have mass, such mass does not support the speculation of cosmologists that neutrinos constitute a portion of the universe's "missing" mass.

Contradicted.

14. Which one of the following titles most completely and accurately expresses the contents of the passage?

This is the same as the last question, just in different form. The title should say that neutrinos may be dark matter.

~~(A)~~ "The Existence of Dark Matter: Arguments For and Against."

This isn't about whether dark matter exists.

(B) "Neutrinos and the Dark Matter Problem: A Partial Solution?"

Exactly.

~~(C)~~ "Too Little, Too Late: Why Neutrinos Do Not Constitute Dark Matter."

Wrong direction.

~~(D)~~ "The Role of Gravity: How Dark Matter Shapes Stars."

What??

~~(E)~~ "The Implications of Oscillation: Do Neutrinos Really Have Mass?"

Super narrow.

15. Based on the passage, the author most likely holds which one of the following views?

Could be anything...

~~(A)~~ Observable matter constitutes at least 90 percent of the mass of the universe.

Opposite.

~~(B)~~ Current theories are incapable of identifying the force that causes all particles in the universe to attract one another.

I'm no Stephen Hawking, but I'm pretty sure that force is called gravity.

~~(C)~~ The key to the problem of dark matter is determining the exact mass of a neutrino.

The key to the problem? No—regardless of their precise mass, they're not the whole solution.

(D) It is unlikely that any force other than gravitation will be required to account for the organization of the universe into galaxies.

I don't know. Is that true?

~~(E)~~ Neutrinos probably account for most of the universe's "missing" mass.

No, 20 percent max.

Hmm, none of the others look good, so let me look for support for (D)... Lines 5–7 say that gravity is believed to shape galaxies—we just don't know where all the gravity is coming from. That's what the rest of the passage is getting at. So gravity seems to be sufficient—we just need to find all the dark matter that's producing it. That fits with (D).

16. As described in the last paragraph of the passage, the cosmologists' approach to solving the dark matter problem is most analogous to which one of the following?

Another analogy. I need to know what the cosmologists' approach is. I know they're checking out different possibilities—neutrinos are a promising start, but more is needed. I'm not sure I know enough specifics about their approach to make an analogy, but let me see what I can knock out.

~~(A)~~ A child seeking information about how to play chess consults a family member and so learns of a book that will instruct her in the game.

I don't see the scientists learning from anyone else. I don't think the universe is supposed to be a family member...

(B) A child seeking to earn money by delivering papers is unable to earn enough money for a bicycle and so decides to buy a skateboard instead.

Does this mean they're abandoning neutrinos for something else? That hasn't happened.

(C) A child hoping to get a dog for his birthday is initially disappointed when his parents bring home a cat but eventually learns to love the animal.

This sounds like they found something they weren't looking for, and I don't see that. These analogies are kind of weird.

(D) A child seeking money to attend a movie is given some of the money by one of his siblings and so decides to go to each of his other siblings to ask for additional money.

They have some of what they want, and now they're looking elsewhere. That could work, since neutrinos are only a partial solution.

(E) A child enjoys playing sports with the neighborhood children but her parents insist that she cannot participate until she has completed her household chores.

What? I have no idea what this stands for. Scientists can't look for neutrinos until they finish saving us from an asteroid? Compared to this, (D) is looking very sensible.

17. The author's attitude towards oscillation can most accurately be characterized as being

Does the author have an attitude about oscillation? It's what gives neutrinos mass, and that's important. Glancing down, I see what the question means—does the author think that oscillation is happening? Yes. The author presents the research in paragraph three as evidence that neutrinos have mass.

(A) satisfied that it occurs and that it suggests that neutrinos have mass.

Looks good.

(B) hopeful that it will be useful in discovering other forms of dark matter.

Other forms? No idea.

(C) concerned that it is often misinterpreted to mean that neutrinos account for all of dark matter.

Don't see this.

(D) skeptical that it occurs until further research can be done.

Opposite.

(E) convinced that it cannot occur outside an experimental setting.

Opposite.

18. Which one of the following phrases could replace the world "cohere" at line 30 without substantively altering the author's meaning?

"Cohere" means stick together. In line 30, it's used to describe how gravity smashes matter together with other matter.

(A) exert gravitational force.

Not quite what I wanted, but it is about gravity.

(B) form galactic structures.

Galactic structures? I don't think so.

(C) oscillate into another type of matter.

More oscillation! Doesn't fit the meaning at all.

(D) become significantly more massive.

Neither does this.

(E) fuse to produce new particles.

"Fuse" sounds like the same thing as "cohere," but I don't think the passage talks about producing new particles.

So what is it, then? I don't love any of them. Looking back, I still don't see anything about making new particles, so (E) is out. Answer (A) is off—gravitational force causes cohesion, not the other way around. The referenced line says that dark matter is making "the huge structures" cohere. What huge structures? Stars, galaxies, etc. Okay, (B) makes sense.

19. The passage states each of the following EXCEPT:

(A) There are more neutrinos in the universe than there are non-neutrinos.

I know there are a lot of neutrinos, but I don't see the passage specifically comparing their numbers to the numbers of everything else. Comparison trap! I think this is it.

(B) Observable matter cannot exert enough gravitational force to account for the present structure of the universe.

That's why we're looking at the neutrinos in the first place—most of the universe seems to be dark matter.

(C) Scientific experiments support the theory of neutrino oscillation.

This is in paragraph three. Yes, the author is down with oscillation.

(D) Neutrinos likely cannot account for all of the universe's "missing" mass.

True, just 20 percent at most.

(E) Dark matter may account for a large portion of the universe's gravitational force.

Yeah, 90 percent.

Leading questions—questions worded in such a way as to suggest a particular answer—can yield unreliable testimony either by design, as when a lawyer tries to trick a witness into affirming a particular (5) version of the evidence of a case, or by accident, when a questioner unintentionally prejudices the witness's response. For this reason, a judge can disallow such questions in the courtroom interrogation of witnesses. But their exclusion from the courtroom by no means (10) eliminates the remote effects of earlier leading questions on eyewitness testimony. Alarmingly, the beliefs about an event that a witness brings to the courtroom may often be adulterated by the effects of leading questions that were introduced intentionally or (15) unintentionally by lawyers, police investigators, reporters, or others with whom the witness has already interacted.

We can control leading questions in the courtroom, but what about interactions that occur prior to the court appearance? Maybe the witness has already been "led."

Recent studies have confirmed the ability of leading questions to alter the details of our memories (20) and have led to a better understanding of how this process occurs and, perhaps, of the conditions that make for greater risks that an eyewitness's memories have been tainted by leading questions. These studies suggest that not all details of our experiences become (25) clearly or stably stored in memory—only those to which we give adequate attention. Moreover, experimental evidence indicates that if subtly introduced new data involving remembered events do not actively conflict with our stored memory data, we (30) tend to process such new data similarly whether they correspond to details as we remember them, or to gaps in those details. In the former case, we often retain the new data as a reinforcement of the corresponding aspect of the memory, and in the latter case, we often (35) retain them as a construction to fill the corresponding gap. An eyewitness who is asked, prior to courtroom testimony, "How fast was the car going when it passed the stop sign?" may respond to the query about speed without addressing the question of the stop sign. But (40) the "stop sign" datum has now been introduced, and when later recalled, perhaps during courtroom testimony, it may be processed as belonging to the original memory even if the witness actually saw no stop sign.

(45) The farther removed from the event, the greater the chance of a vague or incomplete recollection and the greater the likelihood of newly suggested information blending with original memories. Since we can be more easily misled with respect to fainter and more (50) uncertain memories, tangential details are more apt to become constructed out of subsequently introduced information than are more central details. But what is tangential to a witness's original experience of an event may nevertheless be crucial to the courtroom issues (55) that the witness's memories are supposed to resolve. For example, a perpetrator's shirt color or hairstyle might be tangential to one's shocked observance of an armed robbery, but later those factors might be crucial to establishing the identity of the perpetrator.

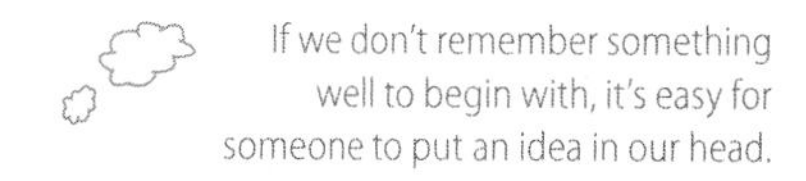

Those "minor details" may turn out to be important.

Hmm, so what's the scale? It seems like the author is just letting us know that leading questions outside of court are something to look out for, and telling us something about how our memory works in the process. There's no real argument here.

The first paragraph says that leading questions aren't just a problem in the courtroom; they can have their effect beforehand. The second tells us how leading questions affect our memory, and the third adds that this is especially true for more uncertain memories. I don't see a real argument, just a warning about leading questions outside of the courtroom and some information about memory.

20. Which one of the following most accurately expresses the main point of the passage?

Leading questions aren't just a problem in the courtroom. People can be influenced pretty heavily by leading questions that are asked before the court appearance.

(A) The unreliability of memories about incidental aspects of observed events makes eyewitness testimony especially questionable in cases in which the witness was not directly involved.

Nothing about leading questions.

(B) Because of the nature of human memory storage and retrieval, the courtroom testimony of eyewitnesses may contain crucial inaccuracies due to leading questions asked prior to the courtroom appearance.

This gets in both elements of the passage—the problem of leading questions before court and the info about memory.

(C) Researchers are surprised to find that courtroom testimony is often dependent on suggestion to fill gaps left by insufficient attention to detail at the time that the incident in question occurred.

This doesn't get directly at leading questions, and I'm not sure it's true, anyway.

(D) Although judges can disallow leading questions from the courtroom, it is virtually impossible to prevent them from being used elsewhere, to the detriment of many cases.

Paragraph one only.

~~(E)~~ Stricter regulation should be placed on lawyers whose leading questions can corrupt witnesses' testimony by introducing inaccurate data prior to the witnesses' appearance in the courtroom.

The author doesn't recommend any regulation.

21. It can be reasonably inferred from the passage that which of the following, if it were effectively implemented, would most increase the justice system's ability to prevent leading questions from causing mistaken court decisions?

It's hard to think of an easy way to solve this problem, since these questions can be introduced by anyone at any point in the process. Let me see what's available...

~~(A)~~ a policy ensuring that witnesses have extra time to answer questions concerning details that are tangential to their original experiences of events

I don't see how extra time would help. Is the memory distorted or not?

~~(B)~~ thorough revision of the criteria for determining which kinds of interrogation may be disallowed in courtroom testimony under the category of "leading questions"

Sure, but the author's point is that a lot of this happens outside the courtroom.

~~(C)~~ increased attention to the nuances of all witnesses' responses to courtroom questions, even those that are not leading questions

This is just in the courtroom again, and I don't see what it would do, anyway.

~~(D)~~ extensive interviewing of witnesses by all lawyers for both sides of a case prior to those witnesses' courtroom appearance

But that's when the leading questions get asked. How will we prevent them?

(E) availability of accurate transcripts of all interrogations of witnesses that occurred prior to those witnesses' appearance in court

Ah, okay, we're not going to be able to prevent the leading questions, but we can know if they've been asked and maybe disallow testimony on that basis. This doesn't seem like a miracle fix, but it's the only one that even comes close.

22. Which one of the following is mentioned in the passage as a way in which new data suggested to a witness by a leading question are sometimes processed?

Where is this? I need to look back. Lines 32–36 say that we use new data to reinforce or fill in gaps in our memories.

(A) They are integrated with current memories as support for those memories.

"Support" sounds like reinforcement. This should be it.

~~(B)~~ They are stored tentatively as conjectural data that fade with time.

Fade with time? No.

~~(C)~~ They stay more vivid in memory than do previously stored memory data.

Not that I know of.

~~(D)~~ They are reinterpreted so as to be compatible with the details already stored in memory.

Reinterpreted?

~~(E)~~ They are retained in memory even when they conflict with previously stored memory data.

It says we store them if they don't conflict.

23. In discussing the tangential details of events, the passage contrasts their original significance to witnesses with their possible significance in the courtroom (lines 52–59). That contrast is most closely analogous to which one of the following?

So maybe a detail isn't important to the witness, but it might turn out to be important to the case.

~~(A)~~ For purposes of flavor and preservation, salt and vinegar are important additions to cucumbers during the process of pickling, but these purposes could be attained by adding other ingredients instead.

The analogies in this section just keep getting weirder! Okay, this says you could get the same result a different way. That has nothing to do with what I'm looking for.

~~(B)~~ For the purpose of adding a mild stimulant effect, caffeine is included in some types of carbonated drinks, but for the purposes of appealing to health-conscious consumers, some types of carbonated drinks are advertised as being caffeine-free.

So this is something that is purposefully used in some cases but not others. That doesn't sound right.

~~(C)~~ For purposes of flavor and tenderness, the skins of apples and some other fruits are removed during preparation for drying, but grape skins are an essential part of raisins, and thus grape skins are not removed.

Again, we get rid of something in some situations but we need to keep it in others. That sounds like there are some cases where it's important to get trivial details and others where it's not. I don't know anything about that.

(D) For purposes of flavor and appearance, wheat germ is not needed in flour and is usually removed during milling, but for purposes of nutrition, the germ is an important part of the grain.

This is kind of like (B) and (C). Eliminate.

~~(E)~~ For purposes of texture and appearance, some fat may be removed from meat when it is ground into sausage, but the removal of fat is also important for purposes of health.

This is describing something that's good to remove for several reasons—there's nothing about usefulness.

Ack! Let me look again. (B)–(D) all look like they're comparing usefulness from one case to another, but on second glance, (D) is talking about how something is discarded even though it turns out to be important. This could be like the detail a witness overlooks (shirt color, hairstyle) that turns out to be important. I'll take it.

24. Which one of the following questions is most directly answered by information in the passage?

This could be anything...

~~(A)~~ In witnessing what types of crimes are people especially likely to pay close attention to circumstantial details?

Hmm, I don't know anything about different types of crimes. Looks like a comparison trap.

~~(B)~~ Which aspects of courtroom interrogation cause witnesses to be especially reluctant to testify in extensive detail?

This isn't about getting people to testify.

~~(C)~~ Can the stress of having to testify in a courtroom situation affect the accuracy of memory storage and retrieval?

Interesting question, but the passage is not talking about this.

~~(D)~~ Do different people tend to possess different capacities for remembering details correctly?

Another comparison trap. There's no comparison of different people's memories.

(E) When is it more likely that a detail of an observed event will be accurately remembered?

This is a comparison the passage actually makes. I think there are a few parts that address this, but offhand, I remember that we're more likely to remember things if we're paying attention. I must have been paying attention during that part!

25. The second paragraph consists primarily of material that

The second paragraph explains how leading questions affect our recall of events.

(A) corroborates and adds detail to a claim made in the first paragraph

Yes—the first paragraph says that leading questions affect our recall and the second paragraph describes how this happens.

(B) provides examples illustrating the applications of a theory discussed in the first paragraph

What theory?

(C) forms an argument in support of a proposal that is made in the final paragraph

Argument? Proposal?

(D) anticipates and provides grounds for the rejection of a theory alluded to by the author in the final paragraph

Rejection of a theory?

(E) explains how newly obtained data favor one of two traditional theories mentioned elsewhere in the second paragraph

More theories?

26. It can be most reasonably inferred from the passage that the author holds that the recent studies discussed in the passage

Where are the recent studies? Looking... Ah, the beginning of the second paragraph. They've given us a better understanding of how leading questions affect our memories.

(A) have produced some unexpected findings regarding the extent of human reliance on external verification of memory details.

I'm not sure if this external verification business is accurate, but I do know that the findings aren't unexpected—they've confirmed what people already knew.

(B) shed new light on a longstanding procedural controversy in the law

I don't see any controversy.

(C) may be of theoretical interest despite their tentative nature and inconclusive findings

No. It's practical and doesn't look tentative or inconclusive.

(D) provide insights into the origins of several disparate types of logically fallacious reasoning

Um, logical fallacies? Where did this come from?

(E) should be of more than abstract academic interest to the legal profession

Oh man, I wish I'd seen this earlier! This is a super understatement. Sure, the author thinks it's going to be of interest to the legal profession—it's really important stuff about the reliability of testimony!

27. Which one of the following can be most reasonably inferred from the information in the passage?

Straight to the answer choices.

(A) The tendency of leading questions to cause unreliable courtroom testimony has no correlation with the extent to which witnesses are emotionally affected by the events that they have observed.

No idea.

(B) Leading questions asked in the process of a courtroom examination of a witness are more likely to cause inaccurate testimony than are leading questions asked outside the courtroom.

Comparison trap again. The point is that both types are a problem.

(C) The memory processes by which newly introduced data tend to reinforce accurately remembered details of events are not relevant to explaining the effects of leading questions.

Yes, they are. That's what the second half of paragraph two is about.

(D) The risk of testimony being inaccurate due to certain other factors tends to increase as an eyewitness's susceptibility to giving inaccurate testimony due to the effects of leading questions increases.

What? This is really involved. Let me skip it for now.

(E) The traditional grounds on which leading questions can be excluded from courtroom interrogation of witnesses have been called into question by the findings of recent studies.

No, the passage doesn't question cutting out leading questions; it shows that they occur outside of the courtroom, too.

Choosing between these last two may take a bit of time—good thing I'm finishing with a few minutes left in the bank! Looking back, I don't see any support for (A), so I'll have to dig into (D). It seems to be saying that when you're more likely to be inaccurate due to leading questions, you're also more likely to be inaccurate for other reasons. So how do leading questions make us inaccurate? Paragraph two says that they often cause us to fill in gaps in our memory. So if we already have gaps, that could lead to inaccuracy. Anything else? Oh yeah, paragraph three spells it out even more. We have vague/incomplete memories of distant events, and so we can be more influenced by leading questions. So basically, the same factors that make us unreliable to begin with also make us more likely to be influenced by leading questions. If we don't remember an event well, either because it happened a long time ago or because we weren't paying attention, we're not going to give great testimony to begin with, and we also have a good chance of getting thrown off by leading questions. Answer (D) is it, and I'm done!

Troubleshooting

We hope that the process of working through this book has molded you into a much more confident and effective test-taker! However, at this point you may be feeling that certain elements of the 170+ approach are just not working out, regardless of how much you practice. Here are a few common concerns, and some actions you might take to overcome them.

I can apply these techniques just fine when I'm interested in the material, but on some passages I have a hard time staying engaged enough to read actively.

We all have our preferences, and no one is going to find every passage equally fascinating. However, a well-prepared test-taker can muster enough interest to get through any passage successfully. Here are a few of our tips:

1. Change your outlook.

Take a moment to look away from the passage, take a few calming breaths, and come back in telling yourself that whatever the content is, you're going to find it positively *absorbing*. Sometimes it even helps to let your body control your mind—work up a smile, lean in to the passage, and treat it like it's the only thing in the universe for a few minutes.

2. Annotate more.

Although not all of us are natural note-takers, putting pencil to paper can keep you more actively engaged with a passage. You may not need this on passages you find genuinely interesting, but it might make all the difference on that harder-to-love passage. Don't mark indiscriminately, but take the time to think about what's most important in what you're reading, and what concepts may play into the bigger picture. Just remembering that there *is* a bigger picture may help to pull you through a particularly dry paragraph.

3. Allow yourself to skip some text.

While we have advocated full-on skimming only as part of an emergency time-saving technique, if you find you're reading words without getting anything out of them, maybe it's time to take a somewhat higher level view. Rather than take the time to digest why two experts disagree on how to categorize a certain kind of doorknob, you might focus on the larger structure: there is general agreement on the different categories of doorknobs, but not on how to place individual doorknobs within those categories. The details can wait!

The scale concept is not working out for me. I have trouble finding two sides of a central scale, and when I do, my results seldom match the scale provided in the explanation.

Remember that the scale is a tool to aid comprehension; it's not essential that your finished scale is the same as ours. Beyond that, though, you may find that you're having trouble finding a scale at all. If that's the case, try these:

1. Focus on the author's opinion.

Even if you don't see a clear two sides to the story, if you have a sense of the author's position, you will be better prepared for the questions and you'll have a frame through which to see the rest of the passage. Why did the author mention particle accelerators? To support her opinion that not all important research can be carried out by corporations. How does this support her position? Because the particle accelerators she mentioned were massive government projects that would not be profitable for individual corporations to take on. Now we can look and see if we can find an opposing position ("Governments should not finance research" or "Government-financed research should still be carried out by corporations."), but even if we don't find it, we at least have a better sense of what the author is doing, and that's the point of the scale.

2. Rely on your passage map.

You're not always going to find a clear scale, or any scale at all. In those cases, the passage map is your best friend. Make sure that you know what is happening in the passage, even if you don't see how it fits into a larger picture. Perhaps the passage is purely informative, or perhaps the various opinions are hard to fit onto a scale but become clear as you map them out one by one. Make sure your methods are serving your overall understanding, and don't agonize over the scale if your passage map gives you a strong sense of the passage.

I feel like I can always get down to two answer choices, and I always pick the wrong one!

This is probably the most frequently voiced student complaint! Sometimes this is just selection bias: people are more likely to examine, and therefore remember, problems they missed, and they don't always pay much attention to all their lucky guesses. However, it's certainly worth spending some time improving your ability to "close the deal" on a question:

1. Slow down.

You may find that the first few wrong answers are easy to eliminate. When you get down to the last two or three, remind yourself to change your pace. There may be tricks ahead, and the last few eliminations can require a different level of attention. This is where the 170+ crowd stands out from the 160's, and you can't rush it.

2. Find the support.

Go back and compare the answers to the passage, not to each other. If you don't see support for either one, take a look around—maybe there is another relevant portion of the passage you forgot to look at. This is where a strong passage map can help.

3. Compare similar answers.

If the answer choices are very similar to each other, perhaps varying only by one word or concept (as in our Similar Answers drill in chapter 6), *do* compare them to each other. Comparing similar answers allows you to see what the question is really testing, and you may be more likely to notice the subtle differences of degree that make one choice right and the other wrong. However, in the end, you will still need to look to the passage to confirm that you've made the right choice.

Sometimes I still like my "wrong" answer the best, even after I've reviewed!

The LSAT is a very well-edited test. We're not saying that the test writers are infallible, but it's very rare to catch them napping when it comes to creating right and wrong answers. Every now and then, a new question turns out to have a slight flaw, but then it is removed from scoring and not included in the eventual PrepTest. If, after all your review, you don't see how the official answer could be right, or you don't see what's wrong with your favorite answer, look for help on our forums. If you understand the reasoning but just have trouble "buying" it, use this as an opportunity to adjust your LSAT mentality. Apparently, the connection you made on your wrong answer is not "legal" on the LSAT, but the move in the right answer is. Make a note to look for other problems that make these same moves. You may find that you catch other mistakes this way.

I do well on individual practice sections, but I always run out of steam when I take a full test.

The most natural advice here is to take more full practice tests, but you probably already thought of that! Although it's important to get plenty of practice with full tests, there are some other factors that might influence your energy level:

1. Make your RC work more routine.

It takes time to make these new techniques comfortable and familiar. During the transition, you may find Reading Comprehension (and perhaps the other sections, as well) even more tiring than you did before you started studying. Work through this pain, however, and you should come out on the other side with a set of techniques that you can apply without a great deal of effort. Keep pushing to routinize your RC process. That doesn't mean treating all the passages as the same, but it does mean approaching each passage with a similar mindset and running through a similar process every time, from reading for the scale through prephrasing the questions to knocking the wrong answers out one after the other. The more comfortable these techniques feel, the less exertion it will take to get through a set of passages.

2. Pull an RC marathon.

Do the occasional back-to-back practice RC sections. This can be a stand-alone, 70-minute experience or you can add an "experimental" RC section to your next PrepTest. Either way, get some practice doing eight RC passages in a row—it will toughen you up! Besides, you never know: because the experimental section can be of any type, this could happen on your real test.

3. Get some sugar in your system.

Of course, long-term you want to take good care of your health—a nutritious diet can certainly help your mental performance—but when it comes to test time, a little sugar at the break can really help your performance. The ability to buckle down and exercise self-control is easily depleted, and studies have shown that some readily available glucose can help in that department. So whether your sugar comes from a banana, a bottle of juice, or a chocolate bar, use your break to give yourself a spike. You can use your practice tests to experiment and find the quick snack that works best for you.

I always seem to run out of time!

If you're still running into timing trouble as test day draws near, it may be time to revisit chapter 7 with an eye toward adjusting your timing strategy. Even last-ditch moves, such as speed skimming or skipping entire passages, work best if you've had a chance to practice them. Remember, sometimes you don't need to dig down that deep to get a workable understanding of the passage. If you get a better sense of when to slow down and when to move on, you'll be able to maximize your return on those precious 35 minutes.

Conclusion

Congratulations! You've made it to the end of what we hope has been a powerful and transformative process that has changed the way you see the world and given you the tools to steer the future of humanity toward peace and prosperity. Well, maybe that will take a few more steps, but give yourself credit for the progress you've made so far! LSAT RC is tough, and you should be proud of the improvement you've made in negotiating the many tensions of high-pressure reading.

Where to go from here depends in part on how close you are to test day and, of course, how you're doing in Reading Comprehension. If you still have a fair amount of time before you take the LSAT, you should continue to address any gaps in your process, using both individual RC sets and full PrepTests. While you may find that in other sections of the test you need to zero in on specific question or game types, such as Match the Reasoning or 3D Ordering, in RC, your success is going to come first and foremost from a strong overall process. Sure, it's important to notice if you're missing a lot of Local Inference questions versus Analogy/Application questions, but the process of finding support and working wrong-to-right is quite similar from one question type to the next—the main difference is simply the type of support you need to find. And, of course, the fundamental skill of reading, understanding, and mapping out a passage is a constant throughout. This allows you to learn a tremendous amount from any passage you do, from the easiest to the craziest. Use every RC experience as a way to strengthen that core process and eliminate any weaknesses. If you had trouble with a passage, don't be too quick to blame the content. Think back to the drills you've done here—how could you have worked around the confusing elements of the text and pulled out a workable scale? How might you have avoided spending so much time on those few confusing answer choices?

If your LSAT is coming up very soon, it's time to focus on the big picture. How's your timing? What kinds of strategic decisions do you need to make to ensure a successful performance? Take a look at some of your past RC sections. What are you doing when you're at your best? How many questions do you miss? If you miss quite a few even at your best, let that thought liberate you—"I know I'm not going to get them all right, so how can I best use my time to maximize my performance?" If you sometimes miss few or none of the questions, what do you think makes the difference? What elements can you have an impact on now? Sometimes it comes down to things that have no direct connection to your reading process. In fact, the closer you get to the test, the more you want to think about personal factors. Are you eating well, exercising, and getting enough sleep? Are you practicing too late at night? Are you studying so hard that you have trouble concentrating? Make sure you are taking good care of yourself, especially in the final days before the exam. By that point, this is the most important thing you can do for your score, so don't try to cram at the last minute. It's normal to feel that urge—even our 99th percentile instructors sometimes have to stifle the impulse to do just a few more practice sets the night before the exam—but you're better off doing something relaxing and calling it a night. You've already learned what you're going to learn—you just need to make sure you're in the best state of mind to apply your well-practiced process!

On the morning of the test, look at something over breakfast just to wake your brain up. It can be a familiar RC passage or something from one of the other sections, but it should serve to remind you of what you can do, not to wear you out or invoke dread. The idea is just to avoid using the first section of your test as a warmup!

So with that, we'll leave you to your studies. Don't forget that there are more drills in your Student Center if you would like to target some of the specific skills we've discussed. When you're all done, drop us a line at results@manhattanslat.com and let us know how your test went!

Good luck on the test, and happy reading!